Please return/renew this item by the last date shown

worcestershire
countycouncil
Libraries & Learning

Everything
You Need to Know
About DJing and Success

Everything You

About DJin

Need to Know

g and Success

Danny Rampling Shares His 20 Years' Experience at the Top

Written with Ben Brophy and Jerry Frempong

First published in 2010 by Aurum Press Ltd
7 Greenland Street
London NW1 0ND
www.aurumpress.co.uk

A catalogue record for this book is available from the British Library.

ISBN 978 1 84513 582 9

10 9 8 7 6 5 4 3 2 1
2015 2014 2013 2012 2011 2010

Text design by Kika Sroka-Miller

Typeset by M Rules

Printed in Singapore

Contents

Contents

Section 2: Danny's Tips for Achieving Your Potential and Succeeding in Life

Section 3: Bonus Resources

Contents

ix

Introduction

Hi, I'm Danny Rampling and I am sincerely thankful that you have taken the step to learn more about DJing and achieving your goals.

My passion for music began at a very young age listening to records at home, developing a fascination with how a vinyl disc could produce such wonderful sounds. My hobby as a kid was collecting records and playing them over and over at full blast on one turntable. These early experiences of music shaped my destiny to become a DJ.

I consider myself blessed to lead the life of my dreams doing something I love. My journey as a DJ has taken me from the bedroom to pirate radio to long-running peak time shows on BBC Radio 1. DJing has also taken me around the world to many of the best clubs, events, festivals and parties, as well as into the music charts and onto international TV as a producer and musician.

I am so grateful to have made so many wonderful friends on these trips worldwide; friends from all walks of life, including many leaders within their respective fields of endeavour. There aren't many DJs that I have not played alongside at some point, and many of my best friends are amazing DJs themselves.

For over twenty years I've been able to remain at the top of my game, rubbing shoulders with many of the world's most inspiring, influential and successful individuals from all walks of life. In this book I am going to share with you everything that I've learned and experienced through this fantastic journey.

On the musical side of things I'll explain all the essentials: from the very basics of collecting music and buying equipment, through all the technicalities of how to DJ, how to promote events and how to embrace online marketing. I will equip you with everything you need to know about how to make it to the top.

As an entrepreneur I will share with you what I have learned about successful people and how to be the best you can be and ensure your best possible chance of success, no matter what area of your life you want to improve.

Having achieved so many of my life's goals (many beyond what I previously believed possible), I now feel a burning desire to pass on my knowledge and experience to you. I want you to be a success and I believe that everyone can create the life of their dreams.

I'm going to share with you the secrets and tools that every successful person uses, irrespective of background or walk of life. Over the course of this book I will give you the tried and tested means for lasting happiness and success, and I will share with you everything that you need to get to the top of your chosen path.

Knowledge alone is not power. APPLIED knowledge is power. Use the pieces of this book that are most relevant to your life and apply them. My personal experience of listening to and reading things is that I always get far more the second and third times around; and often very different things. So I urge you to revisit the material in this book at various times and to take on the parts that jump out for you at that specific time in your life. You don't have to be great to get started, but you do have to get started to be great. By taking the time to learn more about how to advance yourself you are already way ahead in your journey to greatness.

I have had an immense amount of enjoyment putting this resource together for you, and my aim is for at least one piece of my shared insight to help you lead a happier life. If I achieve that, then I have succeeded in my goal.

To see this book now in published form is a dream come true, as it was only a couple of years ago that I was sitting with my partners Ben and Jerry, learning about the potential of internet business at a weekend seminar. We had an inspired idea and concept, applied what we were learning step by step, and held the intention and vision to deliver immense value. Through trial and error an e-book was created, and from there it was picked up by Aurum Press to now offer it as a physical publication in an improved and updated edition around the world.

Thank you for your interest and for investing in yourself. I am confident you will gain some powerful tips within these pages. Please do email me with your success stories, recommendations and insights after applying anything you have learned here and also please let me know how I can improve the book. I'd love to hear from you at http://bit.ly/DannyRamplingBookFeedback.

To your happiness and success.

Danny Rampling
London, 2010

Everything
You Need to Know
About DJing and Success

Section 1:
Becoming a Successful DJ

1 Buying Music and Starting a Collection

To be a true DJ, you need to have a real passion for music and the way it sounds, both in isolation and in a sequence. Many great DJs were cutting and editing DIY tapes well before they ever purchased a set of turntables, just because they were fascinated with the idea of continuous back-to-back music. You are joining a worldwide community of people who spent their school days hanging out in record shops, tuning in to crackly pirate radio stations late into the night, passing around hot mix tapes and desperately searching through piles of records to find the elusive gem at the top of a cherished 'wants' list.

There is an excitement and a hunger for music that must accompany DJing. If you don't have it, then you will not develop that all-important reckless approach to bank balances that a record collection encourages!

For the modern DJ, you have three main options (depending on your equipment choice): vinyl, CD and downloaded MP3/WAV files. It is unhelpful to get caught up in the 'format war', as music is music however you choose to buy it. Seen in an unbiased light, there are pros and cons to all three formats:

Vinyl

> The vinyl format reproduces true analogue sound.

> A well-pressed 12" single sounds phenomenal, particularly in warm lower and lo-mid frequencies.

> Mixing vinyl is hands on and visual.

> Mixing vinyl arguably requires a higher level of skill than using precision CD turntables.

> Vinyl can be ordered online.

> Visiting record shops means you can talk to DJs and staff who can recommend music to you.

> In a record shop you will be able to listen to a whole record before you buy it.

> The physical size, packaging and artwork of vinyl have their own appeal.

> There is no substitute for taking a record out of its sleeve, placing it on the platter and putting the needle on whilst you cue up the groove.

> Waking up in the morning to huge racks of vinyl is enough to put a smile on your face.

BUT . . .

> Vinyl manufacture is an expensive and highly skilled process, making the cost of a record high.

> Much of the music released in the last decade has never been made available on vinyl.

> Constant use of vinyl deteriorates its quality.

> Rarer records can be irreplaceable.

> Vinyl is very heavy to carry around and can be lost, stolen or damaged in transit.

> Airline excess baggage fees are astronomical.

> A box of vinyl screams 'DJ' to customs officials and you may well be put on a return flight if you have no work permit.

> You cannot press a single record of a hot new track without cutting a dub plate, which is expensive and involves specialist equipment. Reggae, Dub and Drum & Bass DJs place an emphasis on cutting dub plates, because of the sound quality, ritual and tradition.

> Vinyl production can be damaging to the environment.

CD

> CDs have a clean, razor-sharp sound and cope with high frequencies better than vinyl.

> CDs do eventually burn through but they don't deteriorate as fast as vinyl unless you are neglectful of them.

> You can store 200 CDs for every 50 records, if not more.

> You can burn extra copies easily and extract CD audio tracks to rearrange or compile custom made set lists.

> Pre-bought CDs result in a visual and tangible collection.

> Often CD booklets give huge amounts of information on the musicians and the production.

> Much lighter than vinyl, two cases of CDs will give you 1,000+ tunes, whilst 200 records will give you backache!

BUT . . .

> Digital sound can sometimes sound a little too processed, too precise.

> Despite some excellent and innovative CD player designs, CDs don't feel the same to play as records.

> Even CDs are viewed by some tech-heads as out of date, as people move into digital downloading.

> It is harder to find the initial cue-point, as you have to skip through the track to locate it.

> DJs are often less careful with their CDs than with their vinyl; many more CDs than records are left or broken at gigs.

> Finding your next CD in a hurry can be difficult if you are sifting through a case of hand-scribbled CDs.

Downloading Music

> Downloading music is the modern way of buying tracks and takes up little space.

> Digital files are cheap and you don't have to buy mixes or tracks that you don't like.

> If you lose or damage a CD, it can be replaced immediately from your computer's library.

> You can also upload sections of your collection to a portable MP3 player without the hassle of manually recording from a record.

> It is convenient to download music from websites such as Traxsource and Beatport.

> You can sort out thousands of digital tracks at the click of a button, rather than pulling out piles of 12"s all over your floor for several hours.

BUT . . .

> MP3s are compressed to save space and some of the frequencies are cropped, resulting in a poorer quality of sound.

> Laptop DJing is less physical and less visual than with vinyl.

> Computers can be fickle things, so you will regularly need to back up your library onto a removable hard drive.

> If you DJ from a laptop, have some physical CDs or records at the ready in case the computer crashes.

> Digital files have no physical product; you will need to provide any CDs and labelling yourself.

I have included a large list of the best record shops, as well as websites for downloading music within the bonus resources section at the end of this book.

Buying Music

It is the sound above all that really makes a DJ: it is about 75% music and 25% mixing skills. Turntable trickery is awesome to watch and you should perfect as many skills as you can, but the music you play is the most important thing.

Music produces a strong emotional response from people, and that response starts with you. If a track doesn't grab your attention, the golden rule is 'don't buy it, and don't play it'. A good DJ shares the same emotional journey as his/her crowd, and should be just as excited about a tune dropping as the rest of the room. There is an energy created between DJ and crowd; a DJ who is enjoying themselves is likely to pick up passengers for the ride. With this in mind, you should become very critical when buying music. Think carefully about whether the track you are checking out has the X factor. Don't ever buy a tune because it is 'alright', only buy a tune that you can't bear to be parted from: one that has you saying 'you're coming home with me!'

Behind every good DJ there's usually a really good record shop. These are the places that have historically been responsible for giving life to huge selections of music that wouldn't have otherwise been picked up by the commercial chain stores. The independent shops are where the real enthusiasts work, the ones who will stock a track which hasn't been on any playlist, hasn't got any obvious commercial potential, and may only sell a few units. Why? Simply because they believe in it, think it's great and want to share it with people.

These are often people who are so passionate about their music that they sacrifice much better paid jobs and careers simply to be engrossed in doing what they love. Now that deserves respect! In recent years it is a real shame that the majority of specialist record shops have closed. The advent of megastores, downloading, CD and digital DJing and file sharing has accelerated the demise of some of the best underground 'institutions' around the world. Good record stores have helped spawn whole music scenes and have traditionally provided a back-bone to musical movements around the world.

Whilst it's true that a small percentage of independent stores can be rather pretentious and snooty about their specialised knowledge, the majority are delighted to share their expertise and passion. Indeed some go beyond the call of duty: citing just one example, Play Music in Leeds was renowned for providing chairs, customer membership (and discounts), drinks and (if you went at the right time) a full-on costumed party club atmosphere with 'name' guest DJs playing surprise sets – obviously in addition to the great music which was the focus first and foremost.

Ultimately the purpose of independent stores has been to 'spread the love' – just as a DJ wants to share his collection. Discovering a shop that supplies music that really does it for you, and then getting to know a member of staff who understands what you're into is one of the best things you can do. More importantly, with their musical knowledge, they will help shape your musical taste and present you with music that you wouldn't otherwise have discovered. One step down this relationship line is where they will start to order music with you specifically in mind, even if it means just getting a single copy because they think it will be up your street. In some instances, if you're a regular and dependable they will even start 'bagging' records for you.

Many high-profile DJs will take a trusted record shop worker's word on a track, even if they don't like it at first. And more often than not a good shop worker will be right: the track may just need some listens to 'grow'.

Everything You Need to Know about DJing and Success

In the resource section I've compiled a list of some of the best stores in the UK and around the world. Even if it means paying a little extra, do your best to help keep them in business – the world without independent record shops will be a worse place.

If you are buying online, be aware that you have an even more daunting shopping experience ahead of you. Scrolling through lists of artists and labels you are unfamiliar with, wondering if you are passing over some hidden gems and trying to make similar judgments on the basis of 30-second clips can be harder still.

File Sharing

It's important to mention the impact and potential ramifications of file sharing. With the advanced technology, software and resources available today, many people increasingly regard it as natural and normal to file share for free. Now, there is the obvious damage file sharing causes to the longevity of the scene by eroding the sustainable income for artists, producers, labels, distributors and those involved in the music business but your first concern should be copyright law. Please note that whilst the following information does not constitute legal advice (you should always consult the actual laws of your territory), it's worth considering these points.

Copyright: What You Need to Know

Copyright and related rights apply in virtually every country, so make sure you know the copyright laws. The following is a brief guide.

> All file sharing is illegal, unless it's done on a licensed service or with the permission of all the rights owners, or unless all the rights have expired. Whether to permit sharing on a peer-to-peer (p2p) network is a matter of choice for the rights owners involved.

> All recordings of music are protected by copyright from the moment of their creation. Rights last for a period of at least 50 years from the making of the recording. Authors (i.e. the songwriters) and music publishers typically retain copyright for 70 years after the death of the author.

> If you want to download a few songs to see if it's worth buying an album, bear in mind that some online music stores (such as Beatport) let you listen to clips from particular songs, or sample a limited download of tracks from their service, as a 'taster' of the music. Some sites (such as Spotify) enable you to listen to all the music you want from

Top Tip:
Listening to other DJs play can be really helpful. Hearing music in the context of a venue gives you a better idea of its sound and its effect on a room full of people. As a DJ, you are never 'off-duty'; always keep one ear open for the music that is going on around you.

7

their catalogues by paying a monthly subscription. Some artist sites promote specific songs by offering free downloads. However, there is no general right or exception that lets you copy before you buy without permission.

> It doesn't make a difference how much you're uploading, technically you're breaking the law. However, the impact on the legitimate music community of what you are doing is more serious the more music you are illegally uploading, and so the penalties are higher.

> Owners of copyright and related rights regularly take action to remove illegal material from the internet and to seek civil or criminal sanctions against copyright infringers. Hundreds of millions of music files are removed from the internet each year through co-operation between internet service providers and the music industry. Civil and criminal lawsuits have been taken against internet infringers in many countries and there have been a few landmark cases where the law has come down exceptionally hard on the file sharers to set an example and make a point. The music industry has announced its intention to step up action against copyright theft of this type, and there is talk of American immigration (who often set the precedent for other Western nations' procedures) stepping up the taking of 'memory swipes' from people's laptops to check them for illegally shared files.

> Another popular misconception is that it's alright to transmit and copy material over the internet if it is marked with 'delete within 24 hours', 'for evaluation purposes', or a similar type of disclaimer. These excuses are not recognised by copyright law.

My personal belief is that music is now cheaper and more accessible than it has ever been and there's no excuse for file sharing. For those who remember spending the equivalent of £7.99 on an import (usually for one track), today's age, where you can easily find a download of most tunes for under £1, seems to make music ridiculously affordable.

Styles of Music

As a DJ, you are likely to be into some styles of music more than others. Nevertheless, it is arguable that some of the best collections are the most eclectic ones. The more open-minded you are, the more all-encompassing your sets will become. As you begin to play out more, you will soon come to realise that different venues, set times, crowds and localities call for many different musical moods. It's likely that a room full of people at a house party are not going to want to hear three hours of dark and tearing Drum & Bass,

Everything You Need to Know about DJing and Success

but dropping a wide-ranging set of Latin party cuts, old club anthems, up-tempo Funk and Boogie will soon have the crowd jumping. It all comes down to knowing the audience.

Legendary Loft DJ David Mancuso went as far as to learn individual clubbers' favourite tracks to keep them on the dancefloor all night long.

History and Heritage

As a young DJ, you should be aware of the vast history that has gone before you. One of the most important pieces of advice that you should take on board is to read extensively on the heritage of dance music (now approaching its 5th decade), which if you genuinely love the music will be fascinating. Starting with last week's releases will give you no understanding of why Drum & Bass (D&B) became as rapid and as hard as it is, or why seasoned DJs still idolise the early club pioneers such as Dave Mancuso, Larry Levan and Ron Hardy.

The golden rule is: 'You need to know where you are coming from in order to know where you are going to.' This is basically the same in all walks of life: you need to know your roots, which then enables you to appreciate, understand and develop who you are. Research the music that you love and trace it back to its roots. Along the way, you will encounter seminal records that had a huge impact on that certain scene. Track these down and buy them. New records are fresh and exciting, but old records unlock memories and emotions for people. If you are looking for an emotional response from a crowd, you need some classic material as well as the upfront tunes.

Always remember that if you embrace a wide scope of music and increase your knowledge, you will improve your DJing skills just as surely as practising the techniques themselves.

Music Genres and Sub-Genres: An Overview

Musicians have a nasty habit of pigeon-holing music into a particular sub-genre, so they can put a recognisable label on it. Most confusingly, these titles are constantly being changed, revised and updated. It's widely known that the media like to help create and hype new genres, which then enables them to market, discuss and reinvent demand. As a DJ, part of your job is to keep up to date with these terminologies, but don't allow them to define you or your music. They should be used to help, not to limit. Good music is what matters most, not the category it falls into.

The list below is designed as a starting point, taking care of some of the principal genres of dance music and what to expect from each one. For reasons of space it is non-exhaustive and new styles and hybrids are constantly being developed. The tempo ranges given in bpm (beats per minute) are an approximate guide. You should go away and do your own research on the history of any style that particularly appeals to you, and learn about the DJs who made that genre what it is today.

House *(Tempo range: 115–130 bpm)*

Pioneered principally by Frankie Knuckles in the latter days of the Disco era (Chicago Warehouse Club), House music is the spinal column of the dance music scene. House is categorised by its '4-to-the-floor' kick drum, which it took directly from Disco, and its continuous looping of instrumental, harmonic, melodic or vocal phrases. Broken Beat refers to House music that deviates from the standard 4-to-the-floor kick drum. Often it sounds similar to up-tempo Jazz Funk, but can also be closely related to Breakbeat. The Bugz In The Attic crew and the Co-Op night were at the helm of this scene.

Deep House employs smooth special pads and strings with atmospheric sounds.

Electro House is somewhat nostalgic for the 1980s synth-based Electric Dance sound. Tiga and David Guetta have been leading protagonists of this sound.

Funky House tends to use effected loops of Disco or Funk cuts. There are often dramatic filters and build-ups. Many of the Hed Kandi and Full Intention club nights and productions are representative of this genre.

Jazz/Latin House is heavily influenced by Latin American Samba rhythms. It often features extended improvised solos from pianos, sax, trumpets and other instruments typical of the Jazz idiom. A lot of emphasis is placed on percussion such as congas, bongos and clave. DJs Louie Vega and Patrick Forge, and Elements of Life and Bah Samba are good reference points.

Minimal House is sparse in its use of percussion, but concentrates on a clean, uncomplicated drum sound. Usually the grooves are left as undecorated as possible, creating plenty of space for subtle sound textures. Richie Hawtin and Ricardo Villalobos, alongside nights such as Circo Loco and Deep, Down & Dirty best represent this style.

Soulful House usually utilises a full vocal structure (similar to US Garage) and sounds like R&B/Soul with a House beat. Dr Bob Jones, Tony Humphries and Masters at Work are a handful of the pioneers of this scene, which culminates in the annual Miami Winter Music Conference and Southport Weekender events and the respected Soul Heaven parties.

Tech House begins to bridge the gap between House and the more persistent locked grooves of Techno. Tech House is often a slightly faster, harder-edged breed of House music. Mr C, Terry Francis, Eddie Richards and Terry Lee Brown Junior helped shape this sound through their residencies, clubs and nights including Fabric and The End.

Garage *(Tempo range: 120–135 bpm)*

Named after the NYC Paradise Garage Club and its infamous helmsman Larry Levan; Garage differs from House mainly in its use of full vocal structure. Both Larry Levan and Frankie Knuckles had been DJs in the Disco era and were close friends from the Continental Baths. The UK Garage scene that rose to fame in the mid-90s moved further and further away from the American model.

Classic US Garage and Soulful House are virtually identical. Full sung vocals, often based on Gospel worship or Soul, are based around typically House grooves. London DJ brothers Bobbi & Steve's Garage City club night was pivotal to this movement, as was Paul 'Trouble' Anderson's The Loft. Both had long-running radio shows on KISS FM, helping to spread this sound.

UK Garage started in the mid-90s with British DJs such as MJ Cole, Matt Jam Lamont and Karl 'Tuff Enuff' Brown speeding up funkier House and Garage records. The term Speed Garage was used to begin with, but as the UK began to tamper with the original US sound more and more, other more appropriate tags were introduced.

2-Step dispenses with the 4-to-the-floor kick drum and replaces it with crisp linear grooves, often using sharp kick and snare sounds. The Dreem Team (DJ Spoony, Timmi Magic and Mikee B) were influential in sharing the sound, as were the hugely popular 'Twice As Nice' events. As the millennium approached, the full vocal element gave way to harder Drum & Bass influences such as Taurus (Reece) basslines and Hip-Hop-esque rhyming.

Drum & Bass *(Tempo range: 160–185 bpm)*

The Drum & Bass scene grew out of the London Pirate Radio sound in the early to mid-90s. Fusing Techno and Breakbeat Hardcore with the Ragga and Hip-Hop that the London community was most into, Drum & Bass emerged as a rapid, high-energy and cutting-edge sound.

Jungle was first used in the early 90s to describe the more Ragga/Hip-Hop influenced Breakbeat sound of London. It is characterised by low sub-bass, pitched up Funk breaks and samples from the Jamaican dancehalls.

D&B is now used as an all-encompassing term for most music in the genre. Mainstream D&B is generally hard-edged with raucous synth bass textures, deep sub lines (low-end frequency bass sounds picked up on larger sound-systems) and rapid 2-Step breaks. Sometimes pitched-up Funk breaks are still used under the main kick and snare, or even as the main beat. Terms such as 'Hard Step', 'Tech Step' and 'Neuro Funk' are sometimes applied to harder D&B. Some of the key players include Grooverider, Goldie, Markus Intalex, Jumpin' Jack Frost and Marky XRS.

Liquid is the newer title for what in the mid-90s was known as 'Intelligent D&B', pioneered by the likes of LTJ Bukem and Fabio. Still running at the same tempo, Liquid concentrates its sound on more overtly musical elements such as Jazz, Latin or vocals. Sometimes Liquid D&B can use similar warm, spatial sounds to Deep House.

Techno *(Tempo range: 125–160 bpm)*

Techno appeared in the late 80s as a more intellectually produced and more electronic version of House. This sound was originally pioneered by Detroit producers Derrick May, Jesse Saunders, Kevin Saunderson and Juan Atkins. Although based on similar 4-to-the-floor kick drum, Techno concerns itself far more with synthesis and electronic grooves that often build gradually over an entire track. Detroit Techno is characterised by its relentless electronic groove. Originally it was pretty much harder than Electronic House, but it has gradually developed to become an entity in its own right.

Acid House is centred on the synthesis of bass loops using a Roland 303, which was created (apparently by accident) by Chicago's DJ Pierre. The unmistakable twittering of extreme filters and rez sweeps gives 'Acid' its distinctive sound.

European Hard House and Gabba. Since the days of Kraftwerk's electronica, European countries, especially Germany, Belgium and Holland have been responsible for some of the harder and more extreme use of synthetic sound. In the early 90s, the UK Hardcore sound and consequently D&B was heavily influenced by the tearing synths and high-energy tempo of European Techno. Gabba in particular pushes this to the limits, pushing the relentless kick drum to speeds of 200 bpm and beyond.

Old Skool/Hardcore *(Tempo Range: 115–145 bpm)*

At the end of the 80s, the UK was greatly influenced by dance music that was coming over from the US. Acid House parties and warehouse raves that popularised House and Techno soon fused with the Big Beat Soul sound, Reggae and Hip-Hop to create Hardcore. This is the music that was directly responsible for Jungle and D&B and despite some sketchy production, and even some banal elements, it is a hugely important part of UK music history.

Acid/Warehouse music was a hybrid of House, Acid House and Techno that was played in British raves from 1987–90.

Bleep & Bass originated in the north of England (Sheffield and Leeds) combining the two extremes of subsonic bass and high bleep-tones. These were usually backed by Techno-esque beats. Pioneered by artists such as Shut Up & Dance, Rebel MC and DJ Hype, the Techno and Acid House elements were accompanied by pitched-up Hip-Hop and Funk breaks.

Darkcore was a reaction against the 'Happy' sound of 1992–3 rave music. Using samples from horror films and menacing synths, this of all the categories of Old Skool led music down the straight path towards Jungle and D&B. Throughout 1992–3 the pace of this music accelerated rapidly from about 130 bpm to 160 bpm. Doc Scott, Goldie and 4 Hero were a few of the figureheads through this phase, and Metalheadz was a legendary club night.

European Rave in 1991–2 gave the British scene a fresh injection of more Techno-based elements. Led by the R&S and XL imprints, the synths and harsh lead sounds were a pre-taste of the hard 'hoover' bass sounds of D&B.

Happy Hardcore, championed by the likes of Vibes and Dougal and their Bonkers events, used high-pitched vocals and samples from children's programmes as a light contrast to the darker pounding Techno backing. It was often ridiculed by ravers who were into the darker side of the scene.

Breaks *(Tempo range: 120–135 bpm)*

The concept of mixing back-to-back breaks stems from the early Block parties of the Brooklyn Hip-Hop scene, but modern Breakbeat music was primarily developed by The Prodigy, The Chemical Brothers, Hybrid and Bentley Rhythm Ace in the mid-90s, and DJs including Adam Freeland and Tayo.

Hip-Hop *(Tempo Range: 70–115 bpm)*

From the Block parties of Brooklyn, DJs such as Kool Herc and Africa Bambaataa a developed a style of mixing back-to-back Funk breaks that came to be known as Hip-Hop. Rapping (rhythmic lyric poetry), particularly describing the 'Ghetto philosophy', soon became a major feature of this genre. Turntablism and scratching pyrotechnics are also characteristic of this style of music.

Old Skool Hip-Hop is now a classic genre, usually incorporating immediately recognisable Funk breaks and samples to accompany the rapping of early MCs.

Gangster Rap comes from two major centres of origin. The East Coast (NYC and New Jersey) and West Coast (LA, California) styles have differed over the years and there has been fierce competition between the two. Gangster Rap's lyric content is often explicitly violent, which has resulted in some fairly bad press over the years.

Instrumental Hip-Hop is often a little more laid back, with Jazz-based grooves and little or no lyric content.

Funk and Rare Groove *(Tempo Range: 70–130 bpm)*

Original Funk from the late 60s and the 70s has been the basis for much of the dance music sound. The breaks from this genre have been sampled extensively by Hip-Hop, R&B, Drum & Bass and House producers over the last three decades. Usually categorised by a driving rhythmic backdrop of drums, bass, keys, guitar and horns. Funk is undoubtedly real party music. Norman Jay's Good Times events and DJ sets have incorporated and championed the best of these sounds, as have DJ Jazzie B and his Soul II Soul parties.

Dancefloor Funk is usually synonymous with James Brown. Sharp, punchy horn lines typical of the LA/Bay Area sound accompany high-energy rhythmic grooves that will have the party jumping.

Rare Library Cuts and **Sound Scores**, often including rare, little-known tracks from vintage films, can be hard to find. Nonetheless, there are some serious collector's items to be found in this genre; often recognisable as the basis for more recent dance records. This site is amazing for helping to identify originals alongside their contemporary or sampled versions: www.inlounge.de/e107_plugins/house_originals/guide.php

Soul and R&B *(Tempo Range: 50–110 bpm)*

Soul concentrates mainly on vocals that are either based on Gospel or subjects such as love, peace, equality or racism. The accompanying instrumental sound usually relies on a strongly rhythmic down tempo groove, rich in both harmony and melody.

Classic Soul and **Motown** tracks come from the early era of Soul (1960s and 70s). From the organ and fat horn-driven Memphis style, to the lush orchestral Philly sound, or the strong rhythmic drive of Detroit Motown, many of the records from this period have become world famous hits and are perfect for beginning or ending the night.

Urban R&B/Hip-Hop Soul gradually developed throughout the 1990s, firstly through Teddy Riley's New Jack Swing sound. Guest Hip-Hop artists were initially brought in to lend a more streetwise element to Soul tracks, but gradually became a permanent feature of this hybrid style.

Neo-Soul was a term first coined by Kedar Massenburg to describe a retrospective Soul sound that coupled the vintage instrumentation of Rhodes/Hammond organ with fresh cutting-edge grooves. Often Neo-Soul has a more detailed and musical approach to the production, sometimes elements of Jazz and Funk are prevalent and occasionally spoken word/poetry is featured. Trevor Nelson, Steve 'Smooth' Sutherland and the BBC 1Xtra network have been pivotal in supporting these soulful forms of music.

This list is limited in its scope, if you want to explore different variations of music in more depth, I recommend you explore the extensive links provided at the back of this book and visit: http://bit.ly/RamplingMusicReadRecommendations

2 Buying Equipment

Getting Started

Getting started as a DJ is the beginning of a journey: a lifelong odyssey that should include an unhealthy obsession with music, equipment and technology. For those of us who have been DJing for some time now, we may well look back with fond nostalgia on the first pair of turntables we owned or the first 12" vinyl that marked the start of our now vast collections.

But in the modern age, with the introduction of so many new technologies for the aspiring DJ, it can be extremely confusing. Where to start?

First and foremost, there is some basic equipment that must be purchased: a pair of turntables/CD decks, a mixer (or a laptop with the appropriate software) and close-backed headphones. You will also need an amplifier or hi-fi unit with an aux/phono input. For the digital DJ there are some other possibilities: either a laptop with mixing software such as Traktor, Serato, or digitally coded vinyls for a program like Vinyl Scratch (the latter requires traditional vinyl turntables and a mixer).

The Budget

When it comes to purchasing the tools for DJing, the budget is your principal concern, but as in all things you really do get what you pay for. If you are serious about becoming a DJ, it is essential to buy good equipment that will last and to choose wisely when it comes to specific models. If you buy really cheap gear, you will simply find yourself having to replace or upgrade; either because the equipment becomes faulty or simply because it does not have the necessary features for you to progress. This is especially important as there are certain brands that have become industry standard and will be found in most clubs and bars. There is nothing worse than adding unfamiliarity of equipment to the performance nerves of playing out for the first time in public.

Everything You Need to Know about DJing and Success

You should allocate around £1,000 for a decent DJ set-up. It seems like a lot of money, but these are your musical instruments. Like any other serious musician, you cannot cut corners on the money side of things if you expect quality and durability.

If money is an issue, it is worth considering finance deals so that the cost is spread over a period of time. Also bear in mind that as soon as you decide to start DJing, everything that you buy, from the turntables and mixer to the records and blank CDs for doing mixes, count as 'expenses' that you can claim off your tax. Of course, you need to look into the specific tax and allowances laws in the country or region in which you live, and you also need to keep all your receipts in a folder for easy accounting.

Vinyl Turntables

Technics SL1210

Vestax PDX2000

Stanton T120c

Figure 2.1

As far as vinyl turntables are concerned there can really be no alternative to the Technics 1200/1210 family. The MKII, MKIII and MK5(G) models only differ in various minor cosmetic details, but the feel of the quartz direct drive platter remains the same. These turntables have been the cornerstone of DJs worldwide for over two decades, and despite some very attractive bids for competition particularly from the Vestax and Stanton models, they are likely to remain so. The Vestax especially do have some really superb features such as control of the break speed and reverse platter, but are rarely to be found in venues.

Although considerably cheaper, belt-drive turntables are not a viable option if you are serious about DJing. The response for cueing and start-up speeds are far too slow, and the pitch control is unreliable.

17

Cartridges, Needles and Slipmats

The necessary head shells, cartridges and needles are usually provided with the turntables at the time of purchase (it is prudent to check on this), but should you wish to switch to using more high-end cartridges, these will be an additional extra. Cartridges come in numerous different designs: usually based on either a head shell-mounted or a concord design. You may want to try several out until you settle on a design that you like and feel comfortable with. One popular myth is that the choice of cartridge is a make-or-break when it comes to scratching. Technique and the actual choice of record (deep and well-cut vinyl) accounts for 90% of scratching success, coupled with correct setting up of the tone-arm and anti-skate. Unless you are unlucky enough to get a dud needle (it happens occasionally), most of the cartridges below sound superb and stay in the groove even during fast scratches. Many retailers also provide felt slipmats for turntables, but if they don't, they are an inexpensive addition.

Figure 2.2

| Stanton 500.V3 | Shure M44-7 | Shure Whitelabel | Ortofon Q.Bert Concorde |

CD Turntables

CD turntables are now a truly viable alternative to playing from vinyl. When it comes to CD turntables, the Pioneer models (the CDJ800 and CDJ1000) have become the industry standard. The Technics DZ1200 is also superb and quite possibly closer to the feel and look of a vinyl turntable, but due to its comparatively late arrival on the market it is not to be found in most clubs or bars. Denon and Numark also make some excellent units; in fact these were some of the first on the market, and often older-style twin CD consoles can be found in bars. Numark's X2 model enables you to play all three mediums; vinyl, CD and MP3, but it does not come cheap for a pair.

Figure 2.3

Denon DN-S3700   Pioneer CDJ-2000   Technics SL-DZ1200

Professional DJ CD players work in a similar way to traditional vinyl turntables with a start/stop button and pitch adjust to change the speed of the track. Some have a platter that rotates like that of a real turntable whereas others, such as the Pioneer CDJ1000, have a pad which senses movement. Many players have additional features such as looping, BPM counters, waveform display and digital effects. It is also possible to store cue points on an SD memory card. Some CD players feature USB memory stick ports so that tracks can be played from these devices and others will play MP3 CDs, which allow more tracks to be stored on a single piece of media.

Mixers

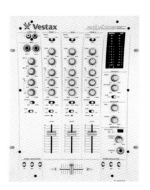

Figure 2.4

Pioneer DJM-600   Vestax PCV-275   Allen & Heath Xone:92

Mixers are less easy to make a decision over. There are hundreds of models on the market at any one time, ranging vastly in their respective prices, quality of build, simplicity and features. Again there are certain mixers that have become industry standard, such as the Pioneer DJM series and the more expensive Allen & Heath XZone series, so it is well worth being familiar with the features of these, even if you don't choose to buy either make. Other brands that are recommended are Vestax, Mackie, Numark, Ecler and Technics.

The minimum features that a mixer should include are as follows:

> Two or more channels capable of taking inputs from either vinyl turntables (phono) or CD (line).

> A crossfader with variable fade shapes from fast cut to gradual blend.

> Independent volume controls and three or more band EQ for each channel (bass, mid and treble).

Any extra features such as filters and on-board effects are a bonus. It is important to bear in mind that if you want easy access between a pair of vinyl turntables and CD decks, or if you wish to add an extra turntable, then two channels will not be sufficient. Also it is essential (particularly for scratching and fast cutting) that the crossfader is well built and smooth to the feel; many mixers have the option of replaceable faders or digital faders to prevent 'bleeding' of channels or static interference.

Software Packages

There are numerous programs available for computer DJing. Crucially, you need to choose a fast and reliable laptop that will be able to run software without any problems (if the laptop crashes, the set will be offline for several minutes which will completely destroy the energy of the dancefloor). Some programs such as Serato or Vinyl Scratch use dummy records to manipulate MP3 files and require a set of vinyl turntables. Others like Traktor will mix music files within the program. We will return to these software packages in a later chapter on digital DJing formats.

Headphones

When purchasing headphones, there are two main considerations. Firstly, they must be close-backed, which means that the shell is enclosed so that the sound is contained and does not allow any external sound to interfere with the sound that is being referenced. Secondly, comfortable padding on the headband and the ear-cups is essential. Pioneer, Technics, Sony and Sennheiser all make some superb models, but there are plenty of other brands to choose from. Have a look at the wealth of headphones available and choose the one that best suits you.

Leads and Cables

There are 3 main types of connecting leads that a DJ should be familiar with: phono (RCA), Jack (3.5mm and 6.3mm) and XLR (3-Pin DIN). Each component, i.e. each turntable or mixer, will need one phono-to-phono cable. Usually these are provided or even built into the piece of equipment. You will need to check the main output of the mixer, however, as there may also be Jack or XLR ports. Newer and more advanced mixers may also have digital/coaxial, optical ins and outs, or USB and firewire ports.

Figure 2.5

Phono (RCA) leads   6.3 mm Jack Cables   XLR (3-pin DIN) cables

3.5–6.3mm Jack converter plug   3.5mm Jack cable

Here is a list of components you can expect to use these leads with:

> **Phono:** Vinyl and CD turntables, mixer outputs, amplifiers.

> **6.3mm Jack:** Mixer main and booth outputs (depending), most headphones, some microphone inputs, instruments such as guitars, keyboards and also rack modules, including FX units.

> **3.5mm Jack:** Personal MP3/minidisk/CD players, some headphones (usually these come with converters to 6.3mm).

> **XLR:** Most microphones, mixer main and booth outputs (depending), outboard rack units, such as compressors, finalisers, etc.

Buying DJ equipment is the same as buying any other electrical goods. The most important thing is to find a retail outlet that offers good value, helpful advice and customer support that is reliable and trustworthy. Always do some careful research to see what deals are being offered. Most retailers have starter packages that include vinyl or CD turntables, mixer, cartridges, slip mats, headphones and leads. These can often be really good bargains, but check the RRPs of each product and do the maths so you don't get hood-winked.

Many people like to buy on the internet. The main piece of advice here is to be careful. It is certainly wise to go into a DJ store and try various models even if you actually end up buying online.

Always make sure that any purchases have manufacturers' warranties and full instruction manuals. It is also well worth taking time to register products on the manufacturers' websites as the customer care and advice they usually offer can prove very helpful.

Second-hand Purchases

Second-hand products are not usually a sensible option, unless you are sure of their history of use. Having said this, there is a wealth of bargains to be had on websites such as eBay. You can often buy second-hand set-ups for less than half price, although you may have to invest time researching the market. When buying second-hand, always contact the seller if you are not 100% sure of the item and its condition. Check the seller's feedback to ensure they have a good track record. Local pick up is also advisable as equipment is less likely to be damaged in transit and you can check that the item is as it was described in the listing. There are a lot of chancers out there, so remember: if it sounds too good to be true, it probably is.

The Booth: Speakers and Amplifiers

Your choice of speakers and amplifier is very important. There are many different solutions; some that are relatively cheap, and others that are considerably more expensive. You should bear in mind that you are buying components that will play a vital role in your ability to reference the sound of the music that you play (and of course mix), so you need to ensure that they are of a decent enough calibre.

The most important thing is to invest in a system that will accurately reproduce the sound from your turntables (or laptop). This means that a well-produced and mixed track should sound good, but a poor one should not. A system that over-compensates certain frequencies, or 'lies' to you is only a disadvantage.

Amplifiers

The amplifier is the piece of equipment that drives the speakers (unless they are active). When you're looking at the specifications on an amp the main thing you need to look at is frequency response (at least 20Hz–20kHz) and the maximum wattage at a 4 ohm load, and at an 8 ohm load. The ohm rating refers to the measurement of the electrical resistance of a given speaker. Anything above 96dB will suffice.

There are three main sorts of amplifier:

> Integrated amplifiers are the most common, as they are an all-inclusive unit.

> Pre-amplifiers boost the incoming audio signal but will not in themselves power the speakers.

> Power amplifiers are designed purely to power speakers, especially ones with a higher wattage.

Figure 2.6

Cambridge Audio Azur 650A

Marantz PM8003

Nad C325BEE

There are quite a few great amplifiers to choose from. The most sensible choice will be a decent integrated amplifier, such as one of the models shown above. It is possible to spend anything from £100 to well in excess of £1,000 on an amplifier depending on the level of sound accuracy you are looking for. Other recommended manufacturers include Denon, Technics, Pioneer, Linn, Arcam, Quad and Cambridge Audio. Whichever style or brand of amplifier you decide to buy, always make sure that you have the tone settings (bass and treble boosts) flat, or you will over colour the speakers. This will give you a misleading representation of the sound.

Speakers and Monitors

When choosing speakers, you have two options: hi-fi speakers and studio monitors.

Hi-fi Speakers

Occasionally, real audiophiles will invest in very expensive high-end speakers, but this is not the norm. The most important thing is to ensure that the speakers are compatible with the amplifier in terms of power handling or watts per channel. You should always use the RMS figure. RMS stands for 'root mean square', and in electrical amplifier terms refers to the amplifier's electrical efficiency; in other words, the ratio between the amplifier's mean output power and mean input power. Amplifiers waste much of their input power in heat, so if you use the RMS figure you will know how much power output it will give, not how much heat it will create. A good rule of thumb is never to let the amplifier exceed the power handling of the speakers, this way you won't blow your speakers up.

The drawback of using hi-fi speakers is that they have a tendency to colour the sound to a certain degree. This means that the characteristics and idiosyncrasies of your speakers will affect the sound of everything you record and mix. If you've used speakers that demonstrate extremes, they may well leave the results of all your efforts sounding far from as intended when your music is played back on any other system.

Studio Monitors

When practising and preparing you should try to recreate a similar sound environment to a club (although not as loud). For this reason, there is a strong argument for using studio monitor speakers with a flat response over all listening frequencies, coupled with an extra sub bass speaker that will give that bass heavy club sound (living conditions-dependent!). If you do decide to buy a separate sub, it is always best to get one that is the same make as the monitors, as they will be purpose-designed to work together.

Studio monitors can be either passive (which require an amplifier) or active (which are self-powered). The advantage of studio monitors is that they don't colour the sound in any way: what you hear is what you get. The main disadvantage is that most people don't listen to music on such a system; certainly not in their home environment.

Buying Speakers and Amplifiers

Like your DJ equipment, your system should be decent quality; an investment in your art. You should always be very careful when buying speakers and amplifiers. Always try to cross-reference different brands and models to compare them. It is wise to take both good quality music productions and also a badly mixed track with you to test. If the system hides the imperfections of a poor mix down, do not buy it. You need to use your most valuable possession as a DJ (your ears) to decide what kind of system sounds best for you. The more you fine-tune your ear to the nuances of different productions, speakers and set-ups, the more you will be able to make subtle and creative changes to your music and improve your sets.

Listening Environment

In order to practise and prepare as a DJ, you will need to set up a 'listening environment', most likely in a room in your own home – at least to begin with. One of the most important things to consider when setting up your listening environment is the positioning of your speakers. You need to achieve the best sound possible with the equipment you have, so it is worth spending a little time getting things just right. Your speakers should be at head height ideally, so that the midpoint between the tweeter and woofer is in line with your ears. You should also make sure that the sound is not being reflected before it gets to your ears. For example if your speakers are sitting flat on a table, sound may be reflected before it gets to your ears causing phasing, making certain frequencies sound quieter and others sound louder.

Now it's time to look at where you and your speakers are in relation to one another. Here we are trying to make sure that you get the best stereo image possible and therefore the best representation of your sound. Your speakers should be an equal distance away from your ears and they should be the same distance away from each other so that you and your speakers make an equilateral triangle. An ideal distance for each side of the triangle in a small studio is just over one metre.

Every room has its own sound depending on its shape, materials and furnishings. There are two different types of environment: live and dead. A live environment is one with a lot of reverberation and sound colouration in the room caused by hard surfaces reflecting sound. A dead environment, which is the ideal environment for creating music, is one without reverberation. This can be achieved with an abundance of soft surfaces which absorb sound and therefore stop reflection.

Standing waves are also a problem in rooms. These occur at certain frequencies when a sound wave reflects between parallel surfaces, and the wave doubles up on its self causing the frequency to sound louder in some areas of the room and cancel out in others. The best way to avoid this is to ensure that none of the walls, ceiling or floor is parallel to one another. In many cases this is impracticable so diffusion is used. A diffuse surface is one that is not flat, an example of which is an egg carton or acoustical foam. Placed on the walls and ceiling around the room, diffuse materials can help break up the sound and stop resonant standing waves. A cheap alternative to expensive acoustical foam is wavy packing foam.

The Importance of Sound Quality

Many audio experts argue that despite all of our advances in digital technology, in today's world the 'general' sound quality is lower than it was twenty-five years ago, suggesting we have, in fact, gone backwards.

Early digital audio was dreadful because of the limitations of the technology and the expense of doing it properly. Add to that the narrow bandwidth of the internet and we now have the ubiquitous MP3 and generations of people who have been deprived of truly top-end sound quality.

So during the development of digital we have either forgotten, neglected or very rarely heard high-quality audio. Despite the fact that we now possess the technology to easily transcend twenty-five-year-old analogue technology, we don't. Of all the formats, vinyl is still the most human.

Many people argue that sound is a more important, deeper sense than sight, for the following reasons:

> We are able to perceive ten octaves of sound, contrasting with only one octave for light, so the spectral range of sound is an order of magnitude greater than the spectral range of vision.

> We perceive sound from every direction in three-dimensional space, whereas vision is a relatively narrow forward-facing cone.

> Our ability to resolve and extract useful information from audio is approximately two thousand times greater than it is from light.

> The atmosphere and mood of a space is largely to do with its acoustic properties.

> Audio perception is always 'on', and probably has more to do with our prehistoric survival than any of our other senses. Incidentally, the inability to switch audio off is the reason we can become tired and irritable in an acoustically annoying environment such as a minimalist, hard-surfaced wine bar.

Why High-quality Sound is Important

Think of the difference between muddy and clear water, or between fog and a clear sunny day. With muddy water only the two-dimensional surface is visible, whereas with clear water one is able to see into it and appreciate three-dimensionally the features within the water. Likewise in fog one can only see a short distance as opposed to having full perspective when it's a clear sunny day. These are appropriate metaphors for contrasting high- and low-quality sound. The latter actually drives the listener away from the experience whereas high quality sound draws the listener into the experience, where the precision of information allows the full bloom of musical feeling.

What is High-quality Sound?

Above all it is clean and clear, allowing instruments and individual sounds to have detail and separation, where they are not smeared together. To achieve high-quality sound production I think it comes down to three fundamentals:

1. The calibre of the equipment.

2. How it is being operated.

3. The nature and quality of the original recordings/samples being employed.

MP3 Quality

To put some perspective on the MP3 format, a CD WAV file at 16 bit 44.1 KHz is not enough information for true audio. Bearing in mind that an MP3 is only ten percent of that gives an indication of the 'sound sacrifice' music enthusiasts are (often unwittingly) foregoing in exchange for convenience.

When you listen to an MP3 version of a CD WAV file closely, you can hear bass with missing low-frequency extension and the notes are also shortened so the 'tails' are missing, which altogether makes it sound a lot weaker. You will also find that the high frequencies are fizzy and crunchy, the opposite of translucent and crystalline. The worst thing however, is the loss of space and dimension depriving the listener of involvement, feeling and spiritual motivation.

High-quality stereo audio generates a three-dimensional left, centre and right sound stage. Anyone who has experienced a high-quality audio experience will understand this, and this is why so many 'audio-acute' producers, DJs and venue owners (the latter are unfortunately in a minority) place so much emphasis on the sound set-up. They understand the effect it has on people and appreciate how much the sound adds to an event, enabling the creation of sonic landscapes in the exquisite detail that humans are capable of experiencing.

When one is deeply, emotionally involved with quality stereo sound a space of light, colour and energy opens up within and the listener 'becomes the sound'. It may sound esoteric but it truly is a place where much can be experienced and learned, and this is why you hear many top-level music professionals 'harp on' about sound quality. And why so many people around the world have moments of clarity, insight and magic when 'lost in the music'.

To an untrained ear, MP3s are ok being used with the internet and iPods, but many argue that they really have no business being used in professional situations such as clubs and shows. A comparison can be taken from the analogy of taking a low-resolution internet picture and then enlarging it to the size of a house wall. Up close it would just look like a pixelated mess. The same thing happens with audio.

If you would like to help improve the quality of your MP3s then the team behind the excellent 'Mixed in Key' software (which we cover later on) have created 'Platinum Notes', which uses studio filters to help improve the pitch and volume of your files, enhancing their sound qualities for playing on systems. You can download it at: www.platinumnotes.com.

Protect Your Hearing

You only get one set of ears, and the one thing most of us in the music industry put at greatest risk is this essential sense. Indeed a whole film plot (*It's All Gone Pete Tong*) was based around the parody of a DJ who loses his hearing. Hearing loss from exposure to loud sound affects millions of people, but it is preventable. Most people do not know for how long they can listen to loud noise without risking hearing damage, so at the back of this book I have provided some essential resources for helping you learn how to protect your most valuable asset as a DJ – your hearing.

3 Setting up a DJ Console

Setting up a home console is well worth taking some time over, as it is the DJ's equivalent of a workstation or office. The surface needs to be flat and sturdy, particularly with vinyl turntables so that the needle does not jump. There are various pre-manufactured units available, but most DJs tend to set up their console on their record cabinets or other home surface. A kitchen work surface is ideal (countless house parties have utilised this set-up).

Although it can vary, the standard console set up has the mixer in the middle of two vinyl or CD turntables *(Fig. 3.1)*. If you wish to use both, it is best to place the CD decks mounted above *(Fig. 3.2)* on brackets, or to the far right and left of the set up *(Fig. 3.3)*.

Figure 3.1

| TURNTABLE A | MIXER | TURNTABLE B |

At this stage it is worth mentioning that if you wish at some stage to add a third turntable for a cappellas and scratching or 3-deck mixing, it is usually put to the right of Turntable B *(Fig. 3.4)* as the vinyl is most often manipulated with the right hand and the crossfader with the left. There is no law enforcing this of course.

30   **Everything You Need to Know about DJing and Success**

Figure 3.2

(CD DECK A)   (CD DECK B)

TURNTABLE A   MIXER   TURNTABLE B

Figure 3.3

CD DECK A   TURNTABLE A   MIXER   TURNTABLE B   CD DECK B

Figure 3.4

TURNTABLE A   MIXER   TURNTABLE B   TURNTABLE C

Getting Connected

The next step to setting up the DJ console is to connect all the leads in the correct way. Fortunately it is usually only the mixer that really varies in its rear panel set-up: the vinyl turntables and CD decks are pretty much standard.

Technics 1200/1210 turntables have three basic leads coming from their rear:

1. A power cable and plug that you should connect to the mains.
2. A phono cable (red and white connectors) that should be plugged into the relevant input channel on the mixer.
3. A thin wire with a small metal hook that is used to earth the turntables and should be attached to the ground connection. If this is left unconnected there will be a humming sound from your speakers.

CD decks (both the Pioneer and Technics models) have just the power lead that connects to the mains and a port for a red and white phono lead to connect the deck to the relevant channel on the mixer.

As previously stated, it is the rear panel of a mixer that varies the most from model to model. However, the terminology is generally the same. Vinyl turntables should be connected to the phono inputs, and CD decks should be connected to line inputs. The connection from

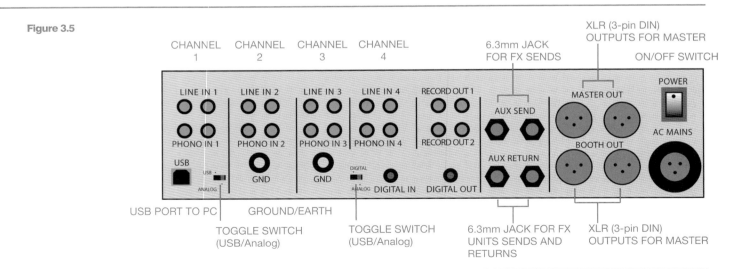

Figure 3.5

the mixer to the amplifier/hi-fi unit is again usually a red and white phono, although some mixers have their main output as XLR (3-pin DIN) or large Jack cable, so it is worth verifying this before purchase. It is possible to convert between these types of connecting leads but it does require buying extra components.

The previous diagram *(Fig. 3.5)* shows the rear panel of a typical mixer. (So that it corresponds to the front of the mixer, this diagram has been rotated left-to-right.)

Mandatory: Basic Set-up

If this was your mixer, you would set it up in the following way:

> Connect vinyl turntables with phono leads to the phono inputs for the desired channels. In theory on this mixer you could have up to four turntables hooked up. (It is important not to connect vinyl turntables to line inputs, as you will get barely any signal at all on the mixer.)

> Connect CD turntables with phono leads to the line inputs for the desired channels. Again on this mixer you could have up to four of these. (It is important not to connect CD turntables to phono inputs, as you will get a distorted and over-loud signal from the mixer.)

> Connect the thin wires with metal hook from the vinyl turntables and screw tight over the GND (GND is an abbreviation for 'ground'). This will make sure that the turntables are connected to an electrical earth and ensures that they do not emit an unpleasant humming sound.

> Connect the outputs from the mixer to the amplifier/hi-fi unit. In this case, you would have the option of using the XLR outs or one of the RECORD outs if you only had a phono input in the rear of your amplifier. The usual input to use on an amplifier is the AUX (auxiliary) input.

> Connect your headphones to the headphone input on the mixer (usually on the front or top panel of the mixer).

Optional: Extra Set-up

Note: some more basic mixers may not have these facilities.

> FX units can be used to add effects such as filter sweeps or delay to your music. If you have an external FX unit you would be able to connect it to the mixer using 6.3mm jack cables. FX units work in a loop so you need to 'send' to the unit and then 'return' to the mixer.

> On the above mixer, you could also connect a USB cable from the mixer to your computer. Often USB mixers enable you to control aspects from a computer. Some mixers also act

Top Tip:
It is advisable to use a good quality four- or six-gang plug extension with in-built circuit breaker to protect your gear from power surges and cuts.

Top Tip:
When powering up, do it in this order: Decks-Mixer-Amp, to avoid a big bump in your speakers. When you power-down, reverse this order.

as a 'sound card', meaning that the USB can be used to record mixes. Your computer may require software drivers to be installed so that it can communicate with your mixer, which can usually be downloaded from the mixer manufacturers' websites.

> If you wanted to have an output to a secondary system such as another amp or recording device, you could use any of the outs still free once the primary output is in use. For example, if you were using the main XLR outs to your main system, you could use one of the record outs to go directly to the secondary device.

> If you wish to use a microphone, it is usually connected by XLR (sometimes by 6.3mm jack) to the microphone input on the top or front panel of the mixer.

With these additional components your full set-up might look something like Figure 3.6 (sorry, but the £1,000 budget wouldn't stretch to a Manley amp).

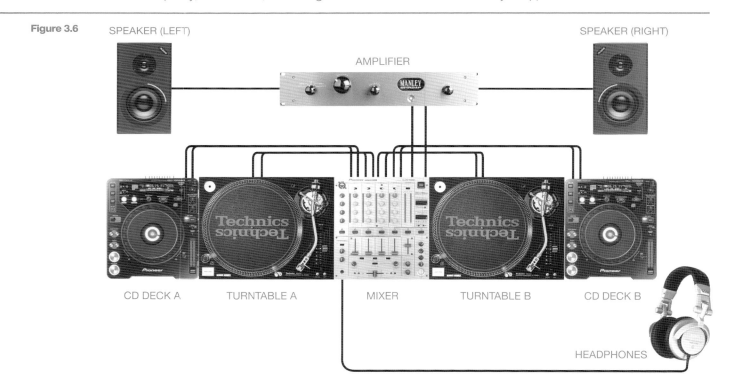

Figure 3.6

SPEAKER (LEFT) SPEAKER (RIGHT)

AMPLIFIER

CD DECK A   TURNTABLE A   MIXER   TURNTABLE B   CD DECK B

HEADPHONES

All that remains is to turn all the devices on and start your career as a DJ. Happy spinning!

Everything You Need to Know about DJing and Success

4 Hearing and Understanding Rhythm

As a DJ, your listening experience becomes more concentrated. You will start to notice rhythmic patterns, sound textures, combinations of instruments, the rise and fall of a track's energy. This type of listening is important for a DJ. You need to develop an ear for how each record is structured.

Time Signatures and Beats of the Bar

You need to be aware of a few basic principles of rhythm. In dance music it is fairly rare to encounter anything that is not in 4/4 time, so all examples have been given in this 'time signature'. Don't worry if Figure 4.1 looks a little like hieroglyphics. It is fairly easy to understand.

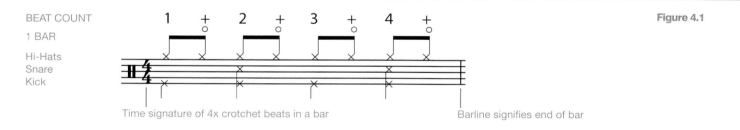

BEAT COUNT

1 BAR

Hi-Hats
Snare
Kick

Time signature of 4x crotchet beats in a bar

Barline signifies end of bar

Figure 4.1

The 'beat count' is quite literally what you would count out loud. There are 4 main 'on' beats with No.1 being the 'down beat'. The 'and' in between each main beat is known as the 'off beat'. In this simple example of a Disco/House/Techno '4-to-the-floor' beat, the kick is sounded on all 4 beats of the bar, the snare (clap) comes on beats 2 and 4 only and the hi-hats come on all 8 'on' and 'off' beats. These are known as 'quavers' (worth ½ a beat) and are written with a beam or tail across the top to distinguish them from 'crotchets' (worth a whole beat). Incidentally, the tiny degree sign above the 'off' beat hats is the symbol for an open rather than a closed hat, so these would sound: *T-TSSS-T-TSSS-T-TSSS-T-TSSS*.

Figure 4.2 shows a different kind of beat known as a 'breakbeat'. Assuming that the tempo of these two beats is exactly the same, you would count along to them in exactly the same way. The extra 'e' and 'a' in between the 'on' and 'off' beats show you a further subdivision known as a 'semiquaver' (worth ¼ of a beat). This is written with an extra beam or tail. In this example, note that the kick only falls on beat 1 and the 'off' beat of beat 3. The snare still comes on beats 2 and 4, but also has two extra skips on the semiquavers 'a' of beat 2 and 'e' of beat 3. This is known as 'syncopation'. The hats remain on all eight 'on' and 'off' beats and would be closed so: *T-T T-T T-T T-T*.

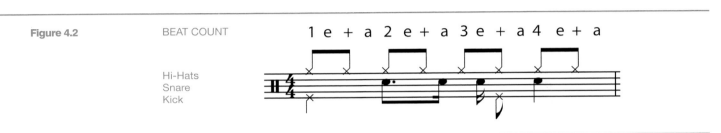

Figure 4.2

If the two beats shown above were on two records, you would be able to beatmatch them perfectly. Try to visualise the way that both downbeat kicks would fall on the first beat of the bar. The snares would synchronise on beats 2 and 4, but the breakbeat would also contribute the extra syncopated hits. The eight hi-hats from each break would be layered together.

Phrases and Rhythmic Structure

As well as the beats of a bar operating in groups of four, you will mostly find that the bars themselves are also grouped in multiples of four. If you think of a simple poem or some song lyrics you will realise that each stanza or verse usually has four lines (often with lines 2 and 4 rhyming). These are known to DJs as phrases *(Fig. 4.3)*, although you should be aware that musicians use this term to mean something slightly different (something resembling a 'sentence' of melody).

Often the start of a phrase is accented on the downbeat with a crash cymbal to highlight the start of that particular section. Minor alterations to the basic groove can draw attention to certain places such as the halfway point and end of each phrase by means of a drum 'fill' or 'edit'. Sometimes a reverse cymbal is also used.

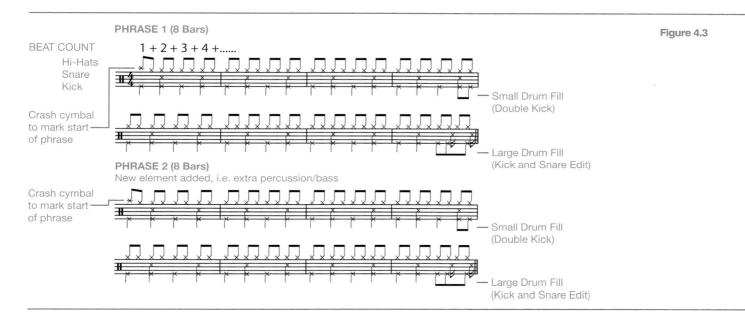

PHRASE 1 (8 Bars)

BEAT COUNT

1 + 2 + 3 + 4 +......

Hi-Hats
Snare
Kick

Crash cymbal to mark start of phrase

Small Drum Fill (Double Kick)

Large Drum Fill (Kick and Snare Edit)

PHRASE 2 (8 Bars)
New element added, i.e. extra percussion/bass

Crash cymbal to mark start of phrase

Small Drum Fill (Double Kick)

Large Drum Fill (Kick and Snare Edit)

Figure 4.3

If you try to introduce a record from the wrong place in the bar, the rhythmic and musical elements of the second record will not enter in the correct way *(Fig. 4.4)*. Even if the beatmatching is tight, the mix will not sit properly and you will have strange things like crash cymbals or basslines coming in the middle of the bar.

If you realise that you have judged the release incorrectly, the simplest thing to do is to re-cue the record and start the mix again.

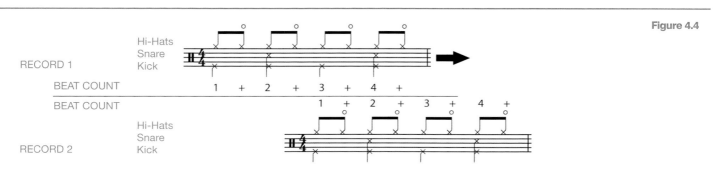

Figure 4.4

RECORD 1

Hi-Hats
Snare
Kick

BEAT COUNT   1   +   2   +   3   +   4   +

BEAT COUNT   1   +   2   +   3   +   4   +

RECORD 2

Hi-Hats
Snare
Kick

5 Starting to Mix

Once you have your DJ console set-up ready, and you have started the never-ending obsession of collecting music, the next step is to become familiar with the basic principles of mixing. The mix is where your audience can hear more than one track being played, even if they don't know it at the time. The idea of mixing is to join records so that the music plays continuously, rather than as separate tracks. To begin with, don't worry too much about beatmatching. Instead, try to get used to the main functions of the turntables and the mixer with the idea of moving between the two selected tracks. Learning to mix is very much an audio and visual experience, so I highly recommend that for improved understanding you utilise the wide selection of DJ tutorial links I have compiled for you in the bonus resources section. Doing so will greatly accelerate your learning.

Cueing Up

Cueing up a record is simply finding the start point from where you can begin mixing. Often this is the first sound you hear, but not always, so it would be wise to choose a simple House record that opens with a strong beat. DJ mixers have channel faders and a crossfader, each channel fader carries one channel of audio, for example the sound signal from a turntable, and the crossfader is used to fade between two individual channel faders.

Listening for the Cue Point *(Fig 5.1)*

> Push the fader up for the channel you are playing on, and the crossfader to the correct side.

> Start the record's rotation with the start/stop button.

> Place the needle on the outer rim of the vinyl surface.

> Wait until the music starts then press start/stop to halt the record's rotation.

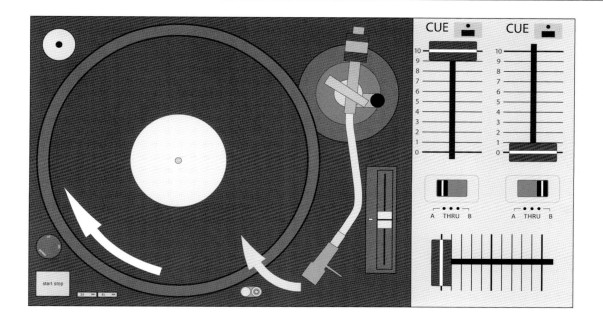

Figure 5.1

Lining up the Cue Point *(Fig. 5.2)*

> Slowly wind the record back until the first beat slips by in reverse.

> Place your hand on the vinyl (usually half way between the outer rim and the label at the 8 o'clock position).

> Without applying too much pressure to the holding hand, use the other hand to start the record's rotation again. The platter should still be spinning without resistance, but the record should be stationary.

> Manually push and pull the vinyl so that it passes back and forth over the first sound (cue point) and then in your own time release in place of one of the forward pushes.

Figure 5.2

Now repeat the same technique, but try to do it without stopping the record's rotation between listening and lining up the cue point so that the platter is in constant motion.

Advanced Cueing

Some records do not start on the down beat, or even with a beat at all. These are harder to use as the cue point is not as easy to define. It is important to listen to a record before you try mixing it so you begin to hear the places where you should try dropping it in.

Anacrusis (Up Beats)

Anything that precedes the down beat is called an anacrusis (up beat). Imagine a record of the children's rhyme The Owl and the Pussy Cat. If you recite this poem, the strong down beat is on 'Owl', not on the first sound which is 'The'. This means that 'The' is an anacrusis. Your cue point here would therefore have to be 'Owl' in order for the rhythm to flow correctly.

Sometimes an anacrusis can have several sounds before the down beat, so listen carefully to where the emphasis falls. Generally in dance music, this is accentuated by the kick drum.

Instrumental Openings

Many records open with rhythmically unaccompanied pads, synth stabs, keyboards or basslines before the entrance of the beat. You can deal with this in two ways. Firstly, play through the intro until the beat comes in, then cue it up to the downbeat. If you are feeling a bit more adventurous, try to listen through the record to see how the instrumental elements fit around the beat when it is present, then return to the start and cue up the record. Imagine the beat of the tune as you remember it, and then release the record in its correct place so that the instrumental groove fits along to the drums that are accompanying it in your mind. (This is obviously much harder to do and will require a keenly developed sense of internal rhythm.)

Fading

On a mixer, you have two main fader options. The channel faders (often called 'up-faders') and the crossfader (Fig. 5.3). The up-faders control the volume of each separate channel, whereas the crossfader moves between the channels, passing from one to another with a 'mix' in the middle. It is probably best at this stage to use the up-faders with their gradual curve from silence to full volume as the 'blending' faders and the crossfader as the more immediate 'switch' between the two channels (assuming your mixer enables you to alter the crossfader curve). This is not a compulsory way of having the mixer set, but if you put a gradual fade on the crossfader, you will have the two kinds of fader doing the same job rather than fulfilling separate roles.

Figure 5.3

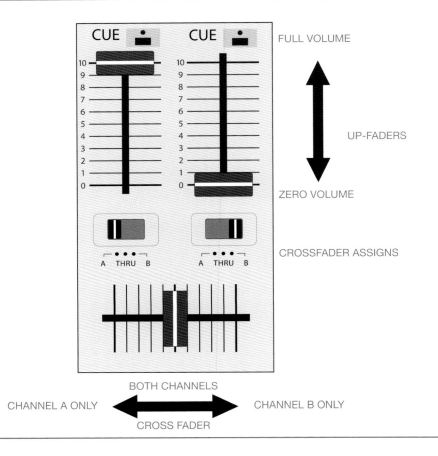

As well as setting your crossfader to a sharp curve, also ensure that the channels are assigned properly to the two sides. On mixers with more than two channels, you will need to designate each channel to a particular side of the crossfader using the crossfader assigns – e.g. channel 1 to the left (A) and channel 2 to the right (B), as in Figure 5.3 above. If you don't do this, or leave the crossfader assigns off, you will not be able to use the crossfader to cut from deck to deck.

Before learning how to beatmatch, you should practise fading between two records in the way that the original DJs did before blending became prevalent. You are likely to encounter some rhythmic clashes (known affectionately as 'train wrecks') whilst perfecting this particular technique, but try not to worry too much about this for the time being.

Fading Between Two Records

Figure 5.4

> Cue up two records (one on each turntable) then start to play the first record with the crossfader over to the relevant side for that channel.

> Bring the up-fader for the second channel down to zero.

RECORD 1
PLAYING

MIXER SET
FOR CHANNEL 1

RECORD 2
STATIONARY (CUED UP
TO START POINT

> When the first record has played for a certain amount of time, move the crossfader into the middle and start playing the second record.

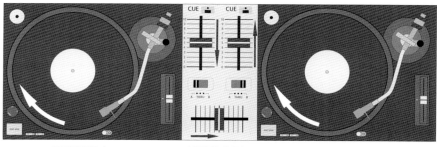

RECORD 1
PLAYING

MIXER SET
FOR BOTH CHANNELS

RECORD 2
PLAYING

> Gradually bring the up-fader for the second channel up whilst simultaneously bringing the up-fader for the first channel down until the second record is all that is left.

> Move the fader over to the relevant side for the second channel and stop the first record.

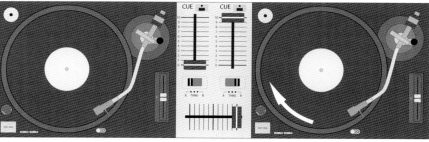

RECORD 1
STOPPED

MIXER SET
FOR CHANNEL 2

RECORD 2
PLAYING

You have just completed your first mix. Now try to cue up a different record on the original turntable and repeat the progress from channel 2 back to channel 1. It is advisable to choose, if possible, sections of a record where the track breaks down to its musical elements only (i.e. no drums, but strings/pads, keys, etc.) for uncomplicated fades. Even without beatmatching, this will result in a more natural blending of the two records.

Beatmatching

Beatmatching was first introduced by the early Disco DJs such as Francis Grasso, Steve D'Aquisto and Nicky Siano. As the equipment improved, this technique, rough at first, became perfect. Another major step in the history of beatmatching was the introduction of music that used beats constructed on a drum machine, rather than live breaks where drummers' beats were subject to fluctuations in tempo.

On modern turntables (both vinyl and CD) and on software programs it is totally possible to beatmatch with 100% precision. This is one of the principal skills that needs real practice in order to perfect. There are very few people (even trained musicians) who succeed the first time, so don't be discouraged by initial failure. You won't be the first or the last person to produce some real 'train wrecks'. Some superb DJs have taken months, or even years, to perfect the technique.

Varispeed Controls on Turntables

Top Tip:
Your progress will be greatly helped if you team up with a friendly and patient DJ who can already beatmatch. This DJ 'buddy' will be able to show you where you are going wrong and how to correct any mistakes.

Figure 5.5 shows you the basic varispeed functions of a typical turntable. DJ turntables enable you to alter the speed within the margin of +8/-8%. Some turntables extend this to +16/–16%, but a record played this far away from its original speed will not sound at all good. The varispeed slider controls the pitch in a smooth gradient between these two extremities. You should start by experimenting with the effect that this has on the sound of a record. The further into the minus speed you go, the slower the record will play. The key will drop (approximately by a whole tone, e.g. G to F) and vocals will sound deeper and more ponderous. In contrast, as you move into the plus speed area, the record will spin faster. The key will move up (again by roughly a whole tone, e.g. from G to A) and vocals will sound higher and chirpier.

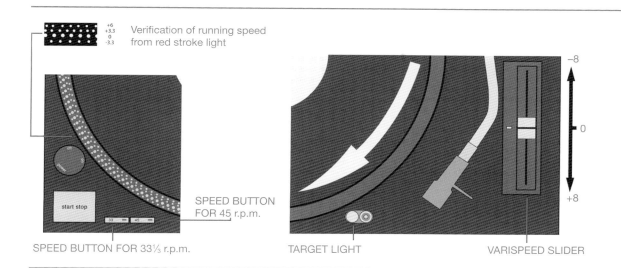

Figure 5.5

Verification of running speed from red stroke light

SPEED BUTTON FOR 45 r.p.m.

SPEED BUTTON FOR 33⅓ r.p.m.

TARGET LIGHT

VARISPEED SLIDER

Beatmatching Two Records

A useful analogy for beatmatching two records is the idea of two cars driving along a motorway. One is a VW Golf, and the other a Peugeot 306 (different makes, but similar vehicles). The aim is for both cars to drive side by side with their front bumpers in parallel. In order to do this, they will each need to concentrate on their speed in comparison to the other. If one starts to pull away, it will need to come back into line or the other will need to edge forwards to match it. Pre-planned acceleration and agreed speed will help, but ultimately it will come to the use of eyes and feel. Now replace these two cars with two records of a similar style (House vs. D&B is like a VW Golf vs. a Ferrari), with one on each turntable. The aim is now to align the beats and bars of the two records so that they are riding in parallel *(Fig. 5.6)*.

The two records below are beatmatched. Notice how the beat count and all the elements of the drums are falling in exactly the same place; kick for kick, snare for snare and hat for hat. Even allowing for variance in the tonal sound of these elements (i.e. Record 1 might have a snappier snare, more hollow kick or tinnier hi-hats) these two beats would mould into one.

Figure 5.6

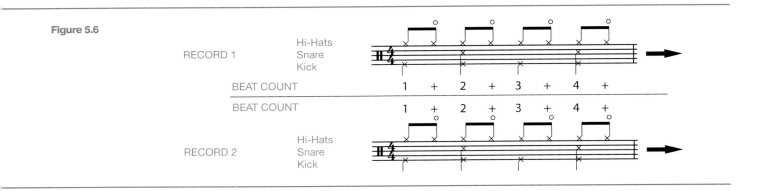

		BEAT COUNT	1	+	2	+	3	+	4	+

Headphone Cueing *(Fig. 5.7)*

> Take two records of a similar style with a strong, simple beat at the start.

> With the crossfader over and the up-fader at full volume for the relevant channel, start to play the first record.

> Switch the headphone cue to the second deck and begin to play the second record.

> Find the cue point for the second record and manually hold the record ready for release.

You will be listening to Record 1 through the speakers, and Record 2 in the headphones. To compare the two, have one headphone cup over one ear but take the other cup off.

Figure 5.7

HEADPHONE CUE FOR RECORD 2   SWITCHED ON

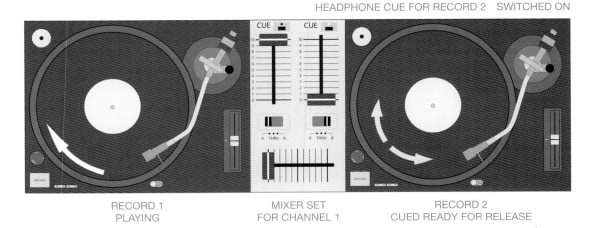

RECORD 1
PLAYING

MIXER SET
FOR CHANNEL 1

RECORD 2
CUED READY FOR RELEASE

Comparing Records Ready for the Mix *(Fig. 5.8)*

> First listen to Record 1 whilst holding Record 2 in readiness (this is a little like a relay runner waiting for their partner to give them the baton before they take off on their own stint).

> Release Record 2 in time with the downbeat from Record 1.

> As the two records spin together listen between 'headphone ear' and 'speaker ear'.

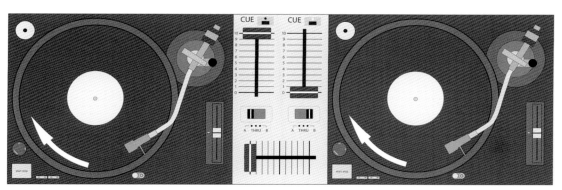

Figure 5.8

| RECORD 1 | MIXER SET | RECORD 2 |
| PLAYING | FOR CHANNEL 1 PLAYING | PLAYING (IN HEADPHONES ONLY) |

Starting to Beatmatch Two Records

If you have chosen two records without exactly the same bpm, there are two possible scenarios:

> **Scenario A:** Record 2 will start to pull ahead of Record 1, which means that it is a faster track.

> **Scenario B:** Record 2 will begin to fall behind Record 1, which means that it is a slower track.

The bpm difference of the two records will decide how quickly this happens. If Record 2 is only 1 bpm faster or slower than Record 1, it will gradually glide out of sync. If the difference is greater, they will fall out even within half a bar. Several seconds later they will be fighting like Tom & Jerry armed with pots and pans.

47

Scenario A: Record 2 is Faster (begins to pull ahead of Record 1)

Figure 5.9 shows you what happens when Record 2 is faster than Record 1. Notice how, despite starting together, Record 2 is moving through the beat count and (consequently its hit-points) faster. By the end of the bar, Record 2 is out of sync with Record 1.

Figure 5.9

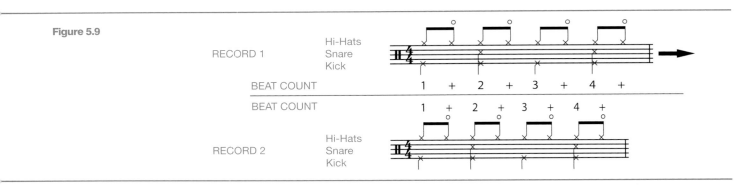

In order to correct this situation, you need to do two things: *(Fig. 5.10)*

> Manually restrain Record 2 so it comes back into line with Record 1.

> Then, move the varispeed slider back so that the record is now spinning a little slower than before. (You have to estimate the amount required. Sometimes you will change the speed too much or not enough, requiring you to repeat the process).

Figure 5.10

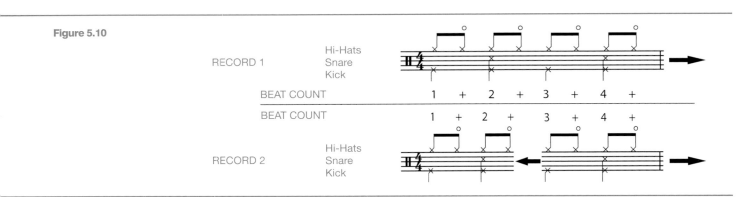

Everything You Need to Know about DJing and Success

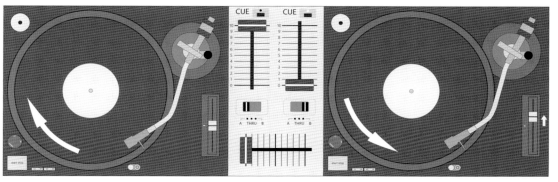

RECORD 1
PLAYING

PULL RECORD 2 BACK TO REALIGN
WITH RECORD 1

DECREASE PITCH
ACCORDINGLY

Scenario B: Record 2 is slower (begins to fall behind Record 1)

Either because it starts out slower, or because you have overstepped the mark in correcting
a faster record, Record 2 may start to fall behind *(Fig. 5.11)*. Notice how, despite starting
together, Record 2 is moving through the beat count (and consequently its hit-points)
slower. By the end of the bar, Record 2 is again out of sync with Record 1.

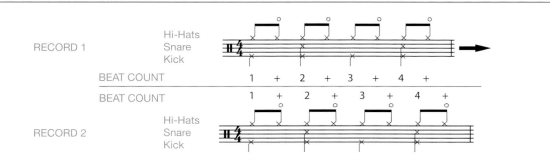

Figure 5.11

In order to correct this situation, you need to do two things *(Fig. 5.12)*:

> Manually push Record 2 forwards so it catches up with Record 1. Gently encourage the record with the flow, don't shove it forwards. Too much push and it will lurch ahead.

> Next, move the varispeed slider forwards so that the record is now also spinning a little faster than before.

Figure 5.12

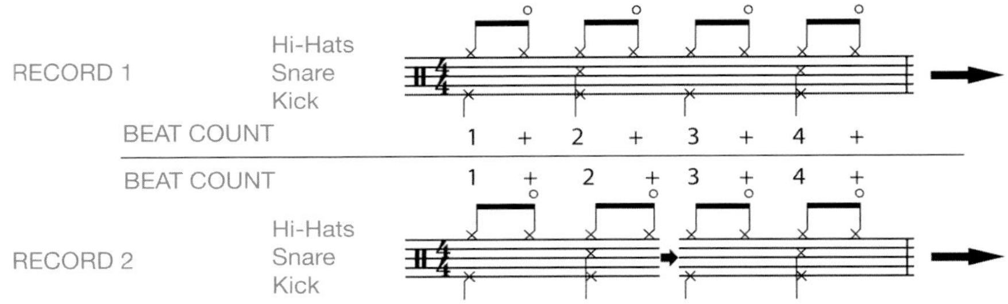

RECORD 1
Hi-Hats
Snare
Kick

BEAT COUNT   1   +   2   +   3   +   4   +

BEAT COUNT   1   +   2   +   3   +   4   +

RECORD 2
Hi-Hats
Snare
Kick

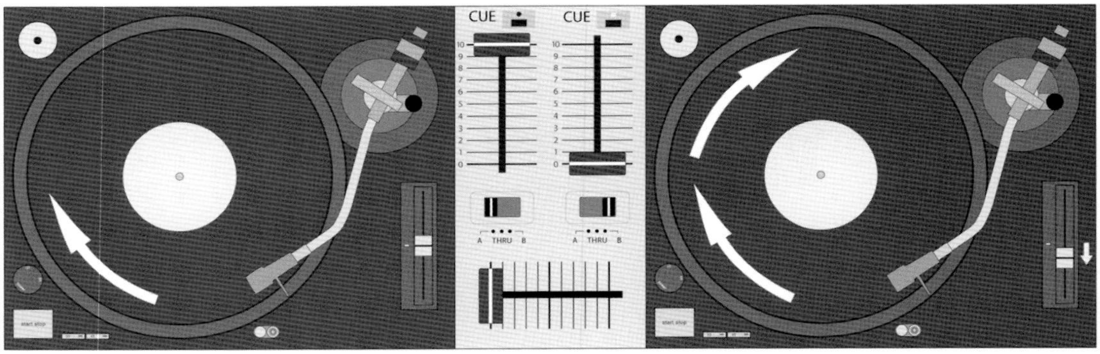

INCREASE PITCH
ACCORDINGLY

RECORD 1
PLAYING

PUSH RECORD 2 FORWARDS TO
CATCH UP WITH RECORD 1

You may need to perform the above steps numerous times; each time becoming more and more accurate until you hit the correct speed. Correcting the speed to match the beats of two records is a process of elimination; trial and error until you have it. Sometimes you will end up with the two turntables spinning 10% away from each other; other times the

Everything You Need to Know about DJing and Success

difference may only be ½%. Even when you think you have the two records running in sync, you will need to keep concentrating on the beat alignment in case one starts to drag behind or pull ahead of the other.

Performing a Mix *(Fig. 5.13)*

When you are happy with the result, bring Record 2 in using the fading technique. If you have got it right, the two records will be mixed as one. If you have got it wrong, they will clash horribly. Every DJ has done this many times, so don't worry. Simply re-cue the records and have another go. Often it is sensible to re-cue anyway so that you can choose a good place to drop your mix.

Figure 5.13

> Bring up-fader for channel 2 up to match channel 1.

> Move crossfader over to centre.

> Mix!

RECORD 1
PLAYING

RECORD 2
PLAYING IN SYNC WITH RECORD 1

It is advisable at all stages to keep the headphones on so you can reference the second record as you mix it in. Many DJs lose a mix because they take their headphones off just as they bring it in. Unless you are very experienced at 'ambient mixing', this is a foolish thing to do. You may well correct the speed of the wrong record if the mix starts to slide out, making the clash worse. Remember, beatmatching is a challenge, so don't be disappointed if you struggle to mix two records at first. It takes time, and when you finally get it, you will have every reason to feel that you have achieved something.

In the Mix

Once you have begun to beatmatch successfully, you will want to develop your mixing vocabulary, so that you have a variety of ways in which to move from one record to another. Fading in from one record to another is the principal method, but there are many other more dramatic ways of mixing two tracks together.

Cutting

Cutting refers to an immediate switch from Record 1 to Record 2 and back again. You can also cut a record into the mix so that Record 2 cuts into Record 1 then cuts out once more *(Fig. 5.14)*. It should be pointed out at this stage that you need to beatmatch two records before starting to cut between them or the cuts will clip each other and become messy.

Figure 5.14

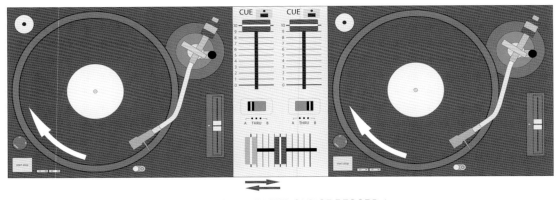

CUT RECORD 2 IN AND OUT OF RECORD 1

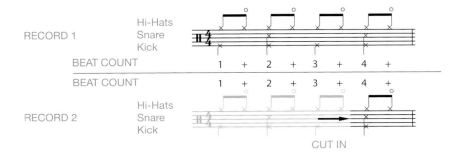

Everything You Need to Know about DJing and Success

Always remember to keep monitoring Record 2 in the headphones as you perform your cuts. This will ensure that the beatmatch stays tight and the cuts remain neat.

You can become very inventive with the way in which you cut between two records. The elements of the chosen records have a big part to play here. Cutting can be used as a 'sneak preview' of the next track (especially if it is a well-known and recognisable riff). You can catch various parts of the drum beat (both on and off beat) using cutting techniques *(Fig. 5.15)*.

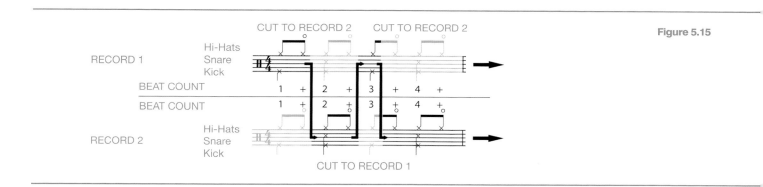

Figure 5.15

Straight Drop/Run in Cut *(Fig. 5.16)*

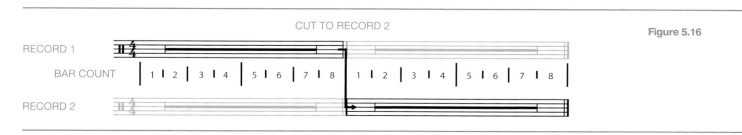

Figure 5.16

The most dramatic cut is the most simple. It is often called a 'straight drop' or 'run in cut', due to the fact that there are no preview cuts from Record 2.

> Beatmatch Record 2 in the headphones.

> Allow Record 1 to complete a phrase.

> Switch the crossfader straight over into Record 2.

This type of cut is the complete opposite to a smooth blend. Although it is very easy to perform, it is hardly subtle. The drop point for Record 2 becomes the make or break factor between total success and total embarrassment.

Bringing Out the Mix

Unless you make one of your cuts a final and decisive move from Record 1 to Record 2, you will need to end the mix at some stage. Again you can use a gradual fade, but you may want to emphasise the transition or even the moment that Record 1 stops. The turntable can be stopped in three different ways; powering down (switching the turntable off), using the stop switch (break) or by manual halting of the platter.

Powering down will cause the record to slow down over a couple of seconds, so in terms of beatmatching, you should not do this if there are any rhythmic elements still left in the track. Stopping will put the brakes on the record fairly rapidly. On some turntables you can alter the brake speed to your taste. Manually stopping the record is usually accompanied by a reverse motion. This can either be a small slip backwards or something a little more radical such as a 'spinback/throwback' or a 'rewind'.

Spinbacks and Rewinds

Spinbacks and rewinds were first introduced by Jamaican Reggae DJs as an effect to hide the joining of unmixed records or to take a really popular record back to the start for a replay. They have both become standard techniques for the modern DJ.

Spinbacks *(Fig 5.17)*

> Mix two records together.

> As you approach the point where you want to perform the spinback, hover your hand around the 10 o'clock position on the relevant record.

> Bring your hand down onto the vinyl at the chosen moment and pull the record sharply towards you in a grabbing motion. (Be careful.)

> Before the record has a chance to recover and resume playing, press the stop button to halt the platter.

Figure 5.17

> Throw the record back from about here

> Hit the Stop button

A good sharp spinback will give a rapid whizzing sound as it reverses through the previous ten seconds of music in about one. Of all the mixing techniques you can learn, this is possibly the one that has been most over-used, so use it sparingly.

Rewinds *(Fig. 5.18)*

> Mix two records together until you approach your chosen drop point (breakdowns are usually the best as there will be no rhythmic elements in the track to conflict with the rewind).

> As Record 2 hits the breakdown, stop Record 1 with either your hand or the stop button.

EITHER

> Perform a gentle spinback allowing the platter to freewheel for a couple of seconds before it naturally comes to a halt. You can help this process by placing your finger on the side of the platter where the strobe dots are.

OR

> Making sure you have stopped the platter, start to play the record backwards, slowly at first then gradually picking up speed as the rewind gathers momentum.

> Bring the up-fader for the rewinding record gradually down so, as it speeds up, it also fades out to zero volume.

For this more rapid style of rewind, you will need to make sure you manipulate the record near to the centre so as not to collide with the needle.

Figure 5.18

> Start rewind from about here

> Manually increase wind speed, or allow platter to freewheel to a stop

Understanding Musical Elements

As you study your records in greater depth you will start to hear how, with each 4, 8 or 16 bars, the music moves from section to section. Various instruments will be introduced or removed *(Fig. 5.19)*, and the beat will gain more energy by adding extra percussion. The more you understand the song structure of a record, the easier you will find it to choose a good place to start a mix.

Once you begin to visualise the music that you hear in this way, you will see where to drop records into a mix. Taking Figure 5.19 as an example, you can see that a second record should enter at the beginning of a phrase rather than at any other point during one. Not only would you have the beats matching, but the building elements of the two records would fit together in a more synchronised fashion.

Figure 5.19

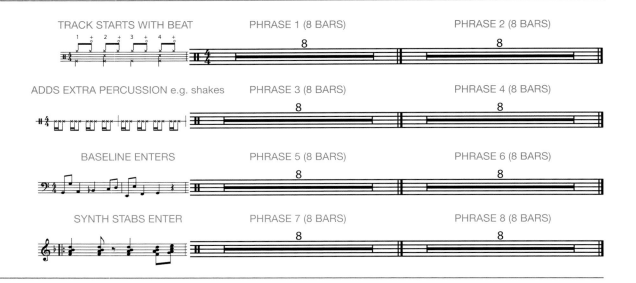

Instrumental Elements

Although many DJs consider rhythm to be the priority, understanding all the other musical elements is just as critical to successful mixing. Each genre of music tends to focus not only on certain styles of rhythmic beats, but also on particular combinations of instruments. One of the main reasons you can tell Heavy Metal from Jazz is its use of distorted guitar, loud 'messy' drum sound and aggressive vocal inflections.

Dance music is no different. House music for example, will run at a certain tempo, have a certain style of beat (usually 4-to-the-floor) and will most likely use particular sounds typical of the genre. You would expect to hear a warm rolling bass, pads/strings or maybe keyboards such as Rhodes or piano, synth melodies or chordal stabs to give extra interest to the groove, vocal phrases, etc.

If a House record suddenly halved its tempo, added snippets of scratching and introduced a strongly rhythmic spoken or rapped verse, it would no longer be House, but Hip-Hop. Similarly, if the speed dramatically increased, changed the 4-to-the-floor to a hard 2-step break and introduced a menacing, rasping synth bass, it would have turned into D&B.

It is important for a DJ to understand what it is that he/she is listening to and the effect that each element is having on the sound and the energy of a track. Classically, there are four different families of standard instruments, as well as further electronic and ethnic categories. You should learn to be familiar with as many of these as possible. As well as listening to pre-recorded music, try to also watch plenty of live music so that you see instruments in action and hear exactly how they sound. Check out everything you can, from orchestral Classical music, to Rock, to big-band Jazz, to Indian music; it will stand you in good stead for your musical understanding.

Melody and Harmony

In order to mix in a more musical way (going beyond matching the rhythm), it helps to understand the role of melody and harmony. Traditionally, playing an instrument or having a musical friend who could demonstrate these techniques were ways to improve your musicality. There are now software tools such as Mixed in Key (discussed later in the book) that can short-cut and assist you in harmonic mixing. Ten minutes of practical listening is better than 10,000 words of explanation, but here is an overview.

> **Melody** is the tune; either the main vocal line or a single line played on another instrument.

> **Harmony** is made up of the musical layers underneath that accompany the melody; backing vocals, strings/pads, chord structures played on guitars, keyboards, etc.

Unless the music uses a collage of unrelated samples, the melody and harmony will most likely work together around a particular tonal centre or 'key'. Some keys are closely related to each other and will work 'in sympathy'; others are more distant and will clash. Blending two records in the same key or a neighbouring one will sound superb, whereas mixing two records that have unrelated tonal centres will clash musically, even if the beats are matched perfectly. Many DJs do not understand this simple fact for all their technical skill, and wonder why the flow of music is not as smooth as it might be.

Finding the tonal centre of a record can be difficult if you do not already play a musical instrument. The easiest way to go about it is to play a keyboard note by note until one of them sits comfortably. There may be several notes that work well in this way, but one will definitely sound stronger than the others. The bassline is a good guide as it usually maps out the key more than any other element of the music. The harmony and melody will also give you what is known as the 'tonality' (major or minor). Often major is described as bright and happy-sounding, whereas minor is sadder or darker.

Figure 5.20

THE CYCLE OF FIFTHS

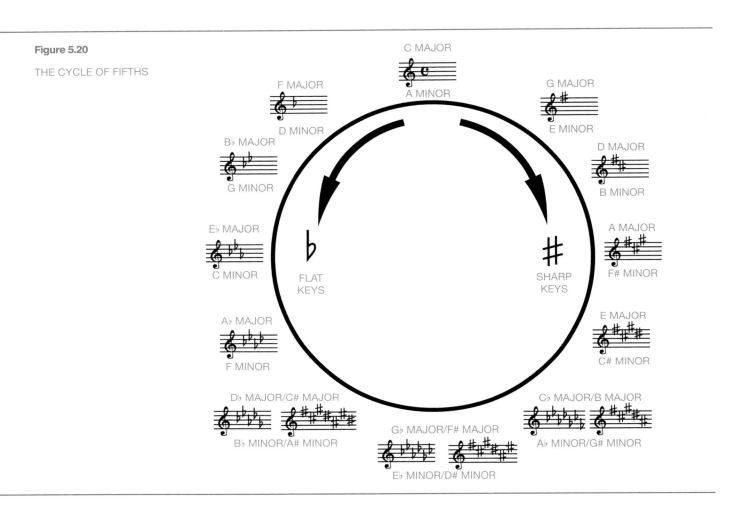

Figure 5.20 shows you the keys arranged in what is known as the 'Cycle of 5ths'. This means that each step around the circle moves key by the interval of a 5th. A 5th is equal to seven semitones, that's seven consecutive notes on the keyboard. Records that are in a key one step away (in either direction) from each other in the cycle will mix harmonically and records that are half way across the circle from each other will clash harmonically. Of course to use this you need to know which musical key each record is in. This can be done using technology such as the Mixed in Key software, discussed in the Digital DJing section. There are also tutorials on my You Tube channel showing how you can ascertain the key of a track without any software: www.youtube.com/user/ramplingmusic.

DJs such as Mark Farina, John Digweed and DJ Sasha have a natural ear for mixing in key. Harmonic mixing means their mixes sound more fluid, natural and effortless as the musical components 'sit' musically next to each other, from one track into the next.

Improved Mixing

Improving your mixing techniques goes hand in hand with the ongoing expansion of your music collection. Remember the ratio of 25% skills to 75% music choice. At this stage in your DJing journey, it is likely that you will be hearing tracks as potential mixes anyway.

You will find yourself in record shops, or searching through online libraries imagining which record in your collection will fit well with the one you are currently listening to. This will make you increasingly more fussy (in a good way) about what you do or don't buy.

As you start to perfect your beatmatching skills you will become more confident that you can sync two records together every time. Developing more inventive vocabulary for bringing mixes in and out, you will also find yourself becoming more creative with the records. You will want to mix 'tighter', 'faster' and 'longer'.

Tighter Mixes

Getting your mixing tighter is really important, in order for you to progress from approximate beatmatching to perfect twinning of the two records. It comes down to practice and experience. You need to listen astutely to all the elements of the two records right down to the smallest shaker or triangle. Your use of the varispeed slider will also become more precise and you will find that the extra half-a-millimetre in either direction will be the difference between a decent mix that you occasionally have to correct and a tight blend that is still synchronising perfectly when you come back from making a cup of coffee. (Yes it is totally possible.)

Some mixes come out better than others for a variety of reasons. Sampled breaks might clip very slightly if the start points or the pitching are not quite right. This is sometimes so minimal that you only notice it when a mix that 'ought' to be perfect keeps slipping out like a naughty eel. Some genres are worse than others when it comes to ropey production. Older, classic tracks made on more primitive studio equipment are often less than perfect. Old Skool Hardcore, early Hip-Hop, House and Techno, can be nothing short of notorious. This does not mean that the records are unmixable; just that you need to be careful. Prepare yourself for unusual phrase lengths, strange key clashes, undefined tonal centres and some pretty scruffy beat samples. The response of a crowd to a classic track is the reason DJs still drop them. They are well-loved old favourites packed with nostalgia. Using a quick mix or even no mix at all is sometimes better than battling to maintain a blend with some of these older tracks. Modern productions are usually less flawed, but don't depend on it. Some Afro-Beat and Latin American music, for example, has live percussion that moves around pretty generously.

Occasionally, you will still find records where the sampling split points are not exact. Producers continue to drop Old Skool breaks that are less than perfect, or use live instrumentalists who don't play with absolute precision. These imperfections do however give music its feel, and especially with electronic music the re-injection of human elements adds to the track, making it sound less 'square' and computerised.

Quick 'On the Fly' Mixing

Getting quicker takes practice and experience. It is a useful skill to develop as you may find yourself running out of time on a record. Beatmatching quickly also allows you to spend more time 'in the mix'. This can either lead to longer mixes known as 'blends', or to a rapid succession of records and a more energetic set. However, do not sacrifice tightness for quick mixes or epic blending. A mix can be like walking a tightrope. The longer the rope or the faster you try to get over it, the more risk there is of falling.

Super-Fast 'Non-Manual' Beatmatching *(Fig. 5.21)*

> Cue up a record ready for the mix and release it at the next available drop point.

> As soon as you assess whether the record needs speeding up or slowing down, use the varispeed in an exaggerated way to rapidly correct the speed.

> Keep correcting by ever smaller degrees till you hit the right speed and the records sync.

> Bring the mix in.

If you get really good at this technique, you can have a record beatmatched and in the mix within ten seconds of it hitting the platter. You don't have to just use the varispeed of course, you are allowed to touch the record too. The advantage of non-manual beatmatching is that your other hand is free to set up the mixer ready to bring the record in.

Everything You Need to Know about DJing and Success

Figure 5.21

FINAL CORRECT
SPEED POINT

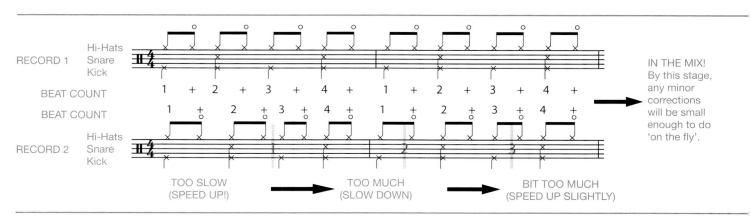

RECORD 1 — Hi-Hats / Snare / Kick

BEAT COUNT   1   +   2   +   3   +   4   +   1   +   2   +   3   +   4   +

BEAT COUNT   1   +   2   +   3   +   4   +   1   +   2   +   3   +   4   +

RECORD 2 — Hi-Hats / Snare / Kick

TOO SLOW
(SPEED UP!)   →   TOO MUCH
(SLOW DOWN)   →   BIT TOO MUCH
(SPEED UP SLIGHTLY)

IN THE MIX!
By this stage,
any minor
corrections
will be small
enough to do
'on the fly'.

63

Long Blends

When two records fit together in a particularly musical way, or you want to gradually introduce a stripped back drum break into the mix, you will need to blend records. This is not a difficult skill technically as you are basically 'riding' the mix, but you will need to consider the various musical aspects of both tracks to create a really successful blend. For long mixes, choose your tracks wisely. Two tracks with full vocals rarely blend well as the double set of lyrics become confused. The only exception to this rule is mixing two different mixes of the same track (i.e. 'Original' and 'Remix' versions). You are, however, more likely to use cutting techniques in this instance.

Instrumental tracks, or one instrumental and one vocal, work far better. Often you will find different elements from each record complimenting each other; merging together to form a collage that begins to create a new track. This is no different from any other musician combining notes to form harmonies and textures.

Two Tracks as One

> Try to pick two records in the same or closely related keys.

> Beatmatch the two records as accurately as you possibly can.

> Bring the second track into the mix using a fade or a cut (a fade will be smoother.)

> Once the two tunes are in the mix, ride them together and listen to how they fit.

> Enjoy the sound of the new 'track' that you have created from the two separate ones.

> After a longer than usual period of time, begin to bring the first record out until the mix is finished.

Figure 5.22 shows two hypothetical records in the middle of a blend. Assuming that these two chosen tracks are in the same or complimentary keys, the various elements from each record will work together to make a newly created piece of music.

Everything You Need to Know about DJing and Success

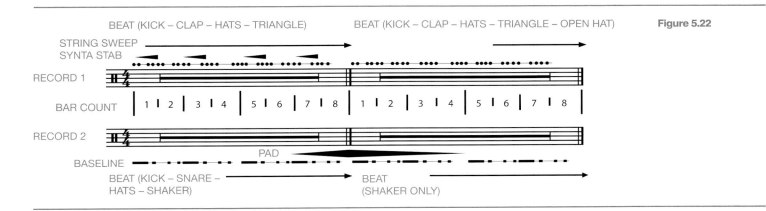

BEAT (KICK – CLAP – HATS – TRIANGLE)   BEAT (KICK – CLAP – HATS – TRIANGLE – OPEN HAT)   **Figure 5.22**

STRING SWEEP
SYNTA STAB
RECORD 1
BAR COUNT   1 1 2 | 3 1 4 | 5 1 6 | 7 1 8   1 1 2 | 3 1 4 | 5 1 6 | 7 1 8
RECORD 2
BASELINE
PAD
BEAT (KICK – SNARE –   BEAT
HATS – SHAKER)   (SHAKER ONLY)

Notice how the two drum tracks contribute to a whole: Record 1 provides a clap and a triangle to go with the snare and shaker from Record 2. The kick and hats would most likely have different qualities too (e.g. Record 1 may have a stronger, deeper kick and sharper hats). Note too how the synth stabs and string sweeps in Record 1 would work with the bassline from Record 2 to build a fuller groove.

You will also see how the pad that arises through bars 7 and 8 of the first 8-bar phrase on Record 2 aids the join into the second 8-bar phrase, where the drums break down to just the shaker. A pad is a soft sounding synthesised note or chord which is sustained over a number of beats or bars. Meanwhile Record 1 picks up some energy in this second half by adding an open hi-hat.

The Role of the Mixer

Your control of the mixer is critical for building long blends. Even though you may be riding two tunes in the mix with the crossfader stationary in the middle, you will need to listen to the way that the elements of the two records are brought in and out of play.

There are two main areas of the mixer that you will be using at this stage; the up-faders and the EQs.

Use of the Up-faders

When you are blending, the end result is still to mix from one record to another. The up-faders will enable you to gradually transfer 'dominance' from the first record to the second one. As the elements of the new track begin to build (especially with the entrance of the bassline) you will want to bring the level of the first record down a little so that the second record begins to take over from it.

Use of EQ

EQ (equalisers) is incredibly important to mixing creatively. Sound is measured in frequency (Hz or kHz for thousands) and there are four main ranges *(Fig. 5.23)*.

Figure 5.23

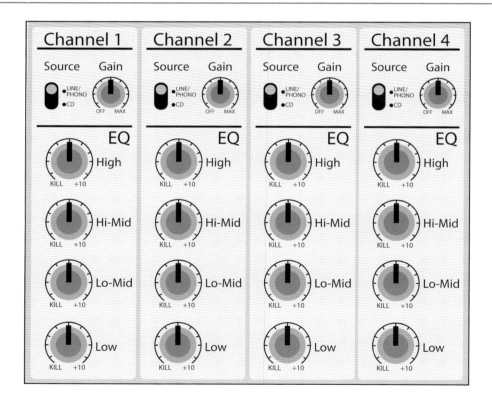

Low refers to the 20–250Hz range. This includes kick drums, basslines and anything that rumbles and hums on the bottom (explosions and booms). Particularly towards the lower extremities of this range, you will hear less precisely, but physically feel vibrations. Your anatomy is set up to experience this as your ribcage vibrates at 80 Hz (so kick drums actually pound your chest).

Lo-Mid refers to the 250–500Hz range. This area is where all the warmth of the kick and bass is. It also includes deep strings, pads, synth chords, richer areas of the vocal range, keyboard and guitar, and lower percussion such as floor toms and congas.

Hi-Mid refers to the 500Hz–3kHz range. This area covers upper vocal ranges, main strings, pads, synth sounds, upper zones of the keyboard and guitar, and higher percussion such as rack toms, bongos, snares and the initial 'body' of some percussion that is mainly found in the High frequencies. Some of the over harmonics of bass instruments and the pop of the kick are also found in the Hi-Mid range.

High refers to the 3kHz–20kHz range. This area covers the 'S' and breath of vocals, high strings, pads, synth sounds, top harmonics of the keyboard and guitar, and high percussion such as hi-hats, shakers, tambourines, triangles and cymbals. Some of the ring of the snare, toms and bongos are also found in the High range. Beyond a certain threshold, the human ear is unable to hear High frequencies. This limit is somewhere between 8–12 kHz (age has an effect on this; younger people have greater ability to hear High frequencies than older people). High frequencies are also more damaging to the ear than any other of the ranges, so protect yourself.

Some mixers only have 3-band EQ (Low, Mid, High), which is fine. 4-band EQ will give you a little more control over the mid-range, but usually only more expensive mixers have it.

Creative use of the EQ will contribute to smoother blending and mixing. Often as you bring a record into the mix, you have the Low frequencies turned down so that it has less kick and bass. As the blend progresses, you gradually strengthen the Low frequencies of the second record whilst weakening them on the first record. This helps to transfer the 'dominance' from Record 1 to Record 2 *(Fig. 5.24)*.

EQ also adds drama to the sound of a mix. You can perform any number of 'EQ filters' by cutting out one range or a combination of ranges. A full cut of one frequency range is known as a 'kill'. Some mixers will also have a switch for an immediate kill of each range. Isolating one particular range will radically alter the sound of a record.

> **Low-Pass Filter** (just the Lows) will give the effect of the music being played underwater as all the detail is removed from the sound.

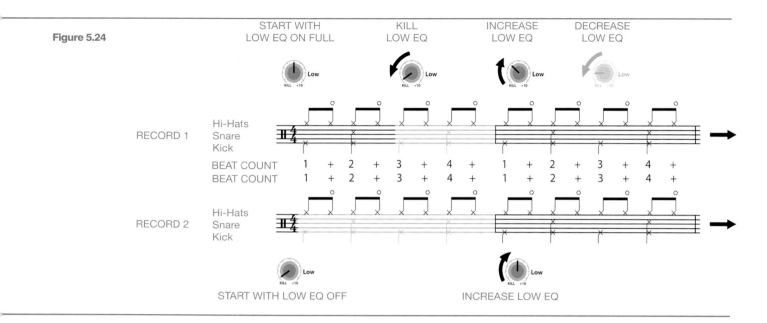

Figure 5.24

	START WITH LOW EQ ON FULL	KILL LOW EQ	INCREASE LOW EQ	DECREASE LOW EQ

RECORD 1 — Hi-Hats / Snare / Kick

BEAT COUNT 1 + 2 + 3 + 4 + 1 + 2 + 3 + 4 +
BEAT COUNT 1 + 2 + 3 + 4 + 1 + 2 + 3 + 4 +

RECORD 2 — Hi-Hats / Snare / Kick

START WITH LOW EQ OFF   INCREASE LOW EQ

Top Tip:
Remember to put the music first. You should never over-EQ a track or over-emphasise particular frequencies. Too much bass will distort, and too much treble is downright painful. Too much EQ filtering will simply annoy the crowd who are ultimately there to hear the music rather than a DJ messing around with it.

> **Band-Pass Filter** (just the mids) will give the effect of the music being played down a telephone. The upper detail and the lower 'bump' will be removed.

> **High-Pass Filter** (just the highs) will give the effect of the music being played in someone else's earphones. All you can hear is a tinny hissing of the top-most details with no substance.

These filters can often have a strong impact on the crowd. The physical presence of the Lows is the major framework and the reason for dance music's pulse. If you remove it, people will automatically anticipate its return. In a similar way, Mid-range and Highs provide all the detail so if you cut them out, the crowd will also await their return to 'complete' the sound spectrum.

Using Sound Effects

Music (especially electronically produced music) often makes use of sonic textures that cannot be compared to any natural acoustic instrument. Early synth pioneers such as Herbie Hancock, Stevie Wonder and Weather Report experimented with twisting sound to produce weird and often wonderful effects. In the same way that sound designers use FX in movies, producers often use sound to accompany the more standard musical elements of harmony, melody and rhythm.

Setting up FX with a DJ Console

Sound effects (FX) are the various methods used to alter sound. Some DJ mixers have built-in FX, others have send outputs and return inputs for use with an external FX unit. Each individual product will operate in a different way, so it seems pointless trying to give operating instructions (you should refer to the operating manual of a particular model) for FX units. The set-up procedure is, however, worth mentioning. You need to set up a loop with the AUX outputs (send) of the mixer connected to the input of the FX unit. Then connect the output of the FX unit to the AUX input (return) on the mixer *(Fig. 5.25)*.

Figure 5.25

6.3mm JACK LEADS

MIXER SEND (OUTPUT) FX UNIT INPUT

MIXER RETURN (INPUT) FX UNIT OUTPUT

If your mixer doesn't have these features, it is possible to run the main outputs to an FX unit in a chain before the amplifier as most of these have a bypass function. FX can usually be controlled by several parameters; 'amount' ('dry' means no effect and 'wet' means full effect), 'frequency' which usually creates a sweep from Low to High EQ ranges and 'resonance' which affects the strength and sharpness of the effect *(Fig. 5.26)*.

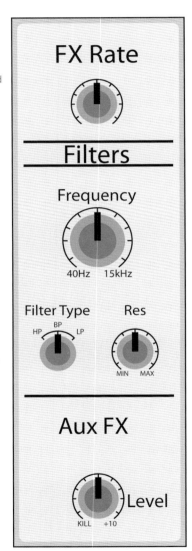

Figure 5.26

Controls the speed
of effect

Controls sweep
from Low to High
frequencies

Res: controls
resonance of
effect

Filter type: selects
desired filter

Controls amount
of effect applied
from external FX
unit

Types of Effect

Filters are the principal effects used by DJs. In addition to the filters that can be performed on the EQs, many mixers also have filters that sweep from the normal sound to hi-pass, lo-pass or band-pass sound. A lo-pass filter only allows low frequencies to be heard, whereas a hi-pass filter only allows high frequencies. A band-pass filter only allows a certain range or band of frequencies to be heard, these would normally be mid-range. It is also possible to get filters that work with an LFO (low frequency oscillation): these add a timeframe in which the filter moves back and forth through the frequencies.

Delay is the kind of echo that is associated with shouting in a mountain range. Sound is bounced and repeated. The 'feedback' of a delay determines how many repetitions you get before the effect finishes, and the 'delay time' affects the regularity of these repetitions.

Reverb is the ambient sound environment that you find in large buildings such as cathedrals or tunnels. You can often control the size of the reverb plate (from small 'ringing' bathroom-style reverb to huge 'booming' caverns) and the length of the 'tail', which will affect the time that the reverb lasts before fading to nothing.

Panning will send the sound to the right or left channel rather than in the centre. Both mono and stereo signals are usually equally divided between left and right. As music moves into the digital age, front and rear panning will also become a possibility for three-dimensional sound (in the same way that home cinema systems play certain sounds from rear speakers).

Flange will sound like a metalising effect on the sound. It works by doubling the waveforms slightly out of sync so that there is a 'rubbing' of the two versions.

Everything You Need to Know about DJing and Success

Phase is an absolute duplication of the waveforms that results in a whooshing sweep through the music. This will make the sound almost entirely disappear as it cancels itself out.

Chorus takes multi-layered sound that is slightly delayed and pitch-shifted to produce a 'choir' effect.

Pitch Shift will change the pitch of the sound in the same way that the varispeed pitch control does. The difference is that this will happen without affecting the length of the waveform by removing or inserting extra parts of the sound. The quality of the sound is noticeably affected if this is done by any more than about ten per cent.

Time Stretch will change the speed of the sound independent of the pitch. This is achieved by duplicating or extracting a certain number of individual waves to make the waveform increase or decrease in length. Like pitch shifting, the sound quality is noticeably affected if this is done by any more than about ten per cent.

Using FX in Mixes

Manipulating the sound by means of FX is very similar to using EQ; a little goes a long way. For example, the dynamic contrast of a breakdown can be enhanced greatly by adding filters, phases or flanges, but you should always return the sound to normal for the re-entry of the track. Reverbs, chorus, panning and delays can also add extra interest to passages of music, but again, it is wise not to overuse these.

Advanced Mixing

As with all skills, the more proficient you become, the more you will want to move on to advanced techniques. However, it is important to remember two vital facts as you start to develop the skills in this section:

1. Trying to attempt advanced mixing techniques before you have fully mastered skills such as cueing, fading, cutting and especially beatmatching is pointless. By all means experiment, but don't expect to succeed until you can do the basics.

2. As you introduce more advanced technical elements into your mixing, fewer people will recognise what you are doing. High levels of skill that go beyond mixing two records together can be like the upper levels of a secret sect to a lot of the crowd (nobody

Top Tip:
You should use FX and EQ to add an extra dimension to the sound, not spoil it by constant repetition.

71

knows what's happening). However, advanced techniques will really impress other DJs and those few people in the know. They also give you immense satisfaction when you perform them (one of the main reasons you want to become a DJ in the first place is to have fun).

A Cappella Mixes

Using unaccompanied vocal tracks (a cappellas) relies heavily on internal rhythmic sense. The other record will provide all the rhythmic elements as a pulse over which you will need to fit the a cappella, but you will need to understand the natural vocal line in order to place it correctly – so you must be familiar with the original track from which the a cappella is taken. This will also help you choose a backing record with similar rhythmic properties (i.e. straight or swing/shuffled groove).

Also, make sure you get to know the a cappella version itself. The vocals are usually separated into verses and choruses with pauses in between, so you may well have to wind forward to find a new cue point for a second verse.

Figure 5.27 shows the alignment of the classic House track 'Bad Habit' by ATFC & Lisa Miller (DFCT19X). Notice how the vocal enters on the first off beat and not on the downbeat. As the a cappella progresses you should set up 'checkpoints' where particular words of the vocal should fall relative to the downbeat of each bar. If you don't know the track well enough, you will be unable to do this. In this example the first checkpoint is where the downbeat of the second bar of the beat record would coincide with the syllable 'rin' of 'ringing'.

Figure 5.27

The technique of mixing a beat over an a cappella is even more complex. The principal is the same but this way round, you have to sync a record to the imaginary drums of the a cappella. As you now have no rhythmic pulse physically present, the task becomes harder. Again, you need to know the original vocal extremely well to accomplish this. Figure 5.28 shows a breakbeat layered over the a cappella from Blu Cantrell's 'Hit 'Em Up Style'. You can see that the break should not be released until the syllable 'sche' of the word 'scheming'. You would then set up your first checkpoint at 'bee' of 'beeming' to make sure that the downbeat of the break fell spot on with this syllable.

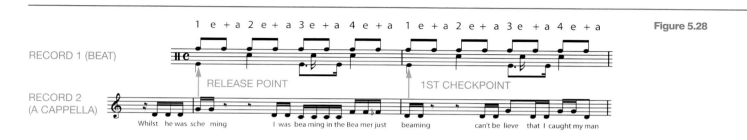

Figure 5.28

Mastering the technique of a cappella mixing will enable you to perform unique 'on-the-spot' remixes. If you choose a classic vocal and mix it with a well-chosen and recognisable instrumental, the effect can be mind-blowing.

Mixing on Three Decks

If beatmatching on two turntables ceases to be a problem and you are up for a challenge, then three-decks mixing is one possible direction you can take. A word of warning; do not attempt this until you are flawless on two turntables. This could be compared to struggling to catch, then trying to juggle three balls. It goes without saying that you will need an extra turntable for this technique. It is very important to set the mixer up carefully before performing a three-deck mix (Fig. 5.29).

You should have Record 1 on one side of the fader and the other two on the opposite side. This is your safety net in case you start to lose the mix. The up-faders for Records 2 and 3 are best kept lower than Record 1; you may also want to take some of the low EQ out too.

Figure 5.29

HEADPHONE CUE FOR RECORD 2 SWITCHED ON

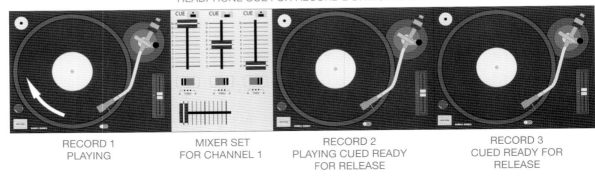

| RECORD 1 PLAYING | MIXER SET FOR CHANNEL 1 | RECORD 2 PLAYING CUED READY FOR RELEASE | RECORD 3 CUED READY FOR RELEASE |

The easiest way to work with three turntables is to work with two of them at a time, so you are mixing Records 1 and 2 and then 1 and 3 as separate pairs. At some stages in the mix, you may have all three at once; sometimes you will want to go back down to two so you can tighten up.

Performing a mix on three turntables:

> Whilst Record 1 is playing, separately cue up and beatmatch Records 2 and 3.

> Re-cue each record (2 and 3) once they are tightly in sync with Record 1.

> Bring Record 2 into the mix using any usual mixing technique (i.e. fade/cut).

> Once you are happy that the blend is tight and can be left unattended, switch the headphone cue over to the channel for Record 3 and drop this third track in. The up-fader for the third deck should remain at zero for now.

> Switch the headphone cue back to Record 2 to check that the mix is still tight. If it has slipped out a little, make the necessary adjustment.

> Return the headphone cue to Record 3 and tighten the mix (if needed) then raise the up-fader and bring the mix in *(Fig. 5.30)*.

> From this point on you will need to focus very hard. Keep toggling between monitoring Record 2 and Record 3 against Record 1. A two bar interval is a recommended timeframe for each mix.

TOGGLE BETWEEN MONITORING RECORDS 2 AND 3

Figure 5.30

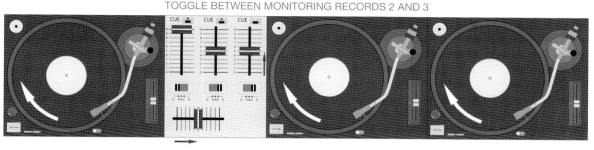

| RECORD 1 PLAYING | MIXER SET TO PLAY RECORDS 1, 2 AND 3 | RECORD 2 IN THE MIX | RECORD 3 IN THE MIX |

Remember if the mix starts to go out, bring the crossfader back over to Record 1 and get out of there quickly.

Needless to say, having three tracks in the mix will sound busier than having two. To avoid a cluttered blend, choose your tracks wisely (more minimal tracks are a safer bet). DJs who use three turntables often keep the third deck reserved for drum tracks, samples, acappellas or scratching. Mixing three full-on tunes is a rarity.

Basic Scratching

The technique of scratching records was developed by early Hip-Hop pioneers such as Grandmaster Flash and Grand Wizard Theodore. The concept of scratching is simple (as soon as you begin cueing records up and moving the record back and forth ready to release, you are actually scratching), but you will quickly realise that the more exotic styles of scratching involve some serious co-ordination between rhythmic manipulation of the vinyl and rhythmic use of the crossfader. Scratching really takes a lot of practice; rather like a skateboard it is easy to get going, but much harder to pull off the really good-looking tricks.

I strongly recommend you explore and utilise the scratch tutorials and web links that I have provided for you at the back of the book; this will prove a much faster method for learning and visually demonstrate the techniques described below.

Modifying the Equipment Set-up

Assuming that you have invested in good equipment, you will only have to make small changes to your set-up to start scratching. Drummers often talk about having their kit 'on their side' so they are working with their kit rather than fighting it. It is amazing how many drummers set up their drums in a totally nonsensical way, and then wonder why they are struggling to get around some of the fills they are attempting. In the same way, if you want to be fast and dexterous on the turntables, you need to bring them in closer.

Figure 5.31 shows a layout known as 'battle style' which is the preferred set-up for scratching and its related techniques. Battle style turns the decks sideways so that the tone-arm and needle are at the top rather than the side. This exposes the greatest portion of the vinyl for easy access.

Figure 5.31

The main disadvantage of this set-up is that you have to reach over the path of the needle in order to use the varispeed for beatmatching. This makes it a bit more awkward for standard mixing.

Everything You Need to Know about DJing and Success

Vestax invests heavily in technological advances for the scratch DJ market. The PDX 3000 is the first turntable with a MIDI input, meaning that a MIDI keyboard can be used to control the speed of the turntable platter, this is great for scratch DJs who scratch with tones, and it means that a DJ can scratch a record whilst also using it to play a melody via the keyboard. The Vestax QFO is another innovative product. Designed by globally respected turntablist DJ Qbert, it features faders on the actual turntable, making a separate scratch mixer unnecessary.

Scratch DJs also recommend various modifications to the standard set-up for the counter-weight, tone-arm and anti-skate *(Fig. 5.32)*. The general principle is to make the needle sit more heavily on the surface of the vinyl so that it doesn't jump. Pennies blu-tacked to the headshell, twisted cartridges and super-elevation of the tone-arm are all a bit excessive but still favoured by some.

Figure 5.32

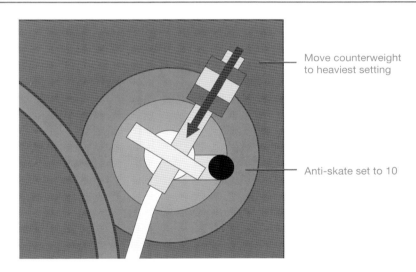

Move counterweight to heaviest setting

Anti-skate set to 10

Scratch Records and Preparing Vinyl

Most slipmats are fine and decent cartridges and needles hold the groove of the record with perfect ease. The thing that will really make a difference is the records themselves. Some records are specifically cut extra deep with widely spaced grooves designed for the sole purpose of scratching. These 'scratch records' are the ideal. There are plenty of titles to choose from, ranging from collections of breaks, vocals and scratches to pure, isolated samples.

77

Some sounds on actual tracks will also lend themselves beautifully to a scratch, but remember that vinyl deteriorates with use. It is not sensible to ruin a tune when there are hundreds of records available purpose-built to get ruined.

Even scratch records need a little bit of preparation. Samples tend to sit better once they are worn in a little as the tiny bumps and pits of the grooves become smoother. If the hole for the spindle is too loose or too tight this will affect the ability to manipulate the record (far more than your choice of slipmat). The hole can be tightened with sticker strips and loosened with rolled-up sandpaper, or even a biro top.

You will also need to get into the habit of marking your vinyl. This will help in terms of seeing where you are in the scratch and seeing the position of the stylus on the record visually, particularly at times where the crossfader is closed and you can't hear the record. How you choose to do this is entirely up to you. A good method is to line the dot or sticker up with a physical aspect of the turntable as it is in your principal field of vision (e.g. the 45 spindle adaptor or the power switch). Another method is to place a sticker on the body surface of the deck next to the platter. You can learn more about all these techniques in the dedicated 'Scratch Tutorial' resources at the back of the book.

Starting to Scratch

Once you have some pre-prepared vinyl, and you have your set-up arranged in a way that feels comfortable, you need to find a sound to scratch with. There are certain famous scratch samples that are pretty much guaranteed to be on most scratch records such as 'ahhhh', 'freeesh' and steady musical tones. Ultimately you are looking for a sound that starts immediately; words with harder vowel and consonant sounds (i.e. 'bad' is better than 'sweet').

It is nigh on impossible to show scratch patterns in pictorial form, so from now on, they will be shown in a notated form that was developed in various stages by Stephen Webber, DJ Radar and John Carluccio *(Fig. 5.33* and *5.34)*. This has been enhanced to include the musical notation of the breakbeat, a visual representation of the scratch sample itself and the crossfader commands where applicable. The grey line in the grid refers to the position of the scratch sound on the record in relation to time. Ghosted areas on the grid show where the crossfader is 'shut' and the sound of the sample's movement is 'hidden'.

Figure 5.33 and Figure 5.34 show:

> Ahhhhh sample played at normal speed
> Crossfader closed and sample rewound to the start
> Ahhhhh sample played at normal speed

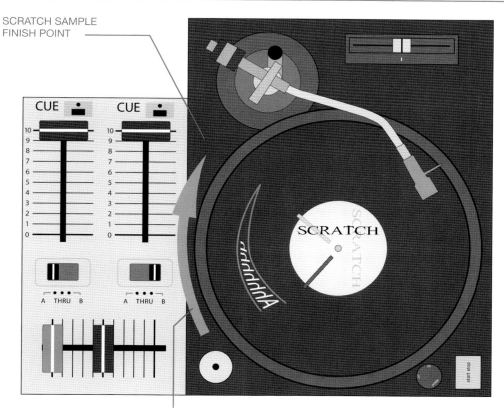

SCRATCH SAMPLE
FINISH POINT

Figure 5.33

SCRATCH SAMPLE START POINT

Figure 5.34

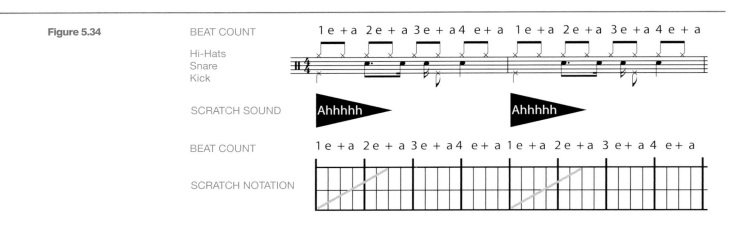

Rubbing/Baby Scratching

The first type of scratch is the 'rub' or 'baby scratch', which you should be doing every time you cue up a record at the start point. This is simply a case of moving the record forwards and backwards over the sample *(Fig. 5.35)*. The only difference is that you should focus far more on returning exactly to the start point. Also, pay more attention to the speed and rhythm of your hand movement. A rub consists of both the 'forward scratch' and the 'back scratch'.

Figure 5.35

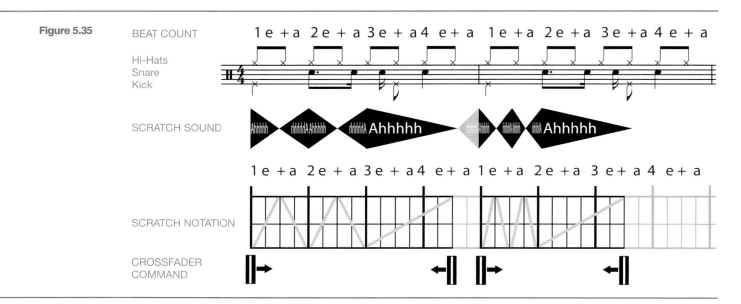

Figure 5.35 shows:

> Ahhhhh sample played and rewound at double speed 2 TIMES

> Ahhhhh sample played at normal speed

> Crossfader closed and sample rewound to the start

> Ahhhhh sample played and rewound at quadruple speed 2 TIMES

> Ahhhhh sample played at normal speed

Do not underestimate the importance of rubbing. Many of the subsequent techniques rely on a tight execution of this simplest of scratches. It is worth spending time developing a large repertoire of rhythmic patterns as well as learning to control the speed (and therefore pitch) of the rubs.

Chops and Chirps

Once you have mastered the baby scratch, you should start to separate the forwards and backwards scratches with the crossfader. A separate front scratch is known as a 'chop' and an isolated back scratch is known as a 'chirp' *(Fig. 5.36)*. The chop will give you a punchy stab as you hit the front of the sample whereas a chirp will give you a whip-back as you quickly reverse the sound.

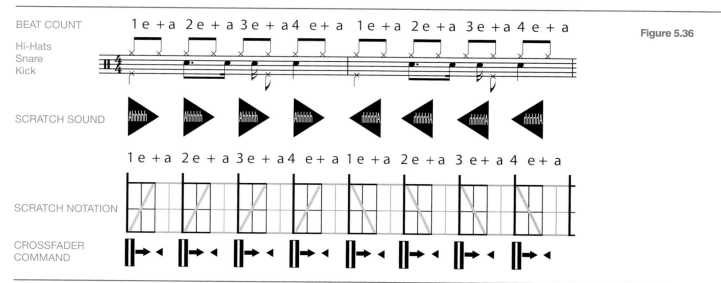

Figure 5.36

Figure 5.36 shows:

>   Ahhhhh sample played at double speed
    Crossfader closed and sample rewound to the start 4 TIMES

>   Crossfader closed

>   Ahhhhh sample rewound at double speed
    Crossfader closed and sample played to the end 4 TIMES

You may also wish to combine the two techniques so you have a pattern that goes chop-chirp-chop-chirp . . . This is effectively a rub with its edges trimmed and neatened up by the crossfader. When you do this, try to give a little more length to the first of each group of 4. Think: 'ca-ter-pi-llar ca-ter-pi-llar'. You will see that the crossfader movement accompanies the scratch movement itself. The crossfader then closes to hide the chirp if you are chopping (and vice versa). This will take a bit of practice to catch cleanly. If the fader movement is not simultaneous with the rub, you will have an overspill in the other direction (the one you are supposed to hide). In this example, the chops and chirps are in time with the 4 main beats of the bar, but you can do them faster!

Drags and Tears

As you begin to progress, you will soon hear how versatile each scratch sound is; quick movement will give a higher, shorter sound whereas slow movement will give you a ponderous longer sound. You should try to develop your control of your vinyl hand. Both 'drags' and 'tears' affect the back scratch. A 'drag' is a basically slurred chirp (starts slow and speeds up) and a 'tear' is a chirp that you split into two halves by stopping midway through the movement (Fig. 5.37).

>   Ahhhhh sample rewound at double speed with slurr
    Ahhhhh sample played at quadruple speed
    4 TIMES

>   Ahhhhh sample rewound at double speed with slurr

>   Ahhhhh sample played at double speed

>   Ahhhhh sample rewound at double speed with stop in the middle
    Ahhhhh sample played at double speed
    4 TIMES

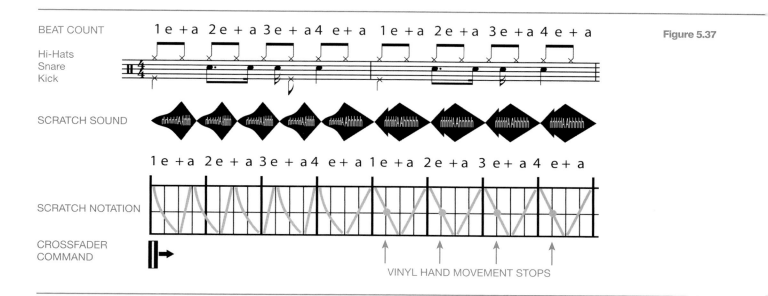

BEAT COUNT

Hi-Hats
Snare
Kick

SCRATCH SOUND

SCRATCH NOTATION

CROSSFADER
COMMAND

VINYL HAND MOVEMENT STOPS

Figure 5.37

Transforming

If you want to improve your scratching, you should take considerable time in mastering the art of 'transforming'. This involves using the crossfader to split the sample into various segments *(Fig. 5.38)*. Transforming is the main skill that will link all your other patterns together so it's well worth investing some serious practice. You should try to use longer samples at first as they give you more time to execute the splits. The crossfader is now your principal rhythmic tool, so try to cut into the beats of the bar (you can also cut in on the off beats and their subdivisions).

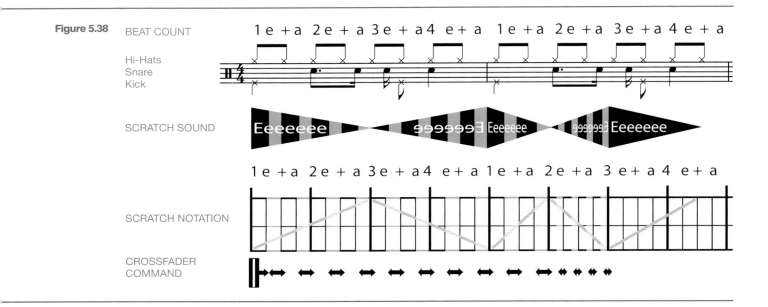

Figure 5.38

BEAT COUNT

Hi-Hats
Snare
Kick

SCRATCH SOUND

SCRATCH NOTATION

CROSSFADER
COMMAND

Advanced Scratching

Rubs, chops, chirps, drags, tears and transforms are sometimes referred to as the 'old school' scratches, as they all work on an older principal of starting with the crossfader open, bringing in the scratch then closing the crossfader. Once you feel that you have mastered these important cornerstones of scratching, you can then explore the possibilities of the 'new school' scratches. It is not advisable to start with these more advanced patterns; not because they are particularly harder (in fact some are actually easier) but simply because the old school techniques will tie your combinations together far more successfully. Some of the 'new school' scratches have a tendency to be performed extremely fast, almost to the point of being messy, so you should intersperse them with solid old school patterns which will make your combinations sound tighter.

Remember to utilise the tuition links at the back of the book to see these techniques demonstrated on camera – you will get a deeper feel for what I'm describing.

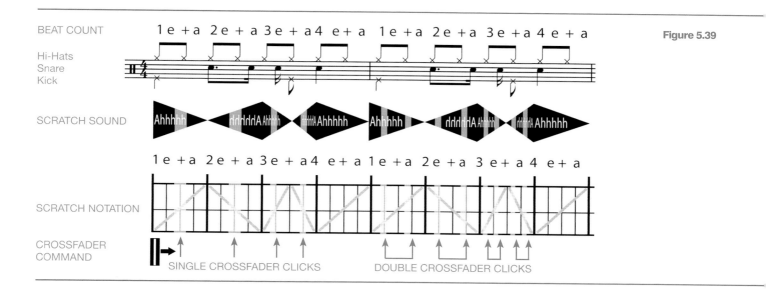

Figure 5.39

Flares and Orbits

The hand movement for a 'flare' and a 'double-click flare' ('orbit') is a back and forth rub. Rather than using the fader to divide the two directions, you put one crossfader click (or two for an orbit) in the middle of each direction *(Fig. 5.39)*. This is often described as an illusion scratch; it gives the impression of more movements than are actually going on. As you hear the change of direction, it serves as an extra 'click' that is not physically performed. It is entirely possible to get a similar scratch sound to both a flare and an orbit using transforming, but there is far more crossfader work involved in the latter.

The main advantage of using flares and orbits is the speed at which they can be rolled out. They both have a natural flow that is a little less 'spitting' than a very quick transform. Both the flare and the orbit start with the fader open so if you are familiar with transforming, the only problem you will have is breaking the habit of cutting the fader in with the change of direction.

Crabs and Twiddles

Pioneered by world-class Turntablist DJ Q-Bert, this finger-style scratch relies on an unorthodox use of the crossfader. The vinyl movement consists of a back and forth rub. It is essential to have absolutely no curve on your crossfader in order to execute clean finger scratches. Only the fastest crossfader will do. You must rapidly tap the crossfader open with three or four of your fingers one after another, using your thumb to quickly close the crossfader after each tap. This motion is performed in a constant cycle.

Hydroplane Rubs

A 'hydroplane rub' is like a shiver. You should use a long sample if possible and play from the end rather than the start. Start dragging the record backwards through the scratch sample, using a finger from the crossfader hand to act as a brake. Pushing down on the record with the right amount of pressure whilst pulling it backwards will make it judder *(Fig. 5.40)*. This could be compared to the continual scuffing of your feet in order to slow a roundabout down to a stop. The result should be a 'purring' of the sound.

Using Other Mixer Functions: Echoes and Bubbles

The two other mixer features used for scratching are the up-faders and the EQs. Some DJs use the up-faders rather than the crossfader (or a mixture of the two) to perform all the other scratches (crabs and twiddles excluded). One particular scratch designed for the up-fader is the 'echo' where you perform a series of cuts that descend in volume *(Fig. 5.41)*.

A back and forth rub, whilst slowly bringing the fader volume down, can be used in a routine to break up different scratch moves.

A 'bubble' scratch is one where the record is rubbed and one EQ band is manipulated between its minimum and maximum setting, whist the other bands are on their minimum setting. The scratch should give you a 'wah wah' type effect. Because most scratch samples are vocal-based sounds, you will find that bubbling is most effective on the middle frequencies.

Using Other Turntable Functions: Tones and Tweaks

The varispeed pitch control and the 33/45 speed controls can be used to alter the tone of a scratch sample. This is most effective with musical samples (bleep tones, horn or string stabs etc.), but can be used with any sample. For example, you could perform a transform pattern with a long whine at 33⅓ rpm, then repeat the same pattern at 45 rpm for a higher pitched (because the platter is rotating at a higher speed) version.

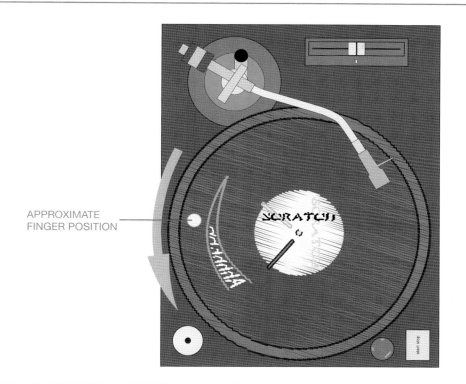

Figure 5.40

APPROXIMATE
FINGER POSITION

The varispeed can be used to actually play melodies. This is limited to a range of 6 different notes (The areas in between -8%, +8% and 0% will not give you notes on the chromatic scale).

Original tone at C
33⅓ rpm: -8% B   0% C   +8% C#
45 rpm: -8% E   0% F   +8% F#

A 'tweak' is any regular scratch performed with the turntable powered down. Because the turntable is turned off the record will not return to its original speed but instead slow down to a halt until you touch it again. This makes the scratch sound sluggish and can be used with a transform or any other pattern on the crossfader. This is a good technique to use for the end of a set of scratch patterns.

Figure 5.41

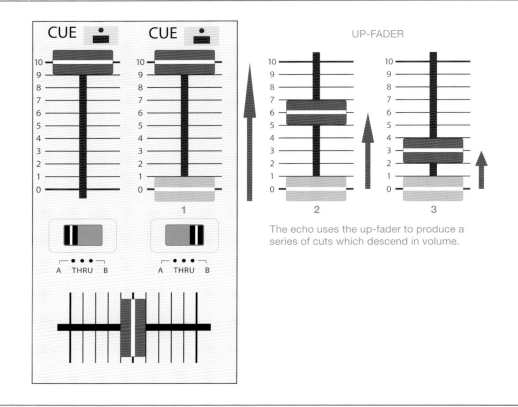

The echo uses the up-fader to produce a series of cuts which descend in volume.

Double Copy Mixing

Hip-Hop DJs in particular buy duplicate copies of every record (twice as expensive, but at least you have a spare) so that they can perform what is known as 'beat juggling'. This term has become an umbrella description for a range of techniques that involve two copies of the same record.

Beatmatching double copies is fairly easy, although be aware that sometimes the exact pitch of the records is sometimes not quite the same (only by a hair's width) due to the turntables' motors being slightly different. You do however need to know the track extremely well so that you can pinpoint where you are in the track at all times. As these techniques usually involve lyrics, you should memorise the vocal lines. You should also prepare the two copies, marking the start of the word(s) that you want to use.

Figure 5.42

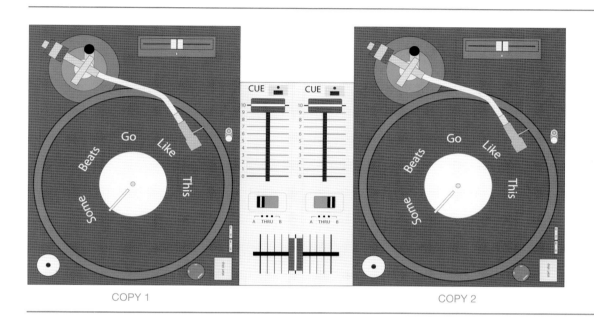

COPY 1   COPY 2

Figure 5.42 shows two records cued to a start point where they will both play exactly the same phrase: 'Some beats go like this'. There are numerous beat juggles that can be performed at this stage.

Flanging and Phasing

When the two records run in sync with each other there is a duplication of sound waveforms. This starts with a flange – described earlier – creating a metalising effect. As the two copies tighten to absolute perfection they will phase, sending a whooshing sweep through the music, sometimes to the extent that the sound will almost entirely disappear as the two records start to cancel each other out. This also happens if you mix two different records that use the same break.

Flanges and phases are easy to perform by playing the records together at the same speed but very slightly out of sync. The moment of total phase will also give you a very strange sonic experience, almost like 3D stereo.

Beat Chasing

Once you have produced some flanges and phases, the next step is to try bouncing between the copies so that they play 'follow-the-leader'. You can beat chase in delay or pre-delay (i.e. you can have Copy 2 one step behind *(Fig. 5.43)* or one step ahead *(Fig. 5.44)* of Copy 1). There are several different methods of setting up a beat chase; you can drop the cue point in early/late or you can slip back out from a phase using a single rub.

Figure 5.43

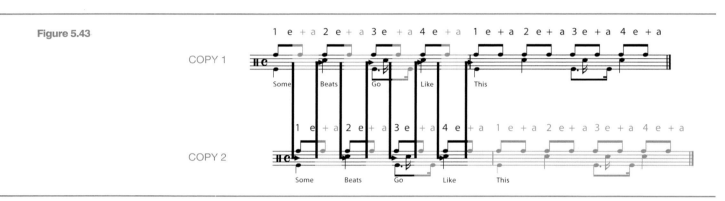

In Figure 5.43, Copy 1 starts the lyrics then bounces to Copy 2 for the repetition. Using black for Copy 1 and Blue for Copy 2, the effect would be: 'Some Some Beats Beats Go Go Like Like This This'. It is important to enter cleanly into Record 1 for the front of the bar line so you would not have the repetition of the word 'this'.

Figure 5.44

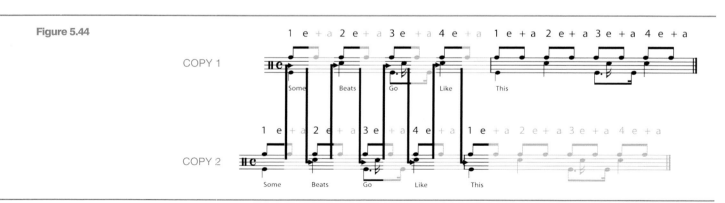

Everything You Need to Know about DJing and Success

In Figure 5.44, Copy 2 starts the lyrics then bounces to Copy 1 for the repetition. Again with the same colour coding, the effect would be: 'Some Some Beats Beats Go Go Like Like This This'. (Notice that you can now fit the extra 'this' before the main bar line of Record 1.)

Incorporating Scratching

Using the 'chop' scratch, you can repeat the first word of the chase over previous lyrics. For example, if the lyrics went:

'Sub blow low lift you off ya feet, Cuttin' and scratchin' DJ's technique
Two turntables in the mix, some beats go like this'

You could scratch the word 'beat' (snare words are better for this particular scratch) from Copy 2 over the first three lines of this verse. A useful pattern to learn for this is the 'Bossa Clave', which is the beat count for the Brazilian Bossa Nova. The Bossa Clave will put the snare on beat 1, the off-beat of 2, and beat 4, then in each second bar, on beat 2 and the off-beat of 3 (Fig. 5.45).

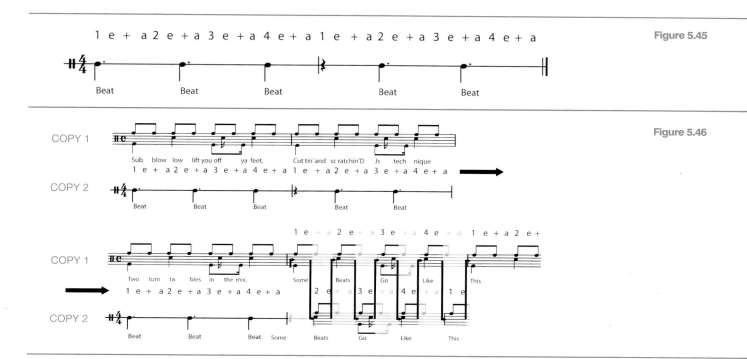

Figure 5.45

Figure 5.46

Figure 5.46 shows how this might fit against the lyrics. The snare that goes with the word 'beat' chops in using the Bossa Clave until the point where Copy 1 is about to say 'beat'. Copy 2 is then released in-between the words 'some' and 'beats' for a pre-delay chase.

Back Cueing

Once you have developed control over slipping the lyrics behind (or in front of) each other on the two copies, you can then move on to 'back cueing' which involves repeating a chosen passage round in a loop. For this technique, you really need to be able to manipulate the vinyl with either hand.

The best way to approach back cueing is to cut between two or even four bars, so using the same example, you would have: *'Some beats go like this-(2-3-4) Some beats go like this-(2-3-4) Some beats go like this-(2-3-4) Some beats go like this-(2-3-4)'* etc.
At this pace, you would be able to use the headphones to re-cue the start of this line, although it is better to do it visually. Try to memorise the amount of vinyl you need to retrace (the marker will help). As you bring the back cueing closer, you will not have time to use the headphones but the visual distance will also decrease *(Fig. 5.47)*: *'Some beats go like Some beats go like Some beats Some beats'* etc.

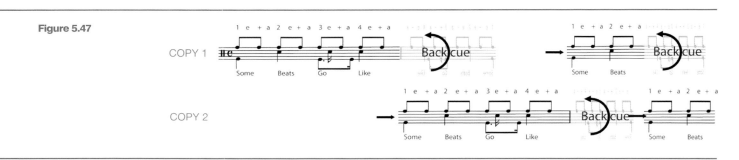

Figure 5.47

DJs such as Cash Money, Jazzy Jeff and Cutmaster Swift who pioneered this technique brought the back cues down to a single word repetition. Again, you can incorporate scratches into this technique, so that each time you back cue, the drop is performed using a scratch. You should also practise using both hands to 'pass' the crossfader to the other side (so left hand passes to the right, and vice versa). In old school Hip-Hop videos, you may also see DJs reversing this technique so the hands cross over each other (sheer madness).

Beat Juggling

'Beat juggling' is to get single pair cuts between each word or part of a drum break. The main difference between beat chasing and beat juggling is that the records are not in continual motion whilst you cut between them. You should start approaching this technique by getting a feel for the 'stops' you need to make for each word or part of the beat (clean non-fussy drum breaks are a good starting point). Use one copy to begin with, isolating each element by stopping the spin of the record in between:

kick-*(Stop)*-*hat*-*(Stop)*-*snare*-*(Stop)*-*hat*-*(Stop)*-*kick*-*(Stop)*-*hat*-*(Stop)*-*snare*-*(Stop)*-*hat*-*(Stop)*

Then start do the same thing with the two records with one record leading the other (*Fig. 5.48*):

kick-*(Stop)*-<u>*kick*-*(Stop)*</u>-*hat*-*(Stop)*-<u>*hat*-*(Stop)*</u>-*snare*-*(Stop)*-<u>*snare*-*(Stop)*</u>-*hat*-*(Stop)*-<u>*hat*-*(Stop)*</u>-*kick*-*(Stop)*-<u>*kick*-*(Stop)*</u>-*hat*-*(Stop)*-<u>*hat*-*(Stop)*</u>-*snare*-*(Stop)*-<u>*snare*-*(Stop)*</u>-*hat*-*(Stop)*-<u>*hat*-*(Stop)*</u>

You will need to pass the crossfader inwards from deck to deck as you perform the cuts. This means developing an acute feel for where each part of the drum break lies on the vinyl, as you will have to back-cue in tiny increments as your hand leaves the vinyl to pass the fader across. This will take many hours of dedicated practice.

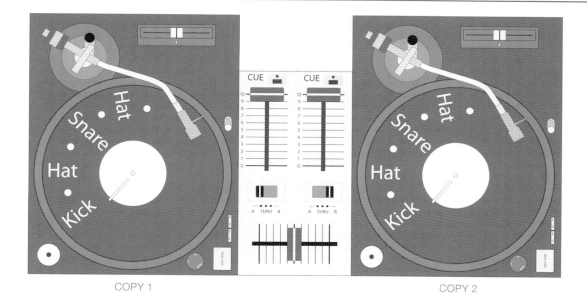

Figure 5.48

COPY 1

COPY 2

Although it is unlikely that you would use techniques such as beat chasing, back-cueing or juggling in the general run of mixing (unless you are mixing Hip-Hop) they are challenging tricks to master. Once you learn how to perfect them, you will have become more than a DJ, you will be a 'Turntablist'.

Lyric Cutting

Lyric cutting is taking lyrics from different tracks and mixing them in such a way that they form a conversation. David Rodriguez, who DJed at the early Disco club The Limelight was known for his ability to tell a story through the music that he played. The technique of lyric cutting takes this one stage further as demonstrated more recently by Danish DMC world champion DJ Noise. The most important requirement for lyric cutting is a good memory for words and sentences.

Depending on your choice of records, you will often find yourself using other techniques such as cutting, scratching, back cueing or beat juggling to execute your lyric cuts. You may need to prepare your records visually by placing a sticker on the surface of the vinyl so that the needle is 'guided' into the correct groove for easy cueing of a particular lyrical phrase. This can be a fiddly piece of preparation, but it is well worth the effort for quick alignment.

Lyric Cutting in Action

To demonstrate an example of this technique, take the Mobb Deep album 'Hell on Earth' on the side with 'Still Shining' and 'Apostles Warning'. 'Apostles Warning' contains the lyrics: *'Here take a toke of this, deadly rhyme vocalist'* – the starting phrase for this particular lyric cut.

> Using the sticker surface cue technique, mark the place on 'Still Shining' where the lyrics are: *'Satisfaction, guaranteed real sh*t'*
> Take Amad Jamal's 'LA City' as your second record, containing the lyrics *'I specialise in writing lyrical jewels so you're rewinding it. See you're possessed and I'm the kind of it'*.
> Start by back cueing between 'Apostles Warning' and the first sentence from 'LA City' then using the second line of the Amad Jamal track, cue up the phrase from 'Still Shining' so: *'Here take a toke of this, deadly rhyme vocalist' 'I specialise in writing lyrical jewels so you're rewinding it'*
> Back cue these two phrases several times, then proceed to the last cut: *'Here take a toke of this, deadly rhyme vocalist' 'I specialise in writing lyrical jewels so you're rewinding it. See you're possessed and I'm the kind of it'*
> Whilst this phrase is playing, cue up 'Still Shining': *'Satisfaction, guaranteed real sh*t'*

Everything You Need to Know about DJing and Success

Notice in the above example that the lyric about rewinding suggests a back cue, so that the initial cut is performed several times before allowing the full phrase from 'LA City' to play. This gives you just enough time to find the cue point for the sentence from 'Still Shining' that should conclude the lyric cut.

Choice of records, and more specifically groups of words and sentences, is everything with lyric cutting. In the above example, you will quickly see that as well as the similarities in the subject matter of these three records, there is an added element created by the rhyming of the sentences. Not only should you listen out for lyrics from records that really speak to each other, but you have to be careful with the EQ and tonal qualities of records. Pay close attention to vocal inflections and backing musical elements, as they may differ too greatly for the cut to be effective (Barry White and Eminem would not sit well together). Beatmatching is sometimes not required to the usual degree of accuracy as you are not actually mixing at any stage, but it is unlikely that two records that run at totally different tempos would work, so the bpms should be approximately the same.

Using CD Turntables

In the modern age of DJing, vinyl has not been entirely replaced by CDs or MP3s, but it has had to make room for the other formats. Some DJs (particularly older ones) have found the introduction of such new technology rather alarming, almost threatening.

Many DJs use all three formats in a set. This does not mean to say that vinyl, CD and MP3 mixing are all the same; they definitely are not.

The Pros and Cons of Using CD Decks

CD turntables are often compared with the industry standard Technics 1200/1210 vinyl turntables in terms of form and function. This is actually not the ideal way to view a CD deck. Although the Technics DZ1200 is closely modelled on its analogue older brother, it is a different machine that offers new functions for a DJ to get stuck into. Seen from a completely unbiased point of view, there are some techniques that are better suited to traditional vinyl decks and others that are exclusive to or far easier to perform on a CD turntable.

Pros
Inbuilt cue-point and looping facilities enable a CD deck to cope with real time re-editing far more successfully, and many models have inbuilt FX even if your mixer does not. With the use of built-in or SD memory cards, CD turntables can store information such as cue-points, loops or even samples. They are also compatible with MP3s without the need for a separate unit.

Top Tips:
> Always keep your scratching tight and in time with the music
> Record your scratching and listen to how it sounds to others
> Avoid scratching over vocals
> Check out other DJs' routines and get inspiration from them
> Make sure that you create your own original technique.

95

Figure 5.49

The Key Features of a CD Turntable

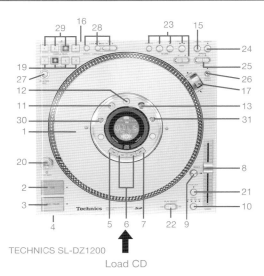

TECHNICS SL-DZ1200

Load CD

PIONEER CDJ-800

Load CD

1 – Platter (rotates on Technics/stationary on Pioneer) – Controls the play of the audio track
2 – Cue button – Locates the beginning of the selected audio track
3 – Start/stop button (brakes on Technics/pauses on Pioneer) – Plays and stops the audio track
4 – Eject button (front panel on Technics/face panel on Pioneer) – Ejects the CD
5 – Track back-skip button – Skips to previous audio track
6 – Track search buttons – Searches though the audio track
7 – Track forward–skip button – Skips to the next audio track
8 – Varispeed controller – Controls the speed at which the audio track plays
9 – Master tempo button – Plays the audio track at its original speed
10 – Varispeed range button – Controls the range of the varispeed controller
11 – Loop in button – Pressed to mark the beginning of a loop
12 – Loop out button – Pressed to mark the end of a loop
13 – Loop exit/re-loop button – Exits a loop or goes back to a previously selected loop
14 – Automated loop length buttons (Pioneer only) – Control the length of the loop
15 – Vinyl simulation button – Allows the audio track to be manipulated like traditional vinyl by using the platter
16 – Vinyl speed control (brake-speed control on Technics) – Controls the reaction speed of the audio track once the platter is released
17 – Reverse platter toggle (motor reverses on Technics) – Plays the audio track in reverse
18 – MP3 folder search functions (Pioneer only)

19 – Cue-point recall functions (Technics only) – Recalls cue points stored in the memory
20 – Power down switch (Technics only) – Has the effect of powering down a vinyl turntable motor
21 – Pitch lock button (Technics only) – Plays the audio track at its original speed
22 – SD/CD toggle (Technics only) – Selects the SD card or CD for audio playback
23 – SD memory edit functions (Technics only) – Allows data from an SD card to be recalled and edited
24 – FX button (Technics only) – Allows platter to be used for effect manipulation
25 – FX scroll (Technics only) – Selects effect type
26 – Instant change button (Technics only) – Lets the audio track play instantly and not in synchronization with the platter
27 – Real time record button (Technics only) – Allows audio to be recorded to the sample pads
28 – Sample edit functions (Technics only) – Edits samples stored in the sample pads
29 – Sample trigger buttons (Technics only) – Sample pads used for storing and triggering samples
30 – Remain/auto cue – Toggles display between the time remaining and time elapsed in the audio track. When held down for two seconds toggles between auto cue on and off
31 – LCD display angle button (Technics only) – Rotates the angle of the display by 90 degrees

Cons

Serious scratching and turntablism skills such as beat juggling (despite some innovative designs) are not really viable options on a CD deck, mainly due to the size of the platter but also because the digital reading of the format does not lend itself to the natural flow and movement required for these techniques. Lyric cutting, beat chasing and back cueing ('looping' if you are a CD DJ) are a great deal easier, but not as visual or as skilful.

Mixing on CD Decks

Many of the mixing techniques discussed in earlier chapters are performed in exactly the same way on a CD turntable. The basic principles of beatmatching, fading, cutting and blending remain unchanged. The technique of cueing, however, takes on a very different roll. Once you have found a cue-point (or even several) you can set this as a bookmark for instant replay. Although the initial search is not as straightforward in that you can't just drop the needle on the record and cue up, re-cueing is instantaneous.

The principal models you will encounter in bars and clubs are Pioneer CDJs (200s/400s/800s or 1000s). You may also come across the Technics DZ1200. Bars occasionally have older 'Mobile DJ-style' Denon or Numark twin consoles, which are capable of the more basic functions only. Figure 5.49 shows both the Pioneer and Technics Model with their functions labelled accordingly.

Diversity of Operation

CD decks can vary greatly in the features that they offer, and unlike vinyl turntables, where you are pretty much always going to be playing on a set of 1200/10s, you can find yourself using a number of different models. Using the jog wheel on a Pioneer CDJ is nothing like using the platter on a Technics DZ1200. Both offer looping facilities, but the top range Pioneers have pre-set time divisions once the loop is set up. The Technics offers different 'needle' simulations, filters and FX that do not work in the same way as any other brand or model.

Even stopping a track is different. The Pioneer does not actually stop but pauses, leaving an audible stuttering effect, and automatically pauses in between tracks. The Technics, once in 'vinyl' mode, will play through the CD like a regular record unless the brake is pressed, so here you have the option of the stop sound of a vinyl turntable (controllable) or an instant cut (the CDJ1000 also has this feature).

Top Tip:
You should learn the basic functions of all the different models of CD turntable so that you will never feel like a piece of equipment is unfamiliar and learn which model is best for you.

6 Digital DJ Formats/Mixing with Computer Software

This section is going to provide you with an overview of digital DJing and help to explain everything, from building your first digital set-up to mastering some of the advanced techniques of the current software and hardware available. 2009 was a monumental year for the digital DJing industry. There were more company collaborations, developing new products; more software enhancements; more MIDI (Musical Instrument Digital Interface) controllers were released; and more DJs were using digital components in their live sets than ever before.

Digital DJing: A Brief History

The move away from analogue, vinyl-based DJing gathered momentum with the introduction of CD turntables. The Pioneer CD turntable, conceived some 15 years ago, became a reality when the CDJ 1000 was released in 2001, quickly becoming the industry standard. In 2009 the fully updated CDJ 2000 was released.

In 2000, Native Instruments, who are now widely recognised as being the original innovators of the digital DJing scene, released the world's first computer-based DJing software: Traktor DJ Studio, now known as Traktor Pro. 2005 saw the release of vinyl and CD emulation technology, giving DJs the ability to play digital tracks on their existing analogue set-ups, via the use of specially designed time-coded vinyl and CDs. The main products offering this technology were Native Instrument's Traktor Scratch, Serato's Scratch Live and Stanton's Final Scratch.

In 2005, we also saw Ableton Live become a credible alternative to the traditional turntable and mixer set-up, with DJs such as DJ Sasha converting to use the software.

Who knows if the future of DJing is digital? What's beyond doubt is that the modern DJ can no longer ignore it.

Digital DJing Pros and Cons

With any new idea or a different way of doing something, there will alway be sceptics, as there have been with digital DJing. However, over the last few years, the digital platform has become the DJing norm, with the majority of top DJs embracing the technology. However, that doesn't mean a digital set up is right for you, to help you decide, we've prepared the following list of Pros and Cons of digital DJing.

Pros

> Ability to be more creative (with your music) when mixing.

> Easy to loop, add effects, slice music and remix on the fly.

> Potential for crossover between certain types of DJing and production software.

> Portability of set up, i.e. laptop and midi-controller versus vinyl decks and mixer.

> Transportation of music, i.e. MP3s versus vinyl records.

> Cheaper cost of MP3s versus vinyl.

> Compatibility with iTunes to manage and store music library.

Cons

> Potential to beatmatch automatically, which diminishes one of the skills of DJing.

> Visual aspects of working with a computer not as 'exciting' as using vinyl decks.

> Absence of vinyl's distinctive sound.

> Potential difficulty in connecting a digital set-up.

Digital DJing: What You Need to Get Started

Digital DJing is essentially the reproduction of an analogue DJ set-up using digital components. These digital components are: a laptop, DJ software, MIDI controller, sound card and MP3 music files. There are numerous alternatives, across a wide range of budgets, to choose from, but the key to your digital set-up is to understand which products best fit your needs.

To Apple Mac or Not

If your budget can stretch to include an Apple Mac Book, then I would strongly advise that you get one. You need a stable operating platform, and it's widely agreed that the most stable belongs to Macs. At the very least you'll need a laptop with a dual-core processor, as the last thing you want is to be in the middle of a killer mix and your entire system to freeze. Having said that, PCs are robust machines, easier to upgrade and, if you're on a budget, are a really good alternative.

Whichever laptop you decide on, I suggest you check out the forums of the software programs you are considering buying. That way you'll find out how current DJs are using their programs, rather than relying on manufacturers' performance specifications.

Choosing your DJing Software

Once you have chosen your laptop, you need to decide on software. Firstly, there are the computer-based, virtual DJ software packages, such as Traktor Pro and Serato ITCH, both of which are controlled with dedicated MIDI controllers.

These programs work by transferring digital music files (e.g. MP3s and WAVs) to virtual turntables, which are then manipulated with the use of the MIDI controller. Audio output is achieved via the sound card.

This type of set up will most likely appeal to new DJs who do not already own vinyl or CD turntables, or those who are restricted in terms of space. A standard set-up will look something like Figure 6.1, including laptop and MIDI controller (with built-in soundcard).

Everything You Need to Know about DJing and Success

Standard Virtual DJing Software Set-up

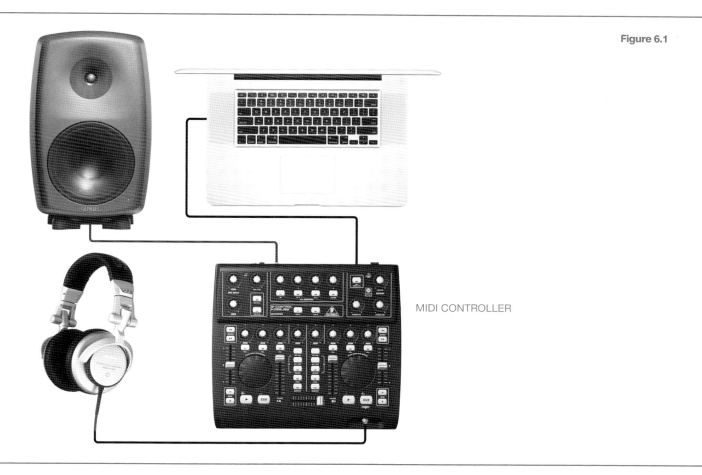

Figure 6.1

MIDI CONTROLLER

The second option is to use vinyl/CD emulation software, where special pieces of time-coded vinyl or CD are used to allow digital music files to be manipulated using a set of vinyl or CD turntables. Traktor Scratch Pro and Serato Scratch Live are two of the leading examples of this type of software. Figures 6.2 and 6.3 show set-up diagrams for each.

Traktor Scratch Pro Set-up

Figure 6.2

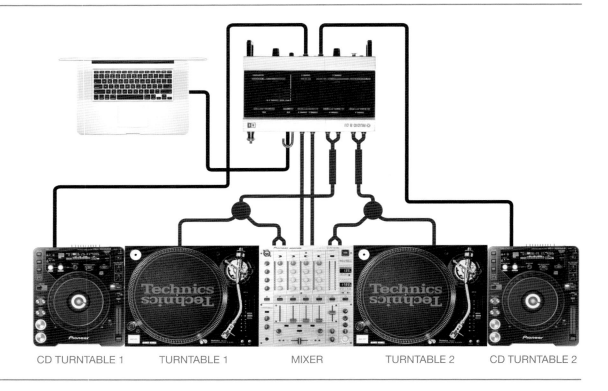

CD TURNTABLE 1   TURNTABLE 1   MIXER   TURNTABLE 2   CD TURNTABLE 2

Serato Scratch Live Set-up

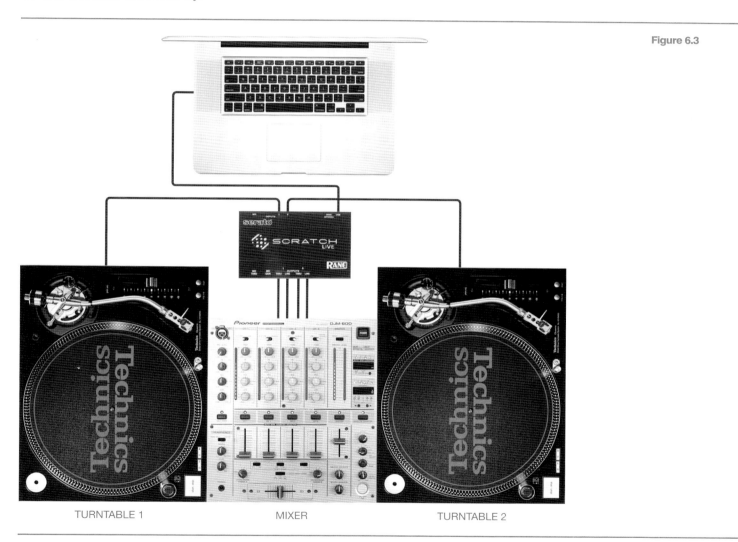

Figure 6.3

TURNTABLE 1   MIXER   TURNTABLE 2

Traktor and Serato in More Detail

The packages offered by Traktor and Serato are fast becoming the industry standard. This is mainly due to their stable operating platforms, cutting-edge features and professional DJ endorsements. The likes of Ritchie Hawtin, Carl Cox and Pete Tong are using Traktor, and DJ Jazzy Jeff, DJ Marky and DJ Yoda using Serato. Arguably, Traktor currently have the edge, due to their tighter time-coded vinyl/CDs and additional features.

Some of Traktor's Top Features
> An intuitive and stylish interface.

> Features 4 playback decks with automatic beat-gridding of tracks, advanced beat detection and Sync Lock for perfect mixing.

> 28 professional effects – tempo sync to any deck or route an external source through the industry-leading effects section.

> Real-time track management with incremental search, Crate Flick artwork browsing, iPod™ and iTunes™ compatibility.

> Play, cue, jog wheel control, hot cues and loop setting/adjusting follow the same intuitive patterns as industry-standard hardware.

> The software interface and features of both Traktor Pro and Traktor Scratch Pro are the same, apart from a small virtual vinyl or CD icon in the Scratch version. This is very useful should you want to swap between the two.

Some of Serato's Top Features
> Integrated 'one-to-one' hardware to software mapping for instant control and minimum set-up time.

> Inter-operable with Scratch Live crates, loops and cue points, and support for iTunes™.

> Clean and simple software user interface with emphasis on hardware controller to display information.

> Auto Tempo Matching, Beat Sync, Optimal Gain and BPM Calculation.

> Uses unique colour waveforms for easy identification of sound.

> Capacity to set and store cue-points.

You can download free demo or full versions of both pieces of software at:

www.native-instruments.com/#/en/products/dj/traktor-pro
www.native-instruments.com/index.php?id=tprodemoversion – Free Demo
www.serato.com
www.serato.com/downloads/itch – Free Demo

However, there are numerous other DJ software packages available, including: M-Audio's Torq Xponent, Stanton's Final Scratch, Numark's Cue, Atomix's Virtual DJ, Fruity Loops' Deckadance, MixMeister's Fusion and MixVibes Cross DJ. You can download or find out more information about them at the following sites:

www.torq-dj.com/forum/viewtopic.php?f=8&t=1521
www.stantondj.com/v2/fs/index.asp
www.numark.com/content1417.html
www.virtualdj.com/download/trial.html
www.deckadance.image-line.com/downloads.html
www.mixmeister.com/download.html
www.mixvibes.com/site/pageeng/page.php?x=demos

When selecting your DJ software, bear in mind the cost, what operating system you'll be running it on, the type of DJ you are and, most importantly, how it feels and responds when you're DJing, rather than just buying products from the big-name software providers.

Ableton

Unlike software such as Traktor Scratch, which is based upon digitising an analogue DJ set-up, Ableton was not specifically designed with DJs in mind.

Ableton is a DAW (Digital Audio Workstation) and music sequencer that has been designed for live performance. A music sequencer essentially provides a framework from which audio and MIDI files can be combined, recorded, manipulated and played back in a specific order. This gives you the ability to create your own music.

The Ableton Live software has really shaken up the way DJs perform, by giving them so much control over their music and the ability to create unique sounds in a live environment, utilising the array of 'instruments' and effects that Ableton has to offer.

In Ableton there are two views: the Arrangement view and Session view. The Session view *(Fig. 6.4)* is unique to Ableton and lends itself to more creative, spontaneous, live performance.

Ableton Session View

Figure 6.4

OVERVIEW   CLIP SHOTS   RETURN TRACKS   SESSION/ARRANGEMENT VIEW SELECTOR

DEVICE BROWSER

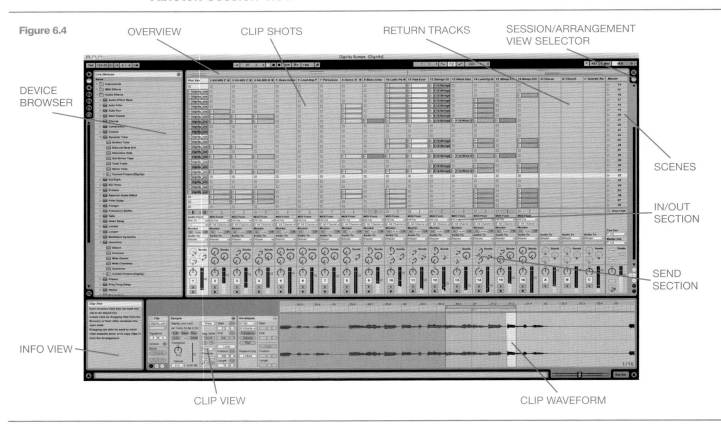

SCENES

IN/OUT SECTION

SEND SECTION

INFO VIEW

CLIP VIEW   CLIP WAVEFORM

Ableton have created their own terminology for describing different elements of the Session view. If you place an audio file or record a MIDI file into the Session view, these become known as 'clips':

> An audio clip could be an entire track imported from iTunes™ or it could be the individual components of a track such as the bass, kick, percussion, lead, pads, etc.

> A MIDI file clip could have been created from playing any one of Ableton's 'instruments'. To play an Ableton instrument you'll need a keyboard, such as M-AUDIO's Oxygen 8. This is a really good, cheap and small keyboard that will keep you entertained for hours.

Everything You Need to Know about DJing and Success

Clips can be organised in horizontal rows, known as a 'scene'. The functionality is then available to either launch one clip at a time or a scene of clips. Add to this as many effects as you like and you have the basis for a really individual DJing performance. One such DJ who has been using Ableton since 2005 is DJ Sasha. Sasha has really helped to push the boundaries of DJing and live performance, using Ableton to compose, arrange and edit audio live, whilst DJing to crowds – creating unique DJ mix sets every time he performs.

Some of Ableton's Top Features

> Multitrack recording up to 32-bit/192 kHz.
> Non-destructive editing with unlimited undo.
> Powerful MIDI sequencing of software and hardware instruments.
> Advanced warping and real-time time-stretching.
> Library with over 1,600 expressive sounds, each with versatile control options.

Another huge benefit of Ableton is that it acts as a tool for composing, arranging and remixing music. If you are interested in making music and are on a budget, it's worth considering Ableton Live, as you can both DJ and compose with the same piece of software, whilst utilising one MIDI controller.

One downside of Ableton is that there is a very steep learning curve – understanding what it does will take time, but don't give up as it's well worth the effort.

To find out more about Ableton, or to download the free demo or buy the full version, visit the links below:

www.ableton.com.
www.ableton.com/downloads – Free Demo

MIDI Controllers

There are numerous MIDI Controllers currently available from all of the big-name manufacturers such as Allen & Heath, Akai, Native Instruments and Vestax. Selecting a MIDI controller is one of the most important decisions you'll make when putting together your digital set-up, as it will largely define the interaction you're able to achieve with the crowd.

You need to pick a controller that is simple and easy to use, whilst giving you the control you need. The last thing you want is to be fumbling around your controller when you should be concentrating on your audience.

Over the last few years hardware and software companies have teamed up to make dedicated controllers. Some examples include Ableton and the Akai (APC 40), and Serato and the Allen & Heath (XONE DX).

The majority of software providers also make their own hardware controllers, such as Native Instrument's Kontrol X1, specifically designed for use with Traktor.

You should decide what you want your controller to do, and then find the one that best meets your requirements – no two controllers are the same. Also, don't be fooled into thinking that you have to buy the latest hardware controller specifically designed for the DJ software you already have. The majority of the leading software includes mappings to the top MIDI controllers, but this is well worth checking before you buy.

Do your research online, read product reviews, watch demonstrations and then (if possible) get yourself to a supplier so that you can have a hands-on demonstration of your selected pieces, to get a feel for what is most suited to you. Remember that shop staff might be on a commission scheme with certain manufacturers which may be reflected in a bias for specific equipment or software. As in any purchasing decision, be informed, educated and alert to any vested interests, and go with what you feel suits your needs best.

Sound Cards

The final piece of hardware you will need to buy, if one is not built in to your MIDI controller, is an external sound card or audio interface.

A sound card is necessary to transfer audio and MIDI sound from your software to your speakers, and to allow monitoring of other audio channels so you can 'cue-up' your next track, loop or audio effect. Sound cards are usually linked to your computer over a Firewire or USB connection. Firewire sound cards tend to be more expensive due to the quicker, more consistent data transfer. However, USB sound cards are robust and a good alternative. Native Instruments, M-Audio and Novation make a variety of sound cards to choose from.

Digital Music Files

The most common formats used are either MP3s or WAV files. WAV files are usually uncompressed data files, having a higher density and better sound quality. However, because of this, they take longer to download and are more expensive. Music can be downloaded from a whole host of websites, and I have included an extensive list of these in the bonus resources section at the back of the book.

Online Resources

If you're confused about any of the points above, there are numerous online websites, video tutorials and forums, where you can find more information. Three of the best websites and forums for Ableton, Traktor and Serato are listed below.

www.native-instruments.com/#/en/products/dj/traktor-pro – Download Traktor Pro
www.native-instruments.com/index.php?id=tprodemoversion – Free Demo of Traktor
www.serato.com – Download Serato Digital DJ software
www.serato.com/downloads/itch – Free Demo of Serato
www.ableton.com – Home of all things Ableton
www.ableton.com/downloads – Free Demo of Ableton

Further expert tuition is recommended at www.FunkNaughty.com, which covers all that is new in the digital DJing and production world. It's packed full of news, reviews, tutorials, tips and tricks and is a useful resource for beginners to advanced users – as are www.macprovideotutorials.com and www.sonicacademy.com.

Harmonic Mixing with 'Mixed in Key'

Although there is no substitute for having a musical ear and knowing what music will work together, there is now a piece of software called 'Mixed in Key' that can automatically tell you what musical key each of your tracks is in and what other keys can sit in harmony in the mix.

The software has received rave reviews from the leading magazines including *DJ* and *I-DJ* as well as from many DJs around the world including Hernan Catteneo and Pete Tong. It enables you to simply add your music to the 'Analyze Songs' window within the software, after which you click 'Start Processing', and Mixed in Key will show you which songs mix together without a key clash, using Mark Davis's Camelot Sound Easymix System, as pictured in Figure 6.5.

The idea of the Camelot Wheel is to give a visual representation of which keys are compatible with each other. On the Camelot Wheel, each key is assigned a key code number from one to twelve, like a clock. Mixed in Key will analyse your digital music and determine the key code of each track.

Top Tip:
Remember: whichever format you decide to use, the music you play and how you interact and entertain a crowd are still the most important aspects to focus on. Don't lose sight of your passion for music, the fun of DJing and keeping the crowd on their toes at all times.

109

Figure 6.5

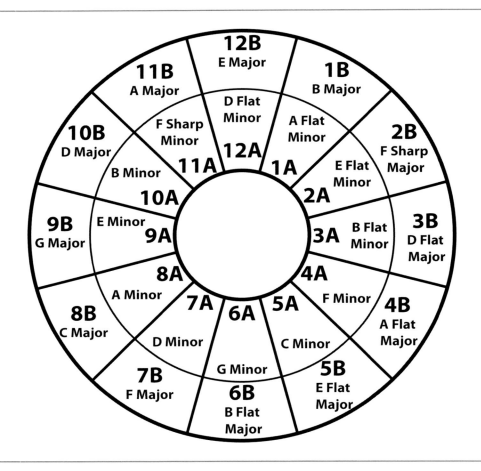

It's worth noting at this point that if you store your music in iTunes™ (or a similar program), you may want to rename the tracks in your library so that they start with the key code. For example Mixed in Key identifies 'I Go Deep – Yass' as being in key 3A, therefore rename it as '3A I Go Deep – Yass'.

This way you can quickly organise your library by key (just click on the 'Name' toolbar in iTunes™, so that all your tracks are listed in key order), which means you can see which tracks flow with each other. You can find other tips on organising your music and CDs on the Mixed in Key website: http://www.mixedinkey.com/Homepage.aspx

Using the analogy of a clock, to select a compatible song for the one you are playing, choose a key code within one 'hour' of your current key code. You can stay in the same hour (in either major or minor), or go back or forward an hour. For example, if you are in 8A, you can play 7A, 8A or 9A next. If you are in 12A, you can play 11A, 12A or 1A. This way your mix will be smooth every time.

You can also mix between inner and outer wheels if you stay in the same 'hour'. For example, you can mix from 8A to 8B (notice the change in melody as you go from Minor to Major) or from 10B to 10A (hear how the melody goes from the 'outer wheel of Major' to the 'inner wheel of Minor').

Harmonic mixing is a simple technique but it opens up a world of creativity. It will enable you to play creative DJ sets and discover interesting song combinations. It's easy to get started with any music genre. Detractors of the software argue that it doesn't deliver 100% accurate results, but on the whole this is proving to be a very able, affordable and successful piece of software that can rapidly accelerate your skill and sound as a DJ. I highly recommend you invest in this bit of kit.

What makes it valuable for many of the world's best DJs is that you can use it to sequence amazing DJ sets which work perfectly harmonically, helping you to stand apart from the competition. The software can also be used alongside digital products like CDs, Ableton Live, Serato, Traktor and other DJ software. If you use the software, get into the habit of listening closely and learn what each musical key sounds like then you can start to mix in key naturally.

At my YouTube channel I have created a short video explaining how Mixed in Key works in more depth: Part 1: www.youtube.com/user/ramplingmusic#p/u/10/FluLeAMe520; Part 2: www.youtube.com/user/ramplingmusic#p/u/9/p25RQT926Ys. You can also learn how to mix harmonically without any software: www.youtube.com/user/rampling#p/u/15/af2-RwNvE3g; http://bit.ly/HowToKeyMatchNaturally

To download a copy of the software visit: www.buymixedinkey.com

7 Putting Together a Professional Demo Mix

Most of the excitement and hype created around underground dance music scenes, particularly in Hip-Hop and Rave, has been due to the circulation of the mix tape. Obviously in the internet and iPod™ age, a cassette is a thing of the past but that does not diminish the importance of putting mixes out to promote your sound to the public.

Preparing a Demo

Putting together a demo mix is an art in itself and requires some attention. The thought process behind constructing a demo CD is different from that of a live set.

Of all the sets that you might play, a demo needs to be well prepared and carefully thought out. There are several factors to consider when choosing the tracks for a demo:

> Every tune should be in the top 10% of your collection, both in terms of quality and your esteem.

> You should pick a good representation of your playing style that showcases your breadth and musical variety.

> The tracks should probably be at least 50–60% upfront material (pre-released tracks and exclusives are also great if you have access to them) but also try to fit in a few classics that display the depth and history of your record collection. A good demo should have a few surprises up its sleeve.

> I would personally recommend that your initial demo mix is no longer than 30 minutes. Promoters often prefer a shorter mix as it's likely that they have stacks to listen through, so it's better to hit them with a tight 30-minute mix and then have a follow up full-length mix you can send them once they have enjoyed your initial taster. Less is often more.

To attract attention to your mix, you need to make your CD stand out by creating an attractive or unusual looking design. Promoters and DJs will be overloaded with demo CDs which all just have basic details on. They all look the same. What's going to help you stand apart? Dare to be different and people are more likely to be drawn towards your demo. The same applies to online download demos. Create a funky page or design to accompany your music, with your picture, biography, ambitions, heroes, influences and musical styles.

After a couple of years of handing everyone demo tapes, I finally got noticed and had my three favourite tracks played on Gordon Mac's London primetime pirate show. This resulted in my radio break when I was given a show on KISS. I was a complete unknown at the time.

Rehearsing the Running Order

The order of play is very important; the mix should flow in the same way as a live set, gradually building to a climax. However, you should be aware that the first few minutes are critical. Most promoters do not have the time or the inclination to listen carefully to a full 80-minute CD, so the first track needs to be something pretty special in order to grab their attention.

A short intro such as an a cappella or sound clip can work nicely at the beginning. You should choose these carefully as they can often set a particular mood and theme for the mix. It is well worth the time to experiment with the way that the selected tracks fit together, both in terms of musicality and energy. Try to get a running order that curves gradually upwards in its energy, but that also nicely blends the tracks together. Working according to a principle known as 'Golden Section' *(Fig. 7.1)*, used by classical composers such as Debussy, try to aim for the ⅔ point for the climax of the mix. This is possibly the most satisfying shape for any art-form, as it allows the concluding ⅓ to serve as a 'cool-down' period, where the mix can be brought back down. In terms of energy, this does not necessarily require you to lose energy but it may mean a change of direction in terms of musical style.

Finally, the last track must make a statement. You may decide to drop this from the top, so make sure that it is a track with a dramatic introduction; a classic from the history of your chosen genre(s) is a good bet.

Recording the Mix

Once you are happy that you have the set worked out, you should record it onto CD or hard disc. As the mixing needs to be completely flawless throughout, be aware you may need to have several attempts, or redo certain mixes, to edit it to perfection.

Figure 7.1

DRAMATIC START   BUILD GRADUALLY   CLIMAX MOMENT   COOL-DOWN PERIOD   END

You should also try to show off as much variety in your mixing technique as you are able without sacrificing the flow of the tracks. Remember that the first mix should be really strong so it is worth rehearsing this one so that you have the ideal drop point pre-planned. Your head-space is just as important for recording a demo mix as it is when playing out. As you have no crowd to feed back on the energy of the selection, this needs to be created by you. Sometimes having a few enthusiastic friends in the room can compensate for this, but if you are flying solo, turn the system up nice and loud and try to get involved in the moment. This is one of the reasons why the track selection needs to be so strong – you need to be excited about playing each tune (especially if you are re-doing the mix for the fifth time) so that your love for the music comes across in your mixing. Use of FX, scratching, double-copy techniques, etc., are all great if you have these skills locked down, but bear in mind that a little goes a long way.

I personally find that it really helps to set the scene and create an environment that is conducive to performing at your best. I like low light, big sound and blue lighting. My first Essential Mix for BBC Radio 1 was done live at Olympic Recording Studios in Barnes. Eddie Gordon set the studio up with UV lighting so that it gave the studio a club feel and we did the mix in one take through the monster studio monitors.

The Finished Mix

After re-editing and tidying up any ropey mixes, burn off a copy and listen to it from start to finish. This is to make a last check that the mixing is as tight as it should be, but also to experience it in a similar way to the people that you are planning to give it to.

If you are truly happy with the end result, burn off some CD copies for distribution. It is worth the effort to design a cover and label, or at least print the track listing to put in with the CD. This should always contain your contact details, including your DJ name, telephone number and/or email address and website details. Duplication software such as Nero often includes cover design templates that will correctly size images for CD sleeves, and many printers come with software that does the same for CD labels (*Fig. 7.2*).

Remember that first impression is all-important, and although the music will ultimately do the talking, it is best to spend time on creating an all round professional image. You can use the online services of companies such as Mixonic (www.mixonic.com), who enable you to upload your artwork and they take care of the rest. If you can't design, use a friend who does graphic design, or go to a local art/design college and put a notice up for someone who wants some experience. This way you can get competent professional artwork at a budget price. There are thousands of willing and able people crying out for exposure and practice.

Figure 7.2

Post-production of the Mix

It is advisable to run your mix through some post-production equipment to give yourself the edge. If you don't already have some audio production software: you can download an excellent free program that is more than fit for purpose at: http://audacity.sourceforge.net/ It's free, open source software for recording and editing sounds in Linux, Mac OS X and other operating systems. There is also Adobe Audition's 'Hard Limiter' function, which many people use.

The two things you want to consider doing in post-production are:

1. Boosting the overall levels of the mix to give it a tighter, punchier sound and to ensure that there is no 'clipping' (audio distortion).

2. Saving two copies of your mix. You can use one that is split up into tracks and one that is not. The trackless version can be used as an MP3 that you can upload onto the internet for people to download. The other 'tracked' copy should be used for the actual promo CD, so that listeners can skip to their favourite tracks easily. Make your mix user-friendly.

Distributing the Demo Mix

Top Tip:
Ultimately, you want to produce a set that makes everybody who hears it sit up, listen and enjoy every minute of it, so the more people you give it to, the more your sphere of influence expands.

The goal is to give your mix out to as many people as possible, so always have some copies with you when you are playing out at a party or event. Promoters and club owners are the obvious choices, but never underestimate the importance of giving mixes to people such as bar staff, doormen and of course punters. Your friends should also get copies, as they will be most likely to actually play it (in their car, at their house party, in front of their friends who may know a promoter, etc.). Shops, bars and restaurants are also good places to get your sound exposed. Many independent boutiques do not have set playlists and may appreciate a well-presented CD which has great music on it. These days, it's also smart to get your mixes up online using resources such as Soundcloud, Podomatic, Mixcloud and iTunes™. Details can be found in the bonus resources section.

8 Preparing a Set to Play Out

Playing out is one of the main reasons that people become DJs. The hours of practice, the vast sums of money spent on music, and the love of the art form itself all point towards that crucial moment when a DJ steps up to a booth and plays in front of a crowd of people.

Once you have a booking lined up, you will need to pull together a set for that particular event. Being well prepared and organised will make a real difference to the way that you play your set, so it is vital to be thorough.

Equipment

You will rarely be required to move your mixing set-up (unless you are playing at a house party) as most bars and clubs have decks and a mixer already installed. It is, however, wise to check out the venue before the night (if possible) so that you know what equipment they have. If you bring a case full of CDs only to discover that they have a pair of vinyl decks and one CDJ, you are going to be in trouble.

Whatever format you choose to play, you will need a bag or flight-case to transport your music *(Fig. 8.1)*. You will also need to provide your own headphones and, more often than not, your own microphone if you use one. For mixing vinyl, it is always sensible to pack your styluses just in case the venue's aren't up to scratch or one breaks. With the pressure of performing, you do not want the added stress of something going wrong that you could have easily rectified.

If you use a laptop to play MP3s and WAVs from, always make sure that you have all the necessary leads with you including your power cables and an extra 4-way plug (there's nothing worse than having the correct cables but no spare plug socket to plug your kit into). In addition, it's wise to take at least a few records or CDs just in case the laptop crashes and you need to reboot. A silent dancefloor is not a good thing.

Figure 8.1

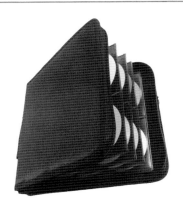

Selecting What Music to Take

You should always consider the venue, night and, most importantly, the crowd. It is important to be case specific each time you play out so that you are adequately prepared for the night. Don't just grab a pile of records at random and hope for the best.

The best piece of advice is to pack for all occasions. Imagine that you are going to this bar or club as a punter, and try to think of what tracks you would want to hear to have a really great night. Even if you know that the venue or event is geared towards a certain style of music, you should always have a few related genres hiding away in your box. Try to pack a range of music from upfront through to the classics. The worst thing that you can do is pack a whole bag full of unknown brand new tracks. The chances are that even the 'heads' in the room won't know them all, and unless you are confident that a particular tune is going to make a real impact, you should consider leaving it at home.

This is one area where different music formats can make a difference. If you play mainly vinyl there will be a physical limit to the amount of music that you will be able to take. This is not necessarily a disadvantage. In a two-hour set, you can only play two hours worth of music, so it is immaterial that you have 2,000 hours of music on your laptop, or 200 CDs in a wallet, the quantity of music played remains the same. However, you will have more of a selection to call upon if you are playing from CD or a laptop and, particularly in the case of the latter, you won't be in a position of regretting not bringing a certain track.

Top Tip:
Be diligent and set up specific playlist folders.

How you organise your box is entirely up to you, but you should be well aware of what you have brought with you, and know where to find each track. There is nothing worse than running out of time on a record as you desperately search for the next tune. If you are playing from CD, make sure that all your discs are labelled clearly, and that you have an accompanying track listing sleeve for each one. The same goes for MP3 and WAV files on your laptop (although computers will tend to organise your files alphabetically).

Some DJs like to have an entire set worked out, others like to rely on their instincts and go with the flow. A happy medium is probably best. Regardless of what you actually end up playing, it is worth putting together at least a skeleton set in your mind. It is a good idea to group small mixes that you know work well together; you can always jump forwards or backwards between these little 'mix chains', especially if you have some interludes or beat/percussion based tracks.

Preparing parts of sets is an important part of creating a successful night's DJing. It's the same as if you were an actor, you would not go onstage without learning your lines. Many of the world's top DJs prepare set content ideas for many hours, such as US DJ Danny Tenaglia, who is renowned for his marathon 20-hour sets. He spends weeks planning his sets for the Miami Winter Music Conference – they are infamous within the industry and ultimately contribute greatly to his worldwide success. The UK's DJ Sasha continues to entertain huge audiences globally, and he clearly spends much time preparing his set and musical parts on Ableton (covered in the Digital DJing section) enabling him to be spontaneous and creative when perfoming.

Generally I spend a few hours ahead of my gigs working on various playlist selections. At present I use Traktor Digital DJ software so that I can prepare my music from my laptop whilst travelling around the world. I, like many international DJs, feel little nostalgia for transporting heavy boxes of vinyl, or spending hours burning CDs to play at gigs. Therefore, by putting the time in with preparation you will generate ideas before your gig, which in turn gives you more time to focus on playing the best sets live in the club.

DJ Gig Checklist

Here's a checklist to help you prepare for your gig, to ensure you don't have any of those 'Damn, I forgot about those' moments. You may need to add or ignore a few elements to suit your personal situation, but this is a good starting point that should see you covered.

Preparation:

> Time, date and location of gig

> Directions and transport to and from gig, time allowed for travel (including buffer for potential delays)

Top Tip:
Be prepared to change musical direction if the atmosphere requires it. Always keep as many musical choices open to you as you possibly can.

Top Tip:
Always consider the venue, the crowd and the promoter of the night. If you keep these three audiences in mind as you pick your tracks, you will be far more likely to play a successful set.

> Accommodation (if required)

> Music policy of the night

> Other DJs playing at what times and likely styles of music played

> Time of set

> Get specifications for the equipment used in the club and preferably have a sound/equipment check beforehand – at the very least ensure you have a working knowledge of the mixer and equipment

> Photo of DJ booth set-up

> Emergency contact phone numbers for the promoter, booking agent and travel agent

> Format: is it vinyl, CD or are there cables/inputs for you to connect your computer?

> Guest list/concessions submitted

> Payment arrangements and any contractual paperwork clearly agreed beforehand

> Any additional equipment/rider agreed and sorted

Equipment and Music:

> Computer, sound card, power cable and any external leads, extensions plus 4-way plugs (if using digital)

> Headphones

> Earplugs to protect your hearing

> Styluses (if you are playing vinyl and have preferred needles and cartridges)

> Slipmats

> Your music selection and your selected formats – if playing digital, take a small CD wallet or a few records as back-up 'just in case'

> A few 'get out of jail' sure-fire mixes and tracks in the set to fall back on

Promotional:

> Business cards with contact details and link to mixes online

> Demo CDs

> Small torch to see in the dark environment

> Permanent marker for any signature requests on fans' flyers, tickets, CDs, etc.

> Towel, change of top, deodorant/aftershave/perfume (if you're prone to sweating and like to freshen up)

> Any personal good-luck charms or rituals you need to make you feel more comfortable and confident

Playing Out to a Crowd

Playing out to a crowd is the true test of a DJ's mettle. All the hours you spend perfecting mixes and technique and the money spent on music can come to nothing if you approach a set with the wrong attitude or perspective. However, the thrill of playing the right music to the right crowd is without a doubt the most satisfying aspect of DJing.

The music must always come first. Remember the all-important formula of 25% skills to 75% music. You could mix the tightest blends, all matched harmonically with flawlessly executed cuts, scratches and spiced with FX all night long. But if the music is wrong, the dancefloor will not pulse with the emotional energy that you are trying to create.

There are several factors that affect how to really rock a dancefloor: the type of crowd, the venue, your set time and the performance itself.

Different Crowds

The crowd is the most important focus for any DJ playing a set. If the crowd enjoys the set, the club-owners, promoters and everybody else will be pleased with the result. The first thing to realise is that the 'crowd' is not a single entity (although at times it seems to become one) but a collection of individual human beings with individual emotions, mind-states and, of course, musical tastes. Whether you are playing to 50 people or 5,000 this is always the case. A dancefloor is I (individuals) X C (capacity of the venue). Whether you are playing at a house party, a bar or a large club, always try to play to individuals and tailor your set towards the music that you observe them enjoying the most. You should always 'pack your bag for all occasions', as you may need to change direction several times before you hit the right flavour for a particular crowd. This has everything to do with watching people and their reactions to the music.

House Parties

House parties are an ideal training ground for playing sets in larger venues. The advantage that you will often have over any other type of crowd is that it will usually be made up of people you know. Naturally, if you are familiar with the people you are playing to, you are far more likely to play a more specifically geared set. Playing at a house party is all about having fun and not taking yourself too seriously. Tight mixing is entirely secondary to playing well-known, funky tracks that will put a smile on everybody's faces. The selection should be eclectic, classic and up-beat.

The likelihood is that you will know specific tracks that are firm favourites for individuals at the party. The age range of the guests will also affect your selection. Always try to play a few 'nostalgic' tracks that will remind friends of great shared moments and experiences.

Bars and Small Clubs

Playing in a bar or a small club can be one of the most difficult and challenging experiences for a DJ. The crowd here consists of people out to spend time with friends, meet new people and have fun. An experienced DJ will understand that there is a long 'soaking period' in a bar where the music serves only as a backdrop to the atmosphere of the venue. For several hours at the start of the evening, the dancefloor will be pretty much non-existent, but the role of the DJ in this time period is to set the mood and gradually build the excitement of the crowd. At a certain point, or more often gradually, people will begin to respond to the music as it begins to take off.

Playing at a bar can therefore be viewed as two separate sets. The first is the warm-up, which should build from a more eclectic, down-tempo vibe. The second is the peak time when people turn their attention more towards the music. At this stage, dance anthems, both current and classic, will usually work best. It is unlikely that a crowd of this sort will want to hear anything too avant-garde. Unless you are sure that the venue attracts clientele who are into harder, more underground music, it is wise to avoid styles of music such as pounding Techno, Drum & Bass or Ragga. It is worth mentioning that some bars hold specialist nights where the crowd will definitely want to hear fresh underground sounds.

If you are playing at one of these, commercial tracks will definitely not be what is required. Towards the end of the night, it is always a good idea to switch your style and play older tracks (this will be about judging the average age of the crowd and playing tunes that you think will conjure up nostalgic and happy memories for them), whether that be early-90s Big Beat, original UK Garage or Funk and Disco. In this respect, the last hour of your bar set becomes more like a house party, where you have the crowd totally on your side and are playing purely for shared enjoyment.

Larger Venues and Big Clubs

Few DJs are able to play successfully to a large crowd without first having had some experience in smaller venues. There are several reasons for this, the principal one being that there are a lot of individuals on the floor. The more people you are playing to, the harder it is to build rapport with individual clubbers, and the harder it is to judge the atmosphere of the dancefloor. When there are 2,000 people in front of you, 200 could walk away before you notice that you are losing energy.

The decisive musical factor on a big dancefloor is drama. In order to play this kind of set you need very specific tracks with a lot of presence and drive. You cannot afford to play a single weak track or 'filler'; in addition, and of all the sets you can play, your mixing really is on show in this environment. Clubs are usually packed with people who know their tunes and their DJs, so tight mixing will be crucial to successfully rocking the crowd.

In a lot of ways, the venue is on your side in a way that it is not in a house or a bar. The sound system will be immense and the lighting will often contribute to providing a party atmosphere. However, it is very important not to rely purely on these elements. The energy must come from you and the music you are playing. You need to be very visual and physical in the way that you play, as you will appear as a tiny figure in the booth from the other side of a 2,000-capacity venue. The downside to this is that you can feel isolated from the clubbers even if you are helping to 'conduct the energy'.

It is important to cultivate as much eye-contact as you can with individuals and to smile, especially with those who are nearest to the booth.

Different Venues

The venue itself can have a large effect on a DJ set in terms of its layout, sound and lighting concepts. Particularly in larger clubs, the DJ booth is often placed high above the dancefloor. You should also be aware of how the club is laid out. Other rooms (and therefore other DJs playing) or separate bar areas/chill-out rooms can alter the dynamic of the night. The energy may fluctuate even if you are playing a fantastic set, as people go to buy drinks (or go outside for a cigarette, etc.), or to check out another DJ for a little while.

The acoustics of a room may not be ideal for the PA (or vice-versa). Be aware that large sound systems are not always good sound systems. Monitor speakers do not have the same sound or EQ as the main rig, so it is advisable to turn the booth off regularly to check the 'house levels', and if necessary leave the booth and hear the music from the dancefloor itself. Often there will be a designated sound engineer who you should always have on your side. If the sound system is not quite set up right it can make your life very difficult, and a disgruntled engineer will not be disposed towards fixing your problems.

Lighting can play a big part in adding or taking away drama on a dancefloor. Lighting engineers also have a responsibility for the energy of the crowd. If you want a certain feel at specific times then it can be worth talking this through beforehand with the lighting technician. For example, you may tell him to lay off too many flashing lights at first, or to keep it 'warm' with red and purple mood lighting, or tell him you want the room blacked out for a certain track. Work together as a team to put the best atmosphere in the room.

Set Times

There is a big difference in playing a warm-up set as opposed to peak-time or after-party. With each type of set, there are certain responsibilities and particular ways of gauging the success of the way you are playing. The crowd's head-space is different in each situation, and you need to understand what your objective is for each one.

Warming Up
It takes a good DJ to hold a floor, but it takes a superb DJ to take an empty dancefloor and successfully ram it to the rafters ready for the next DJ. Warming up takes a lot of skill and personality, as this is the set that the crowd hears as they enter the venue. In order to create the right mood, there are a number of points to consider:

> The music selection needs to be excellent. This is a time to play interesting, attention-grabbing music and to mix it in a stylish way. The programming should have a gentle upwards curve in terms of energy. You should avoid the classic pitfall of playing too hard too soon. Variety is also important. A mixture of slightly rarer classics or alternative versions of well-loved tracks with upfront material is ideal. Try to move smoothly between a number of related genres to give people a taste of things to come.

> The crowd are just starting their musical journey for the night and need easing and teasing into the right frame of mind. As the venue will probably not be very full, this is a good time to talk to anyone that approaches the booth and develop some friendships for later on. Making a point of finding out individual people's tastes and favourite tracks will often provide that essential spark for the dancefloor's fuse. There is a great deal of truth in the saying 'play to the ladies and the men will follow'. Females tend to gravitate towards the dancefloor more readily than men at the start of the night, so play some vocal, soulful and sexier tracks to get the girls moving.

> The mixing needs to be really tight as the volume of the sound system will be lower at this stage of the night and people will have clearer perceptions of how well you are playing. Long blends and smooth musical programming are recommended. Turntable pyrotechnics, scratching and FX should be used sparingly and tastefully or not at all. When done properly, the warm-up set can be incredibly satisfying for even the most experienced DJ. It provides an opportunity to dig back into your collection and play some tracks that you (and the crowd) have not heard for a while. There is also a real sense of achievement when you hand a full room to the next DJ knowing that you started with an empty one.

Peak Time
If you are headlining or playing during the peak-time hours, your main aim is to keep the momentum of the dancefloor going. A warm-up DJ may hand you a packed room ready for lift-off, but it is all too easy to misjudge the mood of the dancefloor and lose the crowd.

> The music selection is extremely important for the peak-time set. The first couple of tracks are critical to setting the pace; they will make a powerful statement about who you are as a DJ, both in terms of your musical approach and your mixing capabilities.

> You will need to take the energy sharply upwards when you take over on the turntables. This is not the time to take risks with unusual experimental tracks, but instead you should concentrate on powerful and dynamic records that have plenty of energy for the crowd to feed off.

> The crowd will be more ready to engage with the music by this stage of the night. Again, it is important to keep your finger on the pulse in terms of reading the crowd (remember that plenty of eye-contact and physical involvement is really key here) and if at all possible, you should observe at least the last ½ hour of the previous set in order to get a feel for the crowd and their particular tastes. Especially with very large venues, keep a sharp eye on the general size of the crowd; if you notice that the numbers are beginning to drop off, you may have to consider the direction of the music that you are playing.

> The mixing for a headline set should be flawless. If an Old Skool anthem sits beautifully on top of an upfront big track, people will enjoy the moment so much that they will forgive a few small errors.

After Hours

The last set of the night is the one that is the hardest to plan in advance. The musical direction will be entirely dependent on what has preceded it. To successfully hold the floor at this stage, you have to judge what the crowd needs to hear next. It is very important to hear the previous DJ to gauge this properly.

> The music selection may need a change of direction, or the energy may need to go up an extra notch if the peak-time set has not been quite hard enough. Towards the end of this set, you may choose to play older, more classic anthems, finishing the night with music that people will go home talking about. Always make the last tune something extra special to round off a great night in style.

> The crowd may diminish during the last set, leaving those who are there for the duration. As the crowd thins out, the advantage is that you will be able to focus more on individuals again. You should be aware of the dynamic of this 'hardcore' group. It will almost certainly contain a mixture of individuals who are real 'heads' who will want to hear some really impressive material from your collection, and people who simply want to carry on dancing regardless of what you play. You will have to judge the proportions for yourself. Real 'heads' will lose interest in your set if you play too much commercial music, so make sure that your selection is credible and sophisticated enough for their tastes.

> The mixing at this stage should be rapid and dramatic. Try to keep the energy of the set fast and furious until you decide to bring the night down (if you decide to do this at all). Many superb last sets are less than perfect in terms of tight mixing but the tunes themselves do most of the talking at this stage.

Programming a Set and Selecting Tracks

A well-prepared DJ should have no problems programming the music for the night, as they will have packed far more music than they need. As most nights work in stages, you should try to select records in groups that pertain to a particular mood or style.

Using a Basic Set Framework

Individual tracks aside, you should have at least a pre-planned framework to work from. For example, if you were playing at a semi-commercial, urban bar where the average age group was 20–30, a basic set plan might look something like:

8:30 p.m.   Deep and soulful, atmospheric and jazzy: Mellow Hip-Hop/Nu-Soul
10:00 p.m.   Move to vocal tracks and solid US Garage
11:00 p.m.   Bring up the pace: upbeat Latin-House, Disco re-edits West-Coast bumping House
12:30 p.m.   Switch to Funk via a well-known classic. Bring up the pace again with a good Disco selection and a few old classic club tracks
1:30 p.m.   Last ½ hour: end with a couple of well-known favourites

In 5½ hours, the bar has been given several different 'sets' by just the one DJ. The plan is a guideline only; respond to the energy in the room and what the crowd is feeling. Without the right preparation, and careful selection of music based on people's reactions, you will be unlikely to play a great set. Your goal is always to cause excitement and create musical moments that the entire crowd can feel in a personal way.

Programming and Pacing Shorter Sets

If you are playing a shorter set (1–2 hours), you will want to make your musical statements in a more intense way. Many DJs make the mistake of thinking that this means simply pushing the energy higher and higher by playing harder or faster. Especially with some styles of music such as Techno and Drum & Bass, there can be no easy return from this kind of intensity. The key is to consider the way in which tracks and sets are parts that make up a whole. In the same way as Babushka dolls fit inside of each other, tracks should work inside a set, and sets should work in the context of a night.

It is great to inspire each other as DJs. A certain amount of friendly competition is fine but you should always bear in mind that you are on the same side. There is little point in playing a set that is impossible to follow. It is far better to spend the last portion of your set preparing the way for the next DJ so that he/she can take over on the turntables without any worry of 'what am I going to play after that?' Always bear in mind the context of your set in the progress of the night. A warm-up DJ should bring the energy of the dancefloor up in order to hand an eager crowd over to the peak-time DJs. Similarly, the headliner should try to leave the late-night DJs with music that best suits their direction *(Fig 8.2)*.

Figure 8.2

WARM-UP DJ   PEAK-TIME DJ   LATE-NIGHT SETS

Figure 8.2 shows an 'ideal' situation, but you cannot depend on other DJs to work in this way. You only have control over the way that you pace your own set. If you take over from a DJ who has not made it easy for you to follow them (particularly one who has played faster than you wanted to start), there are a number of different ways of dealing with this:

> Start your set with a carefully chosen and well-loved classic. A powerful musical memory will completely overshadow any discrepancy in tempo.

> Start with a sound-effect/spoken-word clip to separate the music of the previous set from yours.

> Drop a track that builds from complete silence. By the time the beats enter, the crowd will accept the new tempo even if it is different from the last record.

> Play a totally different style of record regardless, and then build from this like a brand new warm-up. Even if it takes a few records to win the crowd over, you should feel confident enough to bring back the energy of the dancefloor via your own completely different route.

9 Personality, Etiquette and Professionalism

Any professional at the top of his/her game will quickly realise that personality has a huge impact on success. It is very easy for a DJ who is beginning to rock a crowd each time they play to develop an unhealthy ego or attitude towards other people in their environment.

To be a successful and inspirational DJ, always bear in mind a few important points:

> Being a DJ is about guiding and inspiring a crowd to lose themselves in musical moments. This should always start in the booth. A DJ who does not appear involved with the music will not create as much energy as one who is obviously enjoying themselves.

> Always treat people with courtesy and respect. Whether you are talking to an individual from the crowd, another DJ or an engineer at the venue, politeness and a gracious manner will go a long way. A healthy degree of pride in your art and achievements is fine but arrogance, ego and attitude are not. You should never consider yourself to be above anybody else as you may receive a nasty shock. There is always somebody out there who will play better than you, so it's important to have a level of humility. Especially if you are being paid to perform, you should never give any less than your very best. Nobody wants to come into a bar or club and listen to a DJ who is not trying to play well.

Personality Behind the Turntables

When people watch you play a set, they should be able to see your enthusiasm for the music. Energy is infectious and a DJ who is grinning as they drop tunes, nodding their head wildly, abandoning themselves to musical moments or even dancing at the decks will definitely pick up some other people around them for the ride. The reverse also applies. If a DJ looks bored and has no visible reaction to the music, that atmosphere will spread in a similar way.

As you play out more, you will become increasingly confident about the technical aspects of mixing music on a sound system and judging levels. This frees you up to concentrate on the individual members of the crowd. Try to look up as much as possible, and establish eye-contact with the crowd. Rapport is generated far more easily if you are smiling and creating a vibe with people. Never underestimate the power of a friendly and vibrant personality. Too many DJs think being aloof and moody makes them somehow look cooler than anybody else in the room. What these people usually fail to realise is that they simply come across as aloof and moody.

Etiquette

As a DJ you are going to have a lot of contact with people and no amount of technical skill will help you relate better to others. How you conduct yourself, however, will be a key factor in your success as a DJ – or, indeed, in any walk of life.

The Crowd

The venue and style of night will often have an effect on the personal involvement of individuals in your set. In a bar, you can expect people to approach the DJ booth more frequently with requests than in a larger venue where access to the DJ may be restricted. Different crowds have their own dynamics. Remember, people are there to enjoy themselves. At no stage should you offend a member of the crowd by ignoring them or being offhand in your treatment. You should always make sure you are polite, even if a drunken clubber approaches the booth for the tenth time asking for the same record that you haven't brought with you. There is always a diplomatic answer to any request (even if secretly you think it is ridiculous, you should never let this come across in your reaction).

If someone asks you for a record that you don't have, you should be honest and say 'Sorry, I don't have that with me'. Then try to find out what other tracks that person likes, and see if you can choose something that they will enjoy any way.

People will generally understand that a DJ can only carry a certain amount of music. It is always worth asking another DJ if he/she has brought a particular record that has been requested. Remember that you are playing for the crowd, and a request is a direct message to you from them. Even allowing for ridiculous petitions, such as 'Can you play something I can dance to?', it is worth taking recommendations on board as they may trigger more energy on the dancefloor. Never insult anybody.

Other DJs

When it comes to your DJ colleagues, you should tread carefully. Always make sure that you are humble about your own set and complimentary about theirs. Nobody is asking you to lie; if the DJ playing before you has not played particularly well, just try to be positive about some of the tracks they played. If you genuinely didn't enjoy anything about their set, shake their hand and buy them a drink any way. You should be aware of a few unwritten rules about playing alongside other DJs:

> Don't interfere with a DJ who is playing. If you arrive during their set, drop your records off at the booth, quickly say hello and offer to grab them a drink. You can use the time before your set far better by going out onto the dancefloor and hearing the sound system's levels or observing the crowd's reaction to the music, than hanging around the decks.

> Try if possible to arrive early so that you can hear what records are getting played. There is nothing worse than playing a track that the crowd have already heard. Even if it is a very big record, their enthusiasm for it will be dampened the second time around.

> If you are taking over on the turntables, do not mix out of their last record prematurely, or worse still power-down the turntable. This is a truly arrogant way to treat another DJ, and although many famous DJs do this, you should certainly not follow in their footsteps. Instead let the record play through (spending the five minutes or so getting your first few mixes sorted out, or chatting to the last DJ), then fade it gently out and drop your first track or continue with the mix.

Sound and Lighting Engineers

The sound system at a decent venue will probably be set fairly well, but if you hear that it needs some slight adjustment ask politely and humbly whether the engineer can look at the EQ or the levels. Similarly, if they ask you to be careful with the volume, don't push your luck.

Lighting can potentially be used to great effect by enhancing the atmosphere and adding presence to certain musical moments. Make an effort to establish a good relationship with whoever is responsible for visuals or lighting.

Bar Staff, Door Staff and Other Club Personnel

Even if you feel that they are unconnected with the music and your set, be considerate to other staff in the venue.

> Don't push the boundaries with door staff. If they tell you that it is the last tune, you should respect that decision.

> The bar staff can often provide some of the party atmosphere (especially in smaller venues) so don't make their lives difficult. If they are not enjoying themselves, this can easily filter through to the crowd and they are usually still around at the end of the night to give feedback to the promoter/club owner.

Professional Conduct

Top Tip:
Always treat other people as you would wish to be treated yourself.

Because the dance music industry goes hand in hand with partying, it is easy to forget that as a DJ you are doing a job. Naturally you should aim to enjoy yourself when playing your set, but do be aware that your reputation is on the line. This is not purely a case of playing a great set or mixing well, but also about how other people perceive you. Most aspects of professional conduct are common sense (such as not criticising the promoter behind his back) but some have become real grey areas for DJs.

Alcohol and other Substances

The issue of drinking and drug-taking is a delicate one. It is a well-documented fact that drugs have played a major role in the development of dance music (such as the Acid House parties in the late 80s and early 90s). The choices you make with regard to drinking or taking other drugs are your own, as are the responsibilities and penalties that accompany them.

You should be aware that any such substance, legal or otherwise, will affect your judgement. If you are utterly high and totally caught up in the music, you may not be able to make the correct choices about reading the crowd and selecting the best tracks. Similarly, if you are drunk, you may say or do things you regret, or play less well than you are capable of doing. Always bear in mind that we live in the age of camera phones and the internet. If you go on a forum the next day, you may find footage of the previous night. Many DJs set themselves strict rules in terms of keeping straight until they have finished playing their set. This is a good ethos to follow as you will have a sharper and keener awareness of your environment. After the performance, you can make your own decisions.

Long-term heavy use of drink and in particular drugs will cloud your judgment and, worst of all, your own personality. There are many stories, particularly from the golden age of Disco, of DJs collapsing on the turntables, or being too high to even play a set. Bear in mind that this is a sure way to lose a residency or ensure you are never booked by a particular promoter (or many others who hear about the incident) again. There are a number of well-known DJs on the circuit who have 'reputations' and have thus limited their bookings because they are known to promoters as unreliable, or prone to getting wasted and being unable to perform at the level expected. Don't let this be you.

Becoming a Pro DJ

Club Night Residencies

The dance music industry owes much to the early days of resident DJs. In the Disco era of the 1970s, every club had a resident DJ who played week-in, week-out, establishing a particular 'sound' for that venue. Two of the pioneers of the dance music scene, Francis Grasso (The Sanctuary) and David Mancuso (The Loft), provided a blueprint for sets of music that told a story with the way the mixes were crafted. This model was adopted by other DJs around the New York area and further afield, including Nicky Sianno (Studio 54), Steve D'Aquisto (The Gallery) and Larry Levan (Paradise Garage).

Alfredo's Ibiza residency (Amnesia), where he was spinning an eclectic mix of Latin and Italo-House, inspired the first wave of residencies in the UK and the birth of the Acid House and Rave scenes. Other key residencies which have had a major influence on dance music culture include: Norman Jay (High on Hope), Junior Vasquez (The Sound Factory), Tony DeVit (Trade), Carl Cox (Space Ibiza), myself (Shoom), Ian Levine (Heaven), Paul Oakenfold (Cream Courtyard) and Jose Padilla (Café Del Mar), to name but a few. And for every DJ mentioned, there are thousands of working DJs around the world who are the unsung heroes of their local scene for providing great entertainment week-in, week-out.

In the modern age of DJing, residencies at the larger clubs are very hard to come by until you have built up a formidable reputation. The best way to become a resident is at a particular night (often hosted in a bar or smaller club venue). It is very likely that you will be working alongside a syndicate of people to help promote such a night, designing flyers and branding artwork, and designing the concept for the events. Often there are several residents who regularly play at a particular night, each time inviting one or two larger-name guest DJs.

Competition for numbers and venues is fierce, so think very carefully about the name and theme of the night, what it will offer and the quality of the music and atmosphere.

The Benefits of a Residency

A residency is by far the best way to build a community of loyal followers and develop a specific sound and style. Many of the early DJs whose names are now legendary were renowned for mixing a certain style. Frankie Knuckles' reel-to-reel re-edits of older Disco records with their stripped-back grooves provided the essential template for House music, and it was Ron Hardy's fearless experimental approach that first broke the Acid House records of Phuture (DJ Pierre) and the Detroit Techno pioneers Derrick May, Juan Atkins, Jesse Saunders and Kevin 'Reese' Saunderson.

As well as developing musical style, a resident DJ has the freedom to be more experimental, as they are usually playing over a longer period of time. The pressure to play more 'expected' tracks is lifted, and they can be free to explore new musical possibilities. Many DJs have also broken individual tracks that are now intimately associated with them.

Building Community

Perhaps the most important aspect of a residency is the loyalty of the regular crowd. Having a residency gives you the opportunity to build a strong following in a short space of time and the ability to create a strong profile within a local community. Friendships are often built with individual clubbers, and you can really get to know what makes your dancefloor tick. This will inevitably result in truly memorable nights where the sense of involvement and unity on the dancefloor are at their highest levels.

As a resident DJ you will often get to help choose which guest DJs perform. When you perform in front of these guests and show them good hospitality and demonstrate the strength and loyalty of your local following, they will often reciprocate by spreading and strengthening your reputation. By embracing and welcoming a visiting guest DJ to 'your club' you are laying the foundations of a relationship, and as in all relationships, if you give unconditionally, you often receive much in return.

However, it is wise to consider that as you become more successful and in-demand as a DJ, it becomes increasingly difficult to balance the requirements of a weekly residency with offers that may be coming from other venues, clubs and promoters around the world. As tempting as it may be to give up a residency to pursue more enticing offers, it is often advisable to keep your position, even if it means playing less frequently, so that you continue to nurture the relationship with your 'home crowd'.

Being Part of the Crowd

Above all, a resident DJ you should feel like a part of the crowd. New York legend Kerri Chandler is renowned for hanging out at his gigs, getting into the energy of the dancefloor and playing unannounced impromptu sets at after-parties. Clubbers love to feel involved with you, and there's no better way than to 'get a groove on' with them.

10 Contracts and Payment

In addition to being an enjoyable and fulfilling experience, playing a set is a service that should be honoured with a payment. You should remember that the fee you charge for playing a set will take into account the preparation time and the money that you have spent on buying the music, as well as rewarding you for your skills.

The subject of contracts and legal rights is often a complex one, and you should be diligent in ensuring you understand the requirements of your 'territory'. The information provided relates specifically to the UK market. However, there are several important factors to understand.

Offers, Acceptances and Agreements

An offer refers to the proposal made by a venue or promoter to play a set. This will usually be done verbally, i.e. *'Would you like to come and play at my night on July 9th? I can pay you £200.'* The acceptance is where you as a DJ agree to take up the offer, i.e. *'Yes I can come and play that set.'* It may well be that a certain amount of negotiation happens before an offer is accepted. Generally speaking, it is always better to have somebody else (manager or agency) do this for you as their judgement is not clouded by the love of performing a set. If you are doing your own negotiating, you should bear in mind a few important considerations:

> Whether the fee is adequate for your level of skill and reputation.

> Whether you really want to perform for the venue/promoter in question.

> Whether there are any added benefits (exposure, connections with bigger DJs, free drinks etc.)

Once you have negotiated to the point where you are satisfied with the offer and accepted it, an agreement exists between the two parties. This in itself is a contract, whether it is written or verbal.

Revoking Offers and Acceptances

Once an offer is accepted you have a contract, and revocation can only take place with the agreement of both parties. The offer will automatically be revoked after a reasonable period of time if it is not accepted. An acceptance cannot be revoked unless both parties choose to end the agreement.

Contracts

A contract is a binding agreement, either verbal or written. There are two ways an agreement can become binding: either by deed or with consideration. A deed is a technical document which must state that it is a 'deed' and must be witnessed. It is used for more important documents such as mortgages, where the parties concerned do not wish any aspect of the agreement to be left in any doubt. A consideration, on the other hand, is an exchange of something of value. This can be money or goods, or even a service performed (a DJ set is of the latter type). Check out Bonus Resource 12 for a comprehensive and professional DJ contract that you can emulate, or make up your own one bearing in mind that any contract should cover:

> Your name

> Your address, phone and email

> Who the contract is between (you and your employer – and how you are both referred to)

> Date, time and duration of your performance

> Access to the venue one hour before the event for a sound check

> Compensation amount (and in which currency) and payment terms (e.g. 25% on booking, 25% 30 days before and 50% 7 days before event)

> Payment details: your bank account details

> Clause of non-performance: if payment is not made in your terms as outlined above

> If applicable, travel and accommodation arrangements and expenses

> The name under which you may be promoted and what URL, or other contact details you want included on publicity materials

> Copies of all promotional material to be supplied to you

> Your obligations as a DJ: just music or equipment also:

> Employer's obligation: provision of equipment?

> Optional: equipment specification (certain mixers, turntables, etc.)

> Any rider or guest list requirements

> No recording of DJ set unless prior written agreement

> Terms by which the DJ may cancel

> Compensation terms: if DJ and/or venue cancel

> DJ signature with date and employer signature with date

Verbal Contracts

Often, a contract between a DJ and a promoter or venue is a verbal one: a fee for the set is agreed without the presence of a written contract. For small bars or clubs, you should expect this to be the case. Most of the time there is not a problem with getting paid at the end of a night, but you should always remember that venues and proprietors are out to make money just the same as everybody else. Trouble can occur if a night has been quiet and the bar has not taken enough money to 'cover costs'. These costs include the bar staff, door/security personnel and other running costs of the venue. The DJ can suddenly become the last consideration for a promoter or venue owner if the night has not made the expected amount of money. Nonetheless, your fee as a DJ is part of the 'running costs' of the night and failure to honour this is a breach of contract. The problem is that there is no written proof of the agreement in such cases.

Unfortunately there may be some occasions where you will have to make tough decisions about whether you are willing to accept less than the agreed fee. In such instances, the most that you will be able to do is to refuse any further work from such a promoter.

Written Contracts

A written contract is your proof of the terms and conditions of an agreement. Written proof can be gained by simply signing an invoice for the night with the bar/club owner or promoter. See Bonus Resource 13 at the end of this book for a sample invoice template.

Generally speaking, you will need to have a contract agreed prior to the set. Often a contract will include certain clauses (particularly in relation to cancellation) which will safeguard a venue from full payment liability should the event fail to take place. Once such a contract has been signed by both parties, failure to honour the terms on either side will result in a breach of contract.

Breach of Contract

A breach of contract occurs if one of the parties does not fulfil the agreement. It can encompass anything from failure to provide the correct brand of beer for the DJ to cancellation of an event without prior warning, or a DJ failing to turn up to play. Not all breaches terminate the contract, but more serious ones may lead to payment of damages. The risk of damages protects the interests of both parties. It protects the DJ from being paid too little money (or none at all) but it also protects the venue in the instance of a DJ failing to fulfil his/her obligations.

Damages

In the event of a serious breach of contract by your employer, providing there is no cancellation fee and you have a written contract, you should be entitled to the full amount agreed (minus expenses or secondary considerations such as travel, accommodation, food, etc.). In reality, it is often very difficult to obtain damages.

When the contract has failed and the other party won't pay up, you do have the option of claiming through the courts. You can also do this online at: www.moneyclaim.gov.uk: However, bear in mind that the process can be lengthy and you should also consider that if the other party does not have the money to pay, then there is no point pursuing it.

11 Finance and Tax

Before starting out as a professional DJ I strongly recommend that you seek expert advice in relation to all financial and tax matters. I am a DJ, not a financial adviser or lawyer, and the advice given in this book is the product of years of personal experience and mistakes, not expert training in the law or accountancy.

When you become a DJ you generally work for clubs, bars and promoters on a self-employed basis. This means that you become responsible for filing your own tax returns and ensuring anything owed to the government of your country is paid to them by the required deadlines.

Many DJs fall in to the trap of thinking that they can ignore tax as they will be receiving cash in hand on the night and that this form of payment is neither taxable nor traceable. Unfortunately, however, as many DJs have found out to their cost, this is not the case.

By paying all necessary tax you will be able to do the following:

> Report this income to any future providers of essential finance, e.g. mortgages or personal loans.

> Gain access to the full range of state benefits, such as Job Seeker's Allowance, Disability Benefit or your full State Pension entitlement.

> Relax, and not worry about the taxman catching up with you one day.

Top Tip:
Don't bury your head in the sand and hope the taxman will never catch you.

HM Revenue and Customs (and their overseas equivalents) are more savvy than you may think. Believe it or not but many tax inspectors have a life and may even visit a club you are playing at, notice you playing and then check up on you when they return to the office after their weekend – on the off chance of scoring some brownie points from their superiors. It may seem unlikely, but trust me, it happens. That's the harsh reality of things. So declare your earnings correctly and always abide by the law!

Now for a few pointers on how to ensure you don't inadvertently fall foul of the Inland Revenue and to help you to plan financially for your future.

Personal Tax

Once you are registered as self-employed you will need to complete a tax return every year. In the UK the tax year runs from 6 April to 5 April the following year. If you file your return online then you must have it in by 31 January following the end of the tax year. If you file your return on paper, then you only have until 31 October following the end of the tax year. So, for the tax year that runs 6 April 2010 to 5 April 2011, your filing deadlines would be as follows:

> 31 October 2011 for paper returns
> 31 January 2012 for online returns

A tax return will capture all your income for a tax year, and also show any allowable expenses that you can offset against these in order to reduce your tax bill (this will be covered later in this chapter). Once you have completed and filed your return, you will then need to pay any tax that is due. As things stand, there are two required payments each year. Based on our example for the tax year running from 6 April 2010 to 5 April 2011, tax will be due as follows:

> 31 January 2012 Balance of any tax or National Insurance due, plus a payment on account towards the following tax year
>
> 31 July 2012 Payment on account towards the following tax year

VAT

Depending on your income from self-employed work, you may need to become a VAT-registered trader. Once your income goes above a certain limit in any consecutive 12-month period you will need to register for VAT, at which point you will need to also charge VAT on your invoices. At the time of going to press, the threshold for VAT registration in the UK is £70,000, so if your income from self-employed work remains below this for a consecutive 12-month period then you do not need to worry about VAT at all.

Top Tip:
Don't keep putting it off. Once you have your tax sorted out it will be a major weight off your shoulders and you can enjoy your life and career.

National Insurance

It is your National Insurance that goes towards state benefits. Therefore it is important that you keep up with your contributions. As a self-employed DJ you will be required to pay two forms of National Insurance:

1.   **Class 2**
This is payable generally on a quarterly basis, and you will receive a bill from the Inland Revenue on a quarterly basis as well. The rate at time of going to press is £2.40 per week, so each quarter you should receive a bill for £31.20.

2.   **Class 4**
This will be calculated based on your profits for the year, and is currently approximately 8% of your profit. The calculation will be done at the same time as the calculation of your tax liability and payable at the same time.

Expenses

As you are operating your own business, there are costs associated with doing so. When calculating the tax and National Insurance due, you do not look solely at the income of your business. Instead, you calculate it based on the profit made. To arrive at the profit chargeable to tax and National Insurance, you deduct your business related expenses from your income.

There are many areas that you can treat as business-related expenses, and these may include the following (as I said earlier, in practice make sure you check this with an accountant):

>   Equipment, such as decks, lighting, computers, etc.

>   Music, such as downloaded tracks, records, CDs, etc.

>   Travel, such as train tickets to a gig or transport hire

>   Accommodation, such as hotel bills when at a gig

>   Meals, when working away from your usual town of residence

>   Petrol, if using your own car to travel for business purposes

>   Telephone costs

>   Advertising and marketing

>   Stationery

Book-keeping

In order to be able to justify your expense claims, and to be able to prove your income levels, it is important that you keep proper records. This will enable you to accurately complete tax returns and also to provide evidence to HM Revenue and Customs should it be required.

When just starting out, this does not need to be anything fancy or complicated.

In the simplest of forms you should be raising an invoice every time you do a job, and keeping a copy of this for your records, ideally in a file, broken down month by month.

In addition, you should keep a separate file of expenses. Whenever you purchase something that you feel may be tax deductable you should ensure you receive an invoice or till receipt from your supplier. You should then keep all these in a file, again broken down month by month.

You may wish to make things a little easier on yourself and keep a log of all of the income and expenditure on a spreadsheet or a cashbook (which can be obtained from most good stationery outlets).

If you have a large volume of income, expenditure, payments and receipts then you may wish to look into a fully computerised system of accounting, and there are many different products currently on the market that offer such a system, although these can be quite costly so should only be considered if you feel it is totally necessary.

Working Abroad

One of the main perks of becoming a DJ is that you may be asked to work abroad from time to time. This, unfortunately, is an area that manages to catch people out when it comes to tax. Many DJs think that as they're not working in the UK they don't need to worry about paying tax in the UK.

UK tax laws currently state that UK tax may be payable on your worldwide income, depending on whether you are classed as a UK resident in the tax year in question. So, for example, if you were to go and work in Ibiza for three months, you may still need to pay tax on these earnings in the UK.

You should ensure that you speak to an accountant before commencing any work outside of the UK to ensure that you don't get landed with an unexpected tax bill.

> **Top Tip:**
> If tax seems too difficult or time consuming to deal with, an accountant will handle it for a fee, and quite often the tax they can save you will outweigh the fee they charge.

Planning for the Future

The commercial life span of a DJ can be a short one, and many DJs reach the end of their career earlier than they expected and realise they are back where they started with little or no financial security. It is extremely important that you plan for the future to ensure your money works for you. An individual who owns a business may be able to use this as his pension; in other words they can sell the business at the point they wish to retire, and live out the rest of their life on the proceeds. This is not a luxury afforded to DJs as they have nothing to sell on other than their own knowledge and skills.

It is very important that you think very carefully about what you want to do once your career is over. Many top DJs make long-term plans to ensure that their income does not dry up just because they are no longer playing in the world's top clubs.

Top Tip:
Plan for the future, whether that be your next career or your future financial security.

There are businesses out there that can help you with this, whether it be financial planning (making wise investments) or personal coaching (helping you get where you want to be). The services these businesses offer can be invaluable and help to focus your mind on what it means to be a DJ, where it can take you, and how to make the most out of it whilst you can.

12 Promotion and Marketing

Stage Name

Although it is ultimately your music that will do the talking, two very important considerations to bear in mind are your DJ name and image. Yes, we all know that beauty is only skin deep, but the music business can be very fickle, so awareness of how you are portraying yourself is all important, as is the name you choose for yourself.

Your name is what people will know you as for the rest of your career, so it's a major decision. Does your name have a ring to it? Are there any other DJs out there using the same name? Do your research. Is it easy to remember? Is it easy to pronounce? If you have been using your real name, and it is something like 'John Smith,' maybe you should rethink it. Be honest with yourself. Does your name sound OK or is it boring? My advice is to make the stage name simple, yet unique. Many performers across the arts (television, stage, music and creative) change their name to an alias that is more original, exciting and catchy. There is nothing wrong with this. If it helps your career, then embrace it.

Before you choose your name, do your due diligence and Google (and Facebook search) the names. Are there other DJs using the same name elsewhere in the country, continent and world. Are you likely to confuse potential punters? Ultimately, you need to ensure that if someone recommends 'that incredible mix by DJ..........' that it is going to be you they are talking about, and not some other namesake in New York. Always think on a global level.

Whilst you are researching your name (even if you are keeping your own) you should go to www.godaddy.com and type it in (e.g. www.dannyrampling.com) to see if anyone has already registered it. You can register your preferred name within minutes for less than $19 a year.

Image

It's a good recommendation to invest in some professional photography. You are instantly more marketable if you have some high-quality images that promoters can use. Not only does it show people that you have invested in yourself to look professional, but once you have these images you can use them for numerous promotional purposes: business cards, flyers, e-shots, press releases, press kits, CD covers, websites, email attachments.

If you're concerned about price, think creatively. Go to a local university or college and post a notice up on the photography students' board, telling them you are looking for someone who wants good experience, with exposure opportunities and portfolio content, in return for a nominal wage and good reference. Post on a local message board such as www.craigslist.org, www.gumtree.com or utilise a social networking site (MySpace/Facebook, etc.) and reach out for some assistance. You will be pleasantly surprised at how many people are hungry and willing for experience. Make sure that you check the portfolio of the candidate's work. It is also true that on occasion, 'If you pay peanuts you get monkeys'. Ensure the applicants have the skill and ability to create what you want and deserve, and only pay upon satisfactory completion.

It is worth noting that this is also a very good idea if you are looking for any skilled job on a shoestring budget: design, marketing, administration and even accounts. There are always people looking for opportunities to practise their skills: just ensure you do not take advantage of someone's good will and enthusiasm. It must be a win-win agreement for both parties.

Something I'll talk about later on in this book is 'modelling', in terms of emulating people who are getting the results you want to get. Look at the imagery top level performers in any walk of life use. They are usually professional images. An amateur photo of you spinning in your home set-up or in a club somewhere won't position you in the same way as proper 'press shots'.

Have a look at images you like. Where are they? In a studio setting? In an urban cityscape? In a natural landscape? What are the colours and styles used? Give your photographer some parameters to work within, maybe a little direction and possibly some guidance for a few locations. Alternatively, let them work their creative magic and leave it to them. Also have four or five different outfits to hand so that it looks like you've had a number of different shoots taken over a period of time.

Money spent on photos and design is money well spent. You'll get a lot of mileage out of investment in your image. The expression 'the quality remains long after the price is forgotten' holds so true in this context.

Business Cards, Stickers and Design

Continuing on the theme of image, it's essential that you get yourself some business cards made up. Again, use a friend, student, www.madebyanalogue.co.uk, or www.elance.com to source an artist. There are hundreds of places to get stationery printed up very affordably. With many you can design effective cards instantly using their superb free online software. Unlike a promotional CD, you can always carry business cards in your pocket and you should hand them out generously. There's a marketing term called 'Top of Mind Awareness': it's when you're the first thing people think of whenever they think of 'needing a DJ', and you help create this by sending out regular mixes, news and by sowing the seed with a business card.

It's also a thought to get some neatly designed stickers made up. Because of their nature, stickers tend to have a long 'shelf-life' as they get stuck on books, surfaces and bags, ensuring good exposure for very little cost over a sustained period of time.

Promoting Your Own Events

Becoming a DJ in your bedroom is obviously the first stage of your development. Depending on your level of skill and enthusiasm, you will reach a stage where you will want to take your craft onto the road. By now all the demo tapes and CDs that you have given to your friends will give you the confidence to take your new-found DJ skills to the stage.

Many DJs begin to turn on their entrepreneurial genius and start promoting their own parties, which is a fantastic way to get your name heard by local club and bar owners. With the right mindset, it can propel you to a certain level of success. This success is not gained after throwing one party, however, success is a long-term goal and you should never give up and continue to throw parties on a regular basis. By doing this you not only gain experience of playing to the crowd, you also begin to learn how to do business and negotiate deals with venue owners.

Market Research

The first thing that you will need to do is find a good venue that can cater to your needs. If you also find a good bar manager with a good venue, this will be to your advantage as they will help to make your night a success with promotional offers, etc. Find the music hotspots and popular venues in your target area, where people who love your music hang out. It always helps if the people that like your music are already going to your preferred venue, especially in the early stages before you've built your following.

It's always a good idea to spend a few weekends frequenting potential venues to see whether you can 'see yourself' promoting a successful party in each spot. Once you are happy you have found the right place, start making the arrangements to call the venue and ask for the manager or owner of the venue. Make sure that you are talking to a decision-maker: a person with authority, and HAVE CONFIDENCE.

It is advisable to approach venues midweek as opposed to in the evening, or Mondays (which is often a banking, admin and accountancy day) or Fridays (when they will be focused on the pre-weekend build up).

You need to think of various ways to make your event stand out. Perhaps it's an invite-only event, fancy dress, secret venue, themed; anything you can think of that will be appealing to the punters.

It's also a very good idea to think of a brand name and develop a logo that is recognisable and can be identified as your own unique brand. To get inspiration for your own brand and logo, have a look at what the current promoters are doing and spend time considering what you do and don't like from other companies. Its always good to know what the competition is doing.

The book *The Art of The Club Flyer* is dedicated to this whole industry and is a good starting point. To get your brand and logo sorted, look for a graphic designer who has a good track record and is willing to cut a nice deal with you.

Image and Branding

So, now you have your image, brand and logo sorted, it's now time for you to approach your preferred venue and propose a deal to get them to give you a chance at promoting your event.

There are a few things to bear in mind before approaching a venue. The first thing is that bars and clubs are businesses and they require customers to keep the business open. Secondly, the venues may already have successful promoters in place doing a great job, but this does not mean that you can't get a piece of the action: there may be a struggling promoter and the venue may just give you a shot to see if you can do the business.

Striking a Deal

When you have found your venue and you have met the bar manager, you now want to strike a deal that is a win-win. There are various ways that bars will approach a deal. The first deal is the minimum spend deal. Some bars/clubs will suggest that you generate a certain amount of money from drinks/bar sales (generally £1,000), but this greatly depends on the size of the venue. You then want to strike a deal that will give you a percentage bar split once you have hit this minimum spend (often around 10–15%). This deal isn't the greatest as you will only make money once you have hit your target, but if you're confident you can deliver, it may prove lucrative.

The second type of deal is just a straight cut of the bar sale regardless of minimum spend (again around 10–15%). This type of deal is generally popular amongst bars and DJs, and is recommended for you to use. The benefit is that you don't have to hit a target.

The final type of deal involves asking your guests to pay for tickets. At its simplest you keep 100% of ticket sales and the bar keeps 100% of bar spend (or a mutually pre-agreed % split on each). This deal is great as it will pretty much show how well you have performed by the amount of tickets you have sold.

Of all the deals mentioned, the latter two are the best. So put your negotiating skills to the test and go for it.

Negotiating Tips

Always ask for more than your target, even if it may seem ridiculous. For example if you want a 10% commission, initially ask for 15% or 20%. This way when the venue owner says they can strike a 10% deal, it makes them feel like you've conceded. It's an age-old selling formula. Items will always be marked up higher than the vendor expects to sell for, knowing that by allowing a 'margin' to be knocked off in negotiation they will settle for a lesser amount, which makes the buyer believe they have got a good deal.

Here are 10 essential negotiating tips:

1) Listen. Pay attention to what the other side is saying. Don't feel like you have to respond immediately or have an answer right away. Listen, think about what you hear, and then formulate a response. Trust is built through mutual respect, and listening is a way to demonstrate respect. There is an old adage: 'Two ears and one mouth – you should listen twice as much as you talk.'

2) Discuss Interests, Not Positions. Interests are the reasons why you want or need something. Positions are what you want or need. Focusing a discussion around interests transforms the negotiation into a problem-solving exercise. Focusing a discussion on positions makes the negotiation confrontational.

3) Follow Through. Do what you say you are going to do, and do it within the timeframe promised. Another way of phrasing this is, manage expectations effectively. Don't say you'll do something during the negotiation process that you do not then do. If you cannot keep a promise, communicate as early as possible that the promise will not be kept, and provide an alternative way of keeping the promise (e.g. a later delivery date). Recognising the importance of promises, even small promises, builds trust.

4) Step into the Other Side's Shoes. Think about issues both from your perspective and your customer's perspective. What does the other side need? Why do they need it? Be over-helpful and offer solutions to issues your customers might not know they have. Considering issues from the other side demonstrates that you are thinking about things from that person's perspective, which helps build trust.

5) Be Proactive. Think about what issues you'll need to resolve internally, based on the other side's interests, and start working on them early. Even if you cannot provide your customer with everything they want, if you can demonstrate that you have tried and if you can provide reasonable alternatives to address their interests, you will create trust.

6) Credibly Manage the Process. Handle issues in a way that is fair and transparent and show commitment to realistic timetables. Strong deal management demonstrates experience, and meeting deadlines builds a sense of commitment to the transaction.

7) Be Honest. Never lie. It does not matter how big or how small the lie. If you are known for not being true to your word then you instantly lose respect and opportunities, and also attract similarly dishonest people.

8) Be a Straight Shooter. Do not hide tough issues; instead, make them prominent. Show the other side how the issue is being dealt with and provide regular updates. More harm is done trying to hide an issue than is done flat out rejecting it. You don't have to say yes to build trust, but you cannot build trust by saying maybe when you know the answer is no.

9) Be Human. Everyone involved in the negotiation is a human being. To get the deal closed often requires sacrifice from everyone involved. Recognise that and build camaraderie around it. Eat together, discuss non-deal stuff and share stories. Empathy builds trust.

10) Document Everything. At the end of the day, it is important to have documentation that clearly reflects the intentions of both the parties. Hopefully, the trust that is built during the negotiation means that the contract never comes out of the drawer. But if it does have to come out – well, let's just say you want to make sure it's trustworthy.

Contract/Agreement

Before confirming with the venue that you will want to proceed with the promotions, make sure that you confirm a few things before drawing up an agreement. Make sure it is outlined what responsibilities both yourself and the venue have. The venue should be responsible for having a decent sound system and DJ set-up. Most venues provide their own system but in rare cases, you may have to. Preferably, go with a venue that is well equipped unless you aim to increase your fee and charge an extra amount to cover 'hire' of any equipment that you provide.

Make sure that the venue has the appropriate number of bar staff on the night so that your guests get served promptly and are not kept waiting (if there are customers in a venue, great bar staff result in great sales for the business). Lastly, make sure that the venue (if need be) provides some friendly security staff on the entrance and inside. A friendly security presence is always welcomed by guests.

The next thing to do is get everything in writing; don't worry, you don't need a lawyer, just draw up an agreement for both of you to sign. It shows great professionalism and business acumen, and the bar manager will be impressed by your entrepreneurial approach.

Promoting Yourself

Once you've got these ingredients sorted out – that you're happy with the venue and people that run it, that it provides a decent sound system, has great bar staff and that the management have cut you a good deal – it's time for your launch party. So how are you going to get the word out to the people? There are various ways that you can promote to the masses. Firstly, the old school way of spreading the word is by getting some good eye-catching flyers printed and distributed. Generally you should give people at least a month's notice. This will differ on the size and scale of your event. For instance, big festivals and concerts require much more time. However, for smaller scale parties, you should give people at least 30 days' notice. You should go down to the popular venues that play your music and hand out flyers to punters when they leave.

Think of ways and areas where you can get large numbers of people that may be interested in your event, for example, colleges, universities, cool small trendy businesses and so on; just get as creative as possible and the ideas will come. Maybe you can tap into key 'decision makers' and 'opinion formers' within local scenes who have a 'crowd'. Offer them an incentive (such as guest list or VIP entry) to come to your night. This is a form of 'leverage': try to get people who will then 'promote' and spread the word to their friends.

Making party invitations is also a classic and effective way of bringing people to your party. People always love invites and feel special if you have selected them to come to your event. There are hundreds of companies who create very professional wrist bands, tickets and passes at great rates. If you get wristbands made then consider having your web address on it and the date of your next party. Many people will have these on all night and will also keep hold of them as mementos.

If you're doing invites, that means some people will get in for free, so make sure you command a good deal for the drinks sales (no less than 12%). Many beverage companies have budgets for promoting their brand. A good venue/bar manager will have strong links with their suppliers so see how they can work with you to mutual advantage to try and secure some free products from the drinks suppliers.

Most promoters are now turning their hands to promoting their events online, which is a very good way to instantly access thousands (if not millions of people) around the globe. However, as in many walks of life, focus is needed rather than simply casting a 'wide net': it's obvious that if someone in Japan gets to hear about your event, they will probably not attend your party in London, so make sure you know who you are promoting to. If you have a lot of friends on your email list then it would be a good idea to send a blanket email about your event to them.

Promoting online is extremely cost-effective. Ask your designer to send you the flyer design as a 'jpeg' image for you to upload and email around. There are other ways to promote your event online; try websites such as www.facebook.com, www.myspace.com and www.bebo.com, where you can create an event, upload your flyer and info and then invite friends to attend. It's generally a good way to see how busy your night is going to be and it gets the message out there, FAST. There are some great music forums online already. Go onto Google and type in your preferred music genre (i.e. House music forums) and you will find a whole host of forums to join. Also look at the bonus resources section.

Forums are a great way to communicate with people who are truly passionate about specific styles of music. There are also various music specific websites such as www.dontstayin.com and www.tilllate.com where you can promote your events to people who are looking for the next best party to go to – make sure that it's yours.

The Launch Party

So you've done the hard work, you've got your brand name, you have a venue, you've promoted your event through various channels and you've had a great response. Now it's time to showcase your DJ skills. You are bound to be slightly nervous but use and channel this energy into positivity and confidence. It's a good idea to acknowledge as many people as possible so that you can build a rapport and show your appreciation. Get on the microphone at least once to hype up the crowd. Make sure you give the people who are really enjoying the music a promo CD. These are the people who are likely to become fans, listen to the mix and talk about it with others.

Make sure that you've got good photos from any gigs that you play. A good image of you rocking a crowd speaks volumes. It shows you 'delivering the goods' and getting the party bumping, and that will help you get more gigs. Even if your gig isn't full, get a keen photographer to take shots from interesting angles that make it look like it's happening: close-ups of people who are really having a good time, or you locked 'in the zone' on the equipment.

Give out business cards or stickers with your web address on and let people know photos will be uploaded onto the site. It may also be advisable to record the sets from the night, which can then be given away as a gift at future events or online. For a small investment, it's well worth it.

So the night is a success, everyone has had a great time and your efforts have pulled it off. It's very important to take this opportunity to congratulate yourself on this great achievement. Hopefully, the venue manager will be happy with the great business you have done together as well. If so, this is perhaps the perfect opportunity to arrange another meeting to discuss future events.

If all goes as planned, all in all it's a win-win situation; you've had the chance to showcase your DJ skills, the bar has done good business and, more importantly, the punters have had a great time. WELL DONE.

Top Tip:
Get some friends to go up to the manager and bar staff anonymously (make sure they're not seen to be your friends) and get them to say something along the lines of, 'this DJ's really great, is he here every week?' What you're doing here is just creating a little bit of hype around yourself.

Review

It's always a good idea to look back on what went right and what went wrong so that you can evaluate and correct for the next event. Then you can put together a plan of attack for future events. Ask your punters what they thought of the event so you can cater for their needs next time. Likewise, speak with the venue to see what can be done in future to entice more people to come earlier or make your event stand out from the crowd.

You want to ask people for CONSTRUCTIVE FEEDBACK i.e. not negative, destructive comments but ideas of how you might improve. A couple of good questions to ask are:

> 'What do you think went well with the night and what did you like about it?'

> 'How could we improve on the event and make it better?'

Remember to keep your questions positive. Ask a positively phrased question and you'll get a positively slanted answer, whereas if you ask 'what didn't you like about the event' you'll solicit a negative response.

A really important aspect is to 'remove your ego' from the equation, take off the rose-tinted spectacles and be open to honest feedback. Too many people tend to take comments personally. It's a hard thing to do, but the more that you can remove 'yourself' and try not to 'take things personally', the more you are setting yourself up for success. Respect people for being honest with you and make a balanced verdict as to whether their 'constructive feedback' rings true for you. A brilliant tool for creating online surveys is www.surveymonkey.com. I use it to get feedback from my database and I'll be asking you to give me feedback on this book at the end, using this software. It's very quick, simple and powerful.

Also make notes of what records went down well with the crowd so you know to play them in the future. Similarly, don't be afraid to champion new and fresh music; it's always good to be known as an innovator which will get your name out there.

A Few Extra Tips

Be aware of what is going on in the marketplace and what events are on the same night as your own promotion. It may be ill advised to promote your night if a local venue has got a superstar DJ playing at the same time. So make sure you do your homework and find out who's playing where.

If your promotion goes badly, don't all of a sudden turn off the music and go home – stick it out until the end. This shows character and tenacity.

If your event goes well, always, always, always show your appreciation for the guests' support and commitment.

Talk to your guests: don't hide in a back room or office. They've come down to support you and have a good time so be personable.

For future events, think of different themes that are relevant according to the time of year, i.e. summer cocktail party or boat party, Halloween, fancy dress, etc.

Continue to think of ways you may entice punters including free shots or free entry before a certain time.

Consider video marketing, which is a rapidly growing area. Utilising a video camera, some basic software and your computer, you can now be among the first adopting this technology to your advantage for multiple purposes. My team have generated nearly a million views for businesses to great effect using video.

Press Kits

There's no substitute for a simple but effective website that has your important information, mixes, press shots and dates on it. You also want to create a 'press kit' to complement your site. Also known as a PR package, your press kit should contain whatever promotional materials you have.

Create both a physical and electronic press kit. The press kit for a DJ usually consists of a biography, a couple of publicity photos, any imagery you have, business cards and stickers, a copy of a demo mix, and any press from newspapers or nightlife magazines.

You can put a compressed (zipped) electronic version of the kit on your website for people to download or email it to prospective clubs. You can also use a physical press kit to mail directly to club managers or promoters. Keep your biography short, preferably under a page. It should only contain the relevant information. Embrace and promote your strengths but don't be untruthful. If you are not confident with your writing skills then ask a friend or family member if they can help out, as mis-spelling and grammatical errors will make you look unprofessional. Research what other DJs have done for their biographies and model them. Without waffling, it should include how you became a DJ, key influences, what motivates you, notable gigs to date and who you've played alongside.

The packaging of your press kit is also very important. You want it to be neat and easy to navigate. For an electronic version, your biography and press excerpts should be in Microsoft Word format as this is still the most widely used program. Your photos should be at least 300dpi (dots per inch) and in .jpg format, so they may be used on flyers and other print material. The demo should be in MP3 format for easy downloading.

All these elements of your electronic press kit should be separated on your website for easy downloading individually, as well as in a small electronic 'package' using a program like WinZip. This way the whole thing can be downloaded at once and then 'un-compressed', with everything all together in one folder. For a physical press package, you should use a folder containing all the same elements, with your stage name and contact info displayed clearly on the front.

You should ensure that you send the press kit to clubs that you want to spin at, to promoters you want to work with and always follow up. Ask for feedback and follow up by phone to make sure they have received it, listened to the mix and looked at the info. If they respond that they haven't, then ask them when would be a good time to call back. What you want to say is that you really value their feedback and would like to hear their thoughts, so ask them what day would be best to contact them again. This way you subtly put some pressure on them to listen to your mix. If you flood the market with these materials, you are sure to get at least a few calls.

The more press kits you spend time creating and giving out, the better your chances. If the promoter doesn't respond to your calls, send a simple www.surveymonkey.com feedback link to them to show you're embracing new technologies.

Networking

There's a marketing expression called 'being in the corridor'. Basically, if you want to get a name for yourself within a scene, you have to be seen to be in that scene. If nobody knows you or knows your face then you're not going to get invited to play at places.

You'll have to hit the streets quite a bit to make yourself known. There are a couple of different strategies here. If your aim is to 'get your face about' then the first strategy is to target a couple of different clubs that you would like to play at, which best fit your style. Check out the parties at these places frequently, and make sure to say 'hi' to the manager or promoters every time. Don't be pushy, just be friendly and let them know that you are there, supporting the event. Even though you may not see anything happen for a while, you are sowing the seeds at this point. Make a plan to target a couple of venues on Friday and another couple on Saturday. Become a regular and always say hello to the managers, key bar staff, door staff and promoters. People love people who remember information about them, so make sure you remember their names and small details from conversations you've had.

A big 'faux-pas' in your interactions is to talk about yourself all the time. There's no quicker turn off. Ask a lot of questions, be genuinely interested and let them know that you'd like to play at their event at some point. Once you think the promoters or managers know your face, feel free to introduce friends to them. Never go up to anyone who looks extremely busy. Remember, they are working at this time of night. But if they look free, bring your friends over to say hi and show them that you bring people out with you to the party. That is what they are looking for: DJs that can bring a crowd.

Spend more than an hour at the party as anything less than that will make it look like you don't want to be there. If you're contributing to the 'vibe' of the night, the promoter may eventually put you on the guest list, making it much lighter on your wallet.

Another approach is to be totally focused on one gig that you are really after. Make sure that you are consistently at this one night, 'working the venue' and doing the same as above. A laser-like focus on one promoter and DJ gig can work wonders.

The more people that you know and who know that you are a DJ, the more likely you are to get bookings. You should be doing a demo mix at least once a month and getting it into all of the key punters', venue owners' and promoters' hands (as well as posting them up to the main websites and forums). If you're really serious about breaking through, make a point to go out two or three times a week with the sole purpose of networking. Back this up with online networking and relationship development within a scene.

How to Promote Events Using Social Networking Sites

You may be aware of some great social networking websites that are freely available online to use to promote both yourself as a DJ and your events. Facebook is a fantastic way to build your branding. You can easily create events and fan pages to attract people to your gigs. Facebook has a free email facility so that you can contact your friends list and inform them of your events, radio shows, etc. You can also upload event pictures and videos, and this is a great way to show prospective bar/club owners how successful you are as a DJ and the events you host.

Facebook has a great network of people online already connected, meaning that friends of friends of friends may get invited to your party and your name and event gets spread around the online community. And how much does this cost? Nothing.

If you really want to get creative, you can create a whole community of like-minded people by setting up a group to do with the music that you love. By doing this, you create a community for people to chat about music and events, and if you are at the centre of creating the group, you will be seen as a leader, creating a following of people behind you. If you already have a website, it would be a great idea to promote your website link in every email you send out to your target market. This is very effective, especially when you want to build an external database for promoting your events. So make sure you have a website that has an opt-in box (opt-in meaning that someone can input their name and email address to join your database). Use www.aweber.com or www.getresponse.com for this.

One word of warning, please use Facebook sensibly: don't bombard people with the same info every other day, otherwise people may start to perceive you as spam and then you may actually have the opposite effect to that desired. Try to update people with the latest news and developments about once a fortnight and provide value for them; make them want to open your message.

MySpace is a site that many have been using for a few years. It, too, is a great social networking site for promoting yourself as a DJ and your events. Similarly to Facebook, you are able to create gigs/events and invite people to them. You can also create group topics and discussions related to your preferred genre of music. This is a great way to network and get in touch with your target market by finding out what's hot and what's not in the music business.

Building a Website without Breaking the Bank

Do you have a website? If not, then I'd suggest you get a move on and develop an online presence. Having a website is an essential marketing tool and has many advantages:

> Develop your own unique brand.

> Upload your demo mixes for promoters/club owners/fans to download.

> Build your online database of emails so that you can promote your events and announce important news instantaneously.

> Archive successful events in the form of reviews and gallery pictures.

> Provide an easy way for people to contact and book you.

> It's your own 100% personalised global business portfolio, working for you, 24-hours a day, 7 days a week, 365 days a year, for a nominal investment.

In order to achieve online success, you have TWO options:

1. You can seek a good affordable web-designer to develop and host your site. I personally recommend you post your project for free on www.elance.com and get bidders from all over the world pitching for your job.

2. You can develop your own site. Nowadays the need for websites is increasing so programmers have developed easy-to-use templates which allow you to simply upload your text, images and audio yourself. My team are experts in this field and we have provided a cutting-edge list of all the best web-building links in the bonus resources section at the back of this book.

13 Mobile and Function DJing

Setting yourself up in business as a mobile DJ is completely different to being a club DJ.

First and foremost, your clientele will often include people of all ages rather than the more narrow range encountered in a bar or club. This will have a profound effect on the styles of music that you will need to buy and play.

Equipment

As well as requiring either vinyl/CD turntables or a laptop from which to play your music, you will also need to invest in some good PA equipment. For a medium-sized function venue (roughly the size of a school hall), you will need a power amplifier, mid-range speakers, and one or two bass bins. In addition, a mobile DJ is expected to provide some lighting effects, so a few carefully chosen pieces of lighting equipment are also essential.

Figure 13.1 shows a basic PA system and lighting rig. PAs can usually be bought as complete packages, which means that the power amp will correctly drive the speakers in terms of watts per channel. Most systems work in a chain (connecting speaker to speaker), but you should always check the correct way to set up your PA and test that it all operates perfectly before taking on any gigs.

You will also, needless to say, need a reliable vehicle to transport your PA and other equipment to gigs. Make sure that it is regularly serviced as there is nothing worse than being late, or even unable to get to a gig at, all due to transportation problems.

Figure 13.1

Setting up Safely and Efficiently

The golden rule of mobile DJing is to arrive well in advance so that you can set up carefully without neglecting any important details. It is very important to develop a well-rehearsed method for setting up your console and PA, as you will often find yourself working alongside other entertainers (function bands and musicians, etc.) who will also be setting up around you.

At a function, the crowd is usually made up of families, friends or work colleagues. Bearing this in mind, be aware that the presence of a DJ and a dancefloor is merely a contributing factor to the evening's entertainment. The music should never be so loud that guests are put off from having conversations. The ideal set-up, therefore, would be to have the speakers laid out on the four corners of a square dancefloor. This would mean that any guest on the dancefloor would be surrounded by music, but that other people at the function would still be able to socialise without the sound being too obtrusive *(Fig. 13.2)*.

Figure 13.2

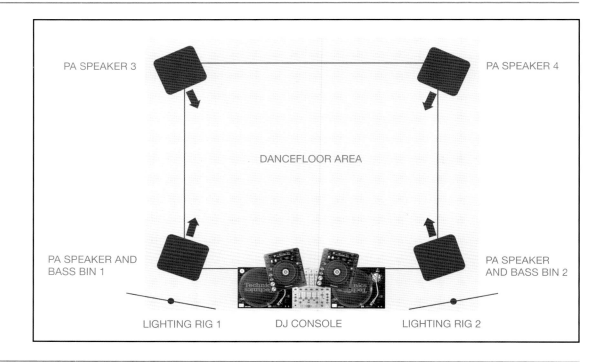

PA SPEAKER 3

PA SPEAKER 4

DANCEFLOOR AREA

PA SPEAKER AND
BASS BIN 1

PA SPEAKER
AND BASS BIN 2

LIGHTING RIG 1   DJ CONSOLE   LIGHTING RIG 2

Once you have set up the PA to your satisfaction, make sure you secure all the wiring to the floor using gaffer tape so that your dancefloor is 100% safe for the guests. Often, dancefloors can be specifically raised sections of sprung board or cork, so cables can run along the edge of these and be gaffered down around the perimeter.

You should also erect the lighting rig behind the DJ booth or speakers so that there is no danger of tripods being knocked over. Similarly, any speakers mounted on stands should be anchored against a bass bin for extra stability. Clearly mark around the boundary of any tripod or stand with a visible tape, as black stand legs can be a hazard in a dark venue. Check the condition of your electrical cables and appliances, and have electrical appliances tested regularly.

Try to restrict the number of people present in the venue when setting up and packing away, become familiar with the positions of the fire exits before the start of the function and regularly inspect equipment such as trolleys and ladders.

Top Tip:
Always ensure that you have all the spare parts and tools that you might require such as spare bulbs for lighting, good working connecting cables, extension leads, etc.

Presentation

Looking professional is extremely important as a mobile DJ. Functions such as weddings, birthdays and corporate work parties are usually events that require smart dress-code, so be sure to wear at least a shirt and tie/bow-tie with smart trousers and shoes if not a full dinner suit.

You should also consider the way that your equipment and console are perceived by guests. Leads should be concealed and all connecting speaker cables should be neatly and safely taped down. The console itself should be tidy and simple. Many mobile DJs buy or construct collapsible workstations that they can mount their console on. The speakers and lighting should all be regularly serviced and well maintained, so that the sound system itself looks professional.

Personality and Etiquette

Although functions may become regular gigs and a source of income, always remember that they are often a once-in-a-lifetime event for the client. You should always make sure that you contribute in a positive way to the occasion by being as friendly and obliging as you possibly can.

> Always remain polite.

> At functions, you can expect a reasonable amount of alcohol consumption, so be particularly careful to respond well to requests from drunken guests.

> Other performers such as function bands, puppeteers or magicians often have their own set-up requirements, and you should try to work around these as best as you can. Everybody's performance will be affected by negative vibes or stress created at this stage of the event.

> Catering staff will be the ones providing you with refreshments so you should try and establish a good rapport.

> Venues and their staff are often in contact with booking agents, so try to make a good impression. Repeat bookings will come from recommendations so focus on giving the best possible service to the guests.

The Performance

As a mobile DJ, you will not necessarily need any mixing skills, although it is certainly fine to use them if you can. The main concern for your performance is to play a wide variety of well-chosen music that will cater for all the guests. You should have a meeting with the client in advance so that you can prepare your selection and tailor it to their requirements. Especially where weddings are concerned, you should ask for a list of tracks that have a special significance for the couple and their family and friends.

You should have as many tracks from the standard repertoire as you can, which includes most of the popular Disco, Soul and Pop from the 1960s onwards. Always try to speak to any other musicians so that you don't end up playing the same tracks. Also, most mobile DJs use a microphone in their performance. This can range from saying just a few words between tracks to plenty of 'witty' banter over the mixes. There is no set code of conduct for using a microphone, but always be sensitive to the occasion. It is best to test the water and judge carefully whether people are responding well to any spoken entertainment from the DJ booth.

Insurance and Financial Aspects

It is imperative that your equipment is insured against damage, and that you also have the correct public liability insurance in case of accidents. Join the Musician's Union, as they offer a range of legal and insurance services connected with public performance. All your equipment should be tested and approved in accordance with public health and safety regulations (some venues will actually check this, and not allow you to use any equipment that does not display a valid and up-to-date certificate).

Always make sure that payment is arranged prior to the performance. Most mobile DJs will do many of their gigs through booking agents who will invoice the client and take a percentage, but any private bookings will require an upfront agreement of fees and a contract. This should stipulate the fee and any other requirements, such as refreshments or changing facilities.

It is important to charge a reasonable amount of money for playing a function. Check against other companies or individuals in the marketplace so that you can put a correct value on your services. As with any business, the initial outlay for your PA and lighting will be recuperated over a period of time and a number of gigs, not all at the outset.

Many DJs offer several different packages to cater for different clients' requirements and budgets. You may include a karaoke service as an additional extra, although bear in mind you will need extra equipment to do this.

Visit DJ Tutor Ellaskins on YouTube: www.youtube.com/user/ellaskins for some great video tutorials from professional mobile DJs, as included in the bonus resources section at the back of the book.

Promotion

Although successful bookings and recommendations will often produce further gigs, you should make sure that you maximise your advertising potential by registering with several booking agents and building a nicely presented website. Your website should give people your contact details, a list of the services you are able to provide and their respective costs, and if possible some references from previous (well-satisfied) clients. Have a stack of business cards or flyers handy to give out to people on the night if asked.

14 Becoming a Radio DJ

Playing a set in a club is a truly hands-on experience; the crowd are physically in front of you, and it is their reaction to your selection that will influence the 'soundtrack' of the night. Playing on the radio is almost the complete opposite, you are alone in a booth playing to a silent, anonymous audience. With a radio broadcast, however, there is the possibility of reaching thousands, maybe millions, of listeners, as well as giving people more of a personal insight into your tastes and character.

Getting on the Air

There are numerous different ways to get into radio, either as a production assistant, producer or DJ. Local hospital and student stations are usually looking for producers and DJs, which gives any budding enthusiast a great opportunity to learn the workings of a radio studio. Podcasting sites make it simpler than ever to share your music.

Another obvious way of getting yourself noticed is to produce a demo that you can send to stations. One of the best things that you can do is to listen to plenty of well-presented shows and try to emulate the way they are produced and structured. Once you have a feel for the way a good show should flow, you will then be able to let your own personality and creativity come through on your own show.

You should accept and embrace any offer of a slot at any time of the day or night, even if it means playing a 'graveyard shift' (a slot that covers the more anti-social times, such as 3 a.m.). My early shows on KISS FM were originally at 1 a.m. on a Tuesday, hardly peak listening time for all the clubbers who'd been out partying all weekend, but I knew it was an opportunity that would help lead me where I wanted to go. You don't go straight to the front of the queue or to the top (at least not in most circumstances), so wait for your time, get your experience and be prepared for when a bigger opportunity arises.

Experience plus knowledge cultivates success. Most famous DJs started by playing at small unknown events or on local radio, so there is no shame in getting broadcasting experience at a local level.

Pete Tong is the classic example of a DJ who started out as a mobile DJ and playing on small-scale radio shows. Taking time to build up his audience, sound, reputation and skills since the late 1970s, he now presents one of the longest running and most influential dance music shows on UK radio. The 'Essential Mix' show on BBC Radio 1 (formerly 'The Soul Sessions' on Capital FM) is a national institution which has been responsible for shaping the sound of the UK Dance scene and for breaking many of the most important artists and tracks over the last 20 years.

Pirate Radio

Although there is a lot of controversy surrounding pirate radio, it is impossible to overlook its significance. The pirate radio scene has been responsible for shaping much of the underground music culture over the past three decades. Many DJs have built international careers after blossoming on pirate radio stations.

The main function of these illegally run stations is to play the fresh, cutting-edge sounds that are not being given airtime on any of the regular radio stations. From the Atlantic Soul of LWR, and the Acid House of Fantasy FM, to the Jungle of Kool FM, the sound of the pirates has had a huge impact, particularly in the inner cities. They have often been responsible for leading the way musically; carving out paths that larger corporate scenes have trodden once a particular musical scene has been broken.

The main consideration for playing on a pirate radio station is the choice of music. Building a reputation has a lot to do with musical style, and although in the early days there were some questionable mixing techniques, it is certainly not true of today's private DJs. Often there are separate MCs booked in (genre depending) to do the talking on pirates, so the DJ's main responsibility is to keep the flow of music going. This tends to be upfront (although the odd older, more classic record is fine) due to the fact that the audience is usually only interested in the hottest new sounds.

There is of course a serious downside to pirate radio. Playing on these carries a far higher risk than it did even a decade ago. Large fines, confiscation of equipment and even jail sentences can await those who are caught trying to broadcast illegally. Nonetheless, it is because of the reputation, following and 'status' of many of the old pirates that the corporate stations have stood up and taken notice.

Internet Radio

The internet has had a huge impact on the way that people listen to broadcasts. People around the world now have immediate access to a goldmine of musical resources. There is now a wave of opportunity to break into radio with the advent of internet stations and fast broadband connections. Anyone with some basic equipment can have access to a global audience, rapidly and relatively cheaply. This is definitely the way forward.

To a certain degree, the introduction of internet radio has dispensed with the need to take the risks that pirate stations incur. Although the buzz of illegal broadcasting is part of the appeal of pirate radio, the internet offers the same opportunity to play with complete freedom, without the risk of heavy fines or loss of equipment.

One of the big problems with the internet is creating public awareness. It is entirely possible to end up playing a superb programme of music driven by great personality, but without a single listener. Marketing your show is a fundamental part of online radio DJing. The regular social networking sites such as MySpace and Facebook are a good way to start but it is also worth trying to strike arrangements with other websites where you exchange advertising space or contact lists on your respective sites.

Top Tip:
Any internet radio shows that you create should be recorded and made permanently available via podcast, or via a platform such as www.soundcloud.com or www.mixcloud.com. (More resources in the Bonus Resources section)

Remuneration

Radio is predominantly about raising your profile, reputation, industry connections and access to new music. It should serve as a platform for sharing your passion for music. It is highly unlikely that you will make any money from radio until you have worked your way up to the higher levels of corporate radio, but it will open doors for you in many ways and these extra gigs, enhanced profile and increased exposure should be what you focus on, as opposed to the direct monetary gain.

Corporate Radio

Working for larger corporate stations will usually require a portfolio of work (recorded shows) as well as a CV that shows you have enough experience. Again, it is a case of working your way up from the bottom. Preparing a show properly is essential to ensuring that the delivery and timing of all your music and features is slick and polished. At the top level, a two-hour radio show will have a minimum of two days' pre-production. That includes research from production assistants, track selection, compiling, pre-mixing, timing of voice links, jingles, interviews and programming. Benji B, the successful BBC 1Xtra radio presenter, honed his skills as a producer on Gilles Peterson's 'Worldwide Show' before he was awarded his own specialist show. See if you can volunteer your services to a desired show or station to learn the ropes.

Dead Air

Dead air (total silence on a radio show) is pretty much a radio DJ's worst nightmare; ten seconds can feel like an eternity. Sometimes due to technical faults it is unavoidable, but there are certain factors that can greatly reduce the likelihood of dead air.

> If you are using jingles, advertisement breaks or over-dubs, double check that they are 'cued up' and ready to go.

> Avoid tampering with anything technical that you are not 100% sure about.

> Make sure that you have the contact details for the station producer immediately to hand, so that you have some professional support in case of a technical emergency.

> In the event of dead air, it is best to stay calm and take action. Never highlight the fault by saying 'we are having a technical problem'. It is far better to get the show back on air as quickly as possible and simply welcome the listeners back.

Microphone Etiquette

Many DJs make the mistake of talking too much, especially early in their careers due to nerves. It is far better to keep vocal links to a minimum, but when you do speak be precise, upbeat and to the point. Authenticity is also important as people soon hear through a façade.

People listen to the radio to hear great music coupled with a sprinkling of your personality. In the same way that you shouldn't mix two vocal records together (unless they are working together synergistically to create something that makes sense and sounds good), you should never speak over vocals. Voice links are best suited to the beginning and end of a track.

It is really important to build your rapport with your listeners by speaking as though you were talking to them individually. Be aware of what the majority of your audience want to hear, talk to them personally and be consistent in your approach. This way you will build up a relationship with your audience and develop a loyal and dedicated following. This is the very best marketing and promotion you could ever hope for.

Top Tip:
You should only open the microphone up if you need to speak; otherwise remember to keep it switched off. There have been many embarrassing incidents where private conversations have been broadcast over the air.

It is usually best to steer away from profanity, blasphemy or insulting people's views or musical tastes on air. Although some people find this kind of approach entertaining, they are vastly outnumbered by people who find it offensive. Remember that when you speak poorly about another person, especially in public, it actually speaks volumes more about you yourself. More importantly, it is totally unprofessional.

Finally, never break the golden rule of DJ etiquette: don't overrun into the next DJ's airtime. Even at the top levels of the music business, there have been incidents where DJs have had serious falling-outs over the lack of respect shown to each other's air time. Every minute is valuable when you're on air, especially when you've got a tight, pre-planned show. Start and finish your show (or DJ slot) promptly, unless otherwise directed. The BBC is a prime example in that all their shows start and finish on schedule (give or take a few seconds). This is mainly down to excellent planning and efficiency, but it is also down to the professionalism of the DJs and producers, who know when to announce that they are out of time and wrap up the show.

Knowing Your Market and Job

With a radio show you should know your target audience and the job you are there to do. You may be able to arrange the style of presentation (entertainment, music, documentary, etc.) with the station; you should work with them to target the desired audience by making sure that you are providing what is expected of you.

As with club DJing, it is good practice to frequently record your shows and sets. Firstly, this gives you a portfolio of your work, but more importantly it will help you to constructively review your performance and look at ways you can improve it. Whether you choose to play the recordings back alone or with some honest, musically inclined friends who are not afraid to give you constructive criticism, it is vital that you evaluate your performance so you know what is working and what is not.

Everything
You Need to Know
About DJing and Success

Section 2:
Danny's Tips for Achieving Your Potential and Succeeding in Life

In Section 1 we covered a lot of the more technical and practical need-to-knows relating to DJing. From here on, I'm going to share with you basic tips and tools that can be applied to ANY area of life to help you achieve your goals: no matter what your background or profession.

It's time to get excited now, because ALL of the points I'm about to run through are common sense, easy to apply, and immensely powerful when combined. I'm summarising what I have distilled from my years of trial and error and discovering what does and doesn't work.

Please congratulate yourself on getting this far. If you apply on a consistent basis what you are about to read, I personally GUARANTEE your life will take on a whole new level of depth, happiness and success. All I ask is that you share this information with others.

As Pete Tong says, 'Without further ado, we continue . . . '

Goal-setting/Know Your Outcome

What do you want to achieve? What's your goal? Is it to release a track? If so, by when, and on what label? Is it to DJ at a specific club? If so, what club, when, and on what night and at what time? If you don't know where you're going, then you're like a boat in the ocean without a rudder. You're going to drift aimlessly. Take control and outline some goals. Here's a tip for setting your goals. Make them S.M.A.R.T.

S: is for Specific/Significant/Stretching. It's not enough to say 'I want more money'. You could find 5p on the floor and that would be 'more money'. 'I'd like to earn an extra £200 per weekend set' is specific.

M: is for Measurable/Meaningful/Motivational. You've got to be able to measure your goal, so you know when you've achieved it. Using the same example, '£200 more per weekend set' is measurable. You know when you've achieved that goal.

A: is for Attainable/Achievable/Acceptable/Action-Oriented. OK, there are mixed views on this, but my personal advice is Aim High. Make your key goals a real stretch for you. Make them so that they are a challenge and something you'll be really proud of once you've achieved them. You know the adage, 'shoot for the stars and if you fall short you'll reach the moon'. dream big, play big. That's where the juice in life is. No leader or figurehead ever got to where they are without first dreaming of it.

R: is for Realistic/Relevant/Reasonable/Rewarding/Results-Oriented. A goal can be both high and realistic.

T: is for Time-Based/Timely/Tangible/Trackable. You've got to put a date on when you want to achieve your goal so that it's not just on the 'never, never'. Parkinson's Law states that a task will expand or contract to fill the time that is designated to it. You need to be realistic to a degree. You can't say 'I want to lose two stone in two days'. That isn't realistic. But you can lose two stone in two months if you're disciplined to do so and take consistent action. Challenge yourself with your goals but make sure that they motivate you also. Make sure they are measurable as well.

'Our deepest fear is not that we are inadequate. Our deepest fear is that we are powerful beyond measure. It is our light, not our darkness that most frightens us. We ask ourselves, who am I to be brilliant, gorgeous, talented, fabulous? Actually, who are you not to be? You are a child of God. Your playing small does not serve the world. There is nothing enlightened about shrinking so that other people won't feel insecure around you. We are all meant to shine, as children do. We were born to make manifest the glory of God that is within us. It's not just in some of us: it is in everyone. And as we let our own light shine, we unconsciously give other people permission to do the same. As we are liberated from our own fear, our presence automatically liberates others'.

Marianne Williamson, quoting Nelson Mandela's inauguration speech.

Ask Yourself WHY, Not HOW to Help Motivate You

It's very important not to ask yourself 'How?' when you are at first envisaging a large goal. It is likely that you will be overwhelmed and come up with limiting thoughts which may prevent you from taking action.

Much more important than asking 'How?' is to ask 'WHY?' you want to achieve what it is you have set yourself. Asking 'Why' will get your mind thinking about all of the reasons that you desire your goal. Don't just think about it. Get some paper, a diary or a book and list as many possible reasons WHY you want your goal.

Brainstorm all of your reasons and get them down on paper. Have fun as you do this: it's a very simple exercise that will help motivate you as well as give you more confidence. More importantly, it helps you to gain clarity of thought and for your sub-conscious mind to start focusing. Once you have got a compelling list of 'whys', continue to brainstorm all of the potential ideas for 'how' you can do it. What are some steps (no matter how small) that you can take right away to move you a step closer?

Some Simple Questions to Help Discover Your Core Values

Three simple questions that have helped me to identify what is of true value to me in my life are:

1.   What would you do if you only had six months left to live?
2.   What would you do if money was no object and you had millions in the bank?
3.   What would you do if failure wasn't an option: if you absolutely couldn't fail?

What are you waiting for?

Focus

Do this exercise: Think of your bedroom at home. Think of your bed, your pillow, your duvet and whatever you have on your walls. Do you have a window? If so, what do you see? OK, what did you just see? Did you see letters and sentences in your mind? Of course you didn't. That's because the mind works in IMAGES: it's visual. So the first thing that you want to do is to be clear about the situations, circumstances and people you want in your life.

A fantastically fun yet powerfully effective exercise is to create a 'treasure map' or 'dream board'. Cut out images from magazines, photos or from the internet (Google Images is good for this) of the things that you want to attract into your life. Cut the pictures out and create a collage/montage, and put them somewhere where you will see them every day. This is all about the 'Law of Attraction', which is the focus of a truly inspiring film that I highly recommend you watch, entitled *The Secret* by Rhonda Byrne.

I thought this was a silly, oversimplified exercise the first time I tried it, but I kept hearing about ultra-successful people who said they had used this method. I did it tongue-in-cheek and I literally attracted all of the things in my images into my reality. This is also known as 'treasure mapping'. Basically what you're doing is impregnating your subconscious mind with clear images of what you want. The sub-conscious works primarily in images, and what you're doing here is not only making something that is nice to look at and reminding you daily of some ideals, but also helping you bring those things about in your life. You can also turn this treasure map into a screen saver or desktop on your computer, or the wallpaper on your phone.

Chunking and Segmenting

You've set yourself a big goal. You now need to look objectively at where you are and where you want to be, look at the 'gap' between the two and then create a plan for closing that gap. The best way to do so is to put pen to paper and make a list of all the things you need to do to get to your goal.

Look at what you want to achieve and break the process down into as many steps as possible. Let's say you want to play at one of the main clubs in a specific town or city, but you're currently only playing at your local bar. Firstly, remember that every DJ who is playing the big spaces will have started off at home, and then progressed up the ranks, gaining experience as they go.

Here's an example of how you can 'chunk and segment' this task:

1. Decide whether you want to set up your own night or whether you want to get a gig at someone else's night.

2. Research all the nights that are on in the area.

3. Identify the musical policies of each and see where your sound may fit.

4. Get business cards and demo mixes posted up online and some CDs pressed up, along with a website.

5. Find out who the decision makers are for the night you want to target. Who's the promoter? Who actually calls the musical shots? How can you contact them?

6. Think about how you can differentiate yourself from all the other people 'chomping at the bit'.

7. You could frequent the targeted night as a punter and stay for the duration, listening to (and watching) how the night works.

8. Can you get your promotional CD/website to the promoter? Have you got their email address? After they've got access to your demo, tell them you'll follow up in a week to see what they think of it.

9. Always follow up and ask for HONEST feedback. They may like your technique but not quite your selection. Therefore, if you still want the gig, you may be able to change your selection to appease the promoter.

> **Top Tip:**
> As in all things in life, whether you think you can or you think you can't, you're right'. Have faith.

You get the idea: you need to take small, doable steps to move you towards your big goal.

Remember the adage 'failing to plan equals planning to fail'. Keep on knocking on that door no matter how many no's you get (and there will be a lot of them, especially in the beginning).

Time Management

There's one thing that we all have in common, and that is that we all get 24 hours in any single day. The homeless person, the prime ministers and presidents of the world, the successful promoters, musicians and DJs, everyone – we all get 24 hours. More so than anything in life, YOUR CHOICE of how you spend your time will determine your success, happiness and outcome. As with all things in life, small actions on a daily basis (either good or bad) will compound themselves and multiply to give you your outcome, for better or for worse.

Top Tip:
Take a bit of paper and log the use of every half hour in your day for one week. This is to bring to your attention where you are spending your time and to eliminate those time-wasting activities that are not helping you achieve your potential and get to where you want to be. Self-awareness is the first big step.

The leading motivator and coach Anthony Robbins has made a couple of extremely poignant statements, profound in their simplicity: 'it's in your moments of decision that your destiny is shaped' and 'sow a thought and you reap an action; sow an action and you reap a habit; sow a habit and you reap a character; sow a character and you reap a destiny.' In essence, your destiny is shaped by the decisions you make through the thoughts you are having on a moment-by-moment basis.

If you're nowhere near where you want to be in life and you're spending three hours a night watching mindless TV or idly chatting, yet you're still dreaming of being a musician, DJ or producer, then maybe you should change your strategy. How about cutting back to two hours or even one hour of TV and putting the other couple of hours into activities that will move you forward.

Remember the power of small steps on a daily basis. A bit of research today, a phone call tomorrow, some emails the next day, planning the mix the day after that, recording the mix the next, etc. These kinds of small steps will have a cumulative effect and begin to build momentum, bringing success and achievement closer to you.

There's a successful author called Steven Covey who wrote a global bestseller called *The 7 Habits of Highly Effective People*. In it he talks about 'putting first things first'. These are the 'important' things that will move you towards your key goals in life. They are usually not 'urgent' so they are often the first to get put on the back burner.

Danny's Tips for Achieving Your Potential and Succeeding in Life
Time Management

Think about all of the activities that fill your life. They come under the categories of:

1. Urgent and Important *(Fire Fighting)* – Requires immediate action with a big consequence. An example would be cramming for a big test or exam.

2. Important but Not Urgent *(Quality Time)* – These things often get neglected in life as they're not urgent, but they're where the real pay-off and reward in life come from. Examples of important things include investing time into your passions, knowledge, skills or health.

3. Urgent but Not Important *(Distraction)* – Over the course of a week, month and year, we can lose so much of our lives to distractions. For example, answering an email as soon as you receive it. It requires answering, therefore is urgent, but very often it isn't important.

4. Neither Urgent nor Important *(Time Wasting)* – People often unconsciously give up their dreams and power when they focus much of their time to activities in this zone. Examples are mindless TV, idle chatter, aimless web surfing and trashy magazine reading, all of which are things that aren't offering any high value to your important life goals.

Having knowledge of these four areas, you can now proactively maximise time spent on non-urgent, important activities. Allocate time in your diary to carry out these tasks when you are at your best. Doing so can reduce the amount of time taken up by fire fighting, since many of these activities may have been 'non urgent but important' activities had they been resolved earlier. An example of this is filling out your tax return in a hurry on the day it's due, as opposed to filling it out a month in advance.

You can also seek to reduce time spent in the urgent but non-important areas of life by improving your systems and processes for dealing with distractions. Finally, if you want to really empower yourself and achieve your goals, seek to eliminate as many of the non-urgent and non-important activities as possible. Remember that 'good habits are hard to form and easy to break, whilst bad habits are easy to form and hard to break'.

Below are some of my favourite quotes relating to time, to act as reminders that it is what you do with your 24 hours more than anything else that will determine your levels of success, happiness and achievement in all areas of your life.

'Never leave until tomorrow that which you can do today.'
Benjamin Franklin

'Lost wealth may be replaced by industry, lost knowledge by study, lost health by temperance or medicine, but lost time is gone forever.'
Samuel Smiles

'In truth, people can generally make time for what they choose to do; it is not really the time but the will that is lacking.'
Sir John Lubbock

'Until we can manage time, we can manage nothing else.'
Peter F. Drucker

'Time is the coin of your life. It isthe only coin you have, and only you can determine how it will be spent. Be careful lest you let other people spend it for you.'
Carl Sandburg

'Focus on the present. Never let yesterday use up today.'
Richard H. Nelson

'You're writing the story of your life one moment at a time.'
Doc Childre and Howard Martin

'Until you value yourself, you will not value your time. Until you value your time, you will not do anything with it.'
M. Scott Peck

'Don't be fooled by the calendar. There are only as many days in the year as you make use of. One man gets only a week's value out of a year while another man gets afull year's value out of a week.'
Charles Richards

'Once you have mastered time, you will understand how true it is that most people overestimate what they can accomplish in a year – and underestimate what they can achieve in a decade.'
Anthony Robbins

'Take care of the minutes and the hours will take care of themselves.'
Lord Chesterfield

'The key is in not spending time, but in investing it.'
Stephen R. Covey

'Time equals life; therefore, waste your time and waste your life, or master your time and master your life.'
Alan Lakein

'Be on time: show that you respect and appreciate both your, and others', time.'
Anon

Setting Priorities and the Pareto Principle (80/20 Rule)

It is commonly recognised that 20% of your activities will account for 80% of your success (the Pareto Principle) i.e. if you have 100 tasks on your task list, it is very likely that about 20 of those will be the key ones that will give you 80% of your results. This principle carries over into many areas of life: 80% of your satisfaction will come from 20% of your friends, 20% of your customers in business will make up 80% of your business (and inversely 80% of your problems or challenges will come from 20% of your customers), 80% of your income will come from a key 20% of your time and efforts etc.

You need to identify what are the key 20% activities that will move you forward to your goal. We all tend to busy ourselves to make ourselves feel or look productive. Simply get into the habit of asking yourself 'What key activities today are most important and influential towards helping me move towards my main goals?' Then prioritise these tasks and make sure that you do them today: preferably first, before other 'distractions' and 'excuses' come up. To help motivate you to take the necessary action, refer back to your list of Whys (all the reasons WHY you want the goal/outcome) and focus on how it will feel to attain the end-result.

You never get back the moment that has just gone, and with each passing day there's less time to live your dreams. If you're not taking action each day towards achieving your dreams, what are you waiting for? 'The road of tomorrow leads you to a town called nowhere.' Take an action NOW, no matter how small it may seem, towards something you'd like to be, have, or achieve in YOUR life. All successful people in the music business have one thing in common. They TAKE ACTION.

As one of my mentors and favourite speakers (Les Brown) famously comments: 'You don't have to be great to get started but you have to get started to be great'.

Attitude and Personality

Have you ever heard the saying 'you are what you associate', or 'birds of a feather flock together'? Well, it's true. This isn't to demean any person or to think anyone is better than anyone else. It is merely a truth that successful people tend to surround themselves with positive, enthusiastic people whilst negative, cynical people tend to attract each other.

One of the keys to achieving what you want in life is to put yourself around the kind of people who are getting the results you want, and to have a support circle of friends or acquaintances who support you in your goals and will hold you accountable for attaining them.

They say 'you can't choose your family, but you can choose your friends'. It's true. Have you got any people in your life that laugh at you or 'rubbish' your ideas? Just be aware of such people, and never ever let anyone tell you what you can or can't be. If you have a vision and genuinely believe in it, then you can achieve it. It may seem a long way off, but if you are dedicated, passionate and committed to achieving it, you can and will achieve it. EVERY person starts out somewhere. What matters is where you are going.

People will treat you the way that you allow them to. In relation to the Law of Attraction, this means that you can set your boundaries so that you will only participate in positive conversations. Feeding into somebody's negative conversation will bring your spirit and attitude down. Decide today to maintain your high vibration and energy and stop feeding into other people's negative vibes. This will go a long way to maintaining your high, positive energy, which will in turn attract other successful people who share similar qualities and aspirations.

Be Likeable and Smile

It's much nicer to be around people who are pleasant and likeable rather than toxic, critical and condescending. A smile speaks a thousand words and triggers off emotions in the body that instantly make you feel better. Smiling at others warms people to you and indicates connection and friendliness, which in turn opens up contact and a platform for opportunities. I love the quote, 'Some people are too tired to give you a smile. Give them one of yours, as none needs a smile as much as he who has no more to give.'

Attitude and Enthusiasm

Who would you rather be around: negative, condescending people who put other people down and focus on all the bad things in their lives, or enthusiastic, positive people who enjoy complimenting other people and sharing the good things that are happening in each other's lives?

If you decide to adopt a positive outlook in life and you approach any situation with enthusiasm, doors and opportunities will open themselves to you. Do you know people who always seem to 'land on their feet' or 'be in the right place at the right time'? From my experience in business and life, I would ALWAYS choose to work with someone who has the right attitude, even if they didn't have the aptitude, over someone who has the right aptitude but the wrong attitude. Why? Because someone with the right attitude can always be taught the necessary skills so that their aptitude increases. On the other hand, it's very hard to change someone's attitude, and a negative attitude is not pleasant to be around.

I'd say that a large part of my success as a global DJ, producer and radio presenter has been because I've always treated people in the way that I'd like to be treated (also known as 'the Golden Rule'). Being friendly, polite and helpful to everyone (irrelevant of position, status or connections) costs nothing but has far-reaching ripple effects. More importantly, it makes for a happier, more peaceful world.

One of my favourite teachers, Dr Wayne Dyer, famously states: 'When you change the way you look at things, the things you look at change.' It's all a matter of perspective and attitude.

Ask for What You Want

We've all heard of 'ask and ye shall receive', 'knock on the door and the door will be opened' and 'everything will come to he who asks'. Do you know people who don't necessarily have the best skills for a job, but have got it ahead of other more competent people? Often, these are the vocal, assertive people who are not afraid of asking for what they want.

Think of something that you would like in your life. Now think of someone who can help you to get this in one way or another: someone who can introduce you to someone, someone who has a skill set or information you would like to know more about. OK, so here's your challenge. ASK them for their help. What's the worst possible outcome? The person says no, politely declines or, very worst case, refuses to help you. BIG DEAL. You're in no worse a place than you were before you asked and at least you 'grew' because you tried.

If you ask for help in a sincere manner then almost all positive people are happy to do what they can to assist you. Think about yourself. If a person asks you for help, what is your natural reaction? It feels good to give and it feels good to help others.

Think of someone you can ask for something now: advice, contacts, information or assistance. Push your comfort zone TODAY (not tomorrow, next week, or sometime in the future) and ask them politely and sincerely for what you would like . . . and see what happens!

Modelling: Don't Reinvent the Wheel

Do you want to fast track your success? Here's one of the smartest things you can do. MODEL someone who has achieved the results that you want. If you want to learn to make music, isn't it wise to invest in a teacher or course that teaches you how to get the results you want? If you want to learn to engineer a studio, then go somewhere and spend some money on learning from someone who is an expert in that field: there are loads of options, invest in a course, a book, online training, a coach, etc.

Likewise, if you want to spin like a certain DJ, listen to how they play, how they structure their sets, how they select their tunes, how they mix. Think of it as a recipe for success: if you want to learn to cook like a professional who has dedicated their life to learning, then pick up a Gordon Ramsay or Jamie Oliver book. What do they do in the book? They tell you step-by-step how to prepare and put the ingredients together, how long to cook it, in what style and at what temperature. What have you just done? You've been smart, invested in learning from an expert, and cut your learning time by years.

If you've got any doubts, get rid of them. There is no one in life who doesn't learn from others. For you to fast track yourself, emulate those who are doing what (and getting the results) you want. Put your own creative slant on your field of endeavour (whether it is music, DJing or otherwise), but take lessons and note from leaders in your chosen field.

In the DJing field, why not arrange an informal, part-time 'mentorship'? Exchange some of your time to get under the wing of someone you want to learn from. What can you offer them for free? A few examples include driving them to gigs, help carrying or setting up their equipment, help in the office with the admin or assisting with their promotion or social networking. In return you get to be around their expertise, the power of association, to see how the business works and you get to know these people well. You also get to prove your worth so that you can then charge for your services and time down the line.

This is one of the best ways to accelerate your growth in any arena. Who wouldn't want an enthusiastic and passionate volunteer helper around to assist in their day-to-day activities? Just a couple of examples include Tristan DaCunha, who volunteered to help out at Ralph Lawson's 20:20 Vision record label one day a week. From this opening he went on to become A&R manager for the label, manager of another label and was mentored by Ralph as a resident at the infamous Back 2 Basics club in Leeds. He now plays at the best clubs the world over.

Another example is Mat Playford, who threw his infectious enthusiasm into helping Angel Moraes, Sandy Rivera and Tim Deluxe doing whatever needed doing. In return he learned the industry ropes, made contacts, earned their 'ear and support' and picked up insider tips. He now enjoys residencies at world leading clubs such as Space in Ibiza, as well as having multiple best-selling productions. All this, simply through offering his time up-front in a win-win arrangement, with the ability to see the opportunity and pay-off in the bigger picture.

Leverage

There's a word you may or may not have come across: leverage. It means using resources around you to get bigger results from your efforts. For example, the power of the internet gives you leverage to communicate with many people quickly and cheaply. Similarly, to shorten your learning time and experience, you can gain leverage by speaking with people who have achieved the results you want and seeking their advice to help propel you forward. This is also why teams can work so well; when individual members have complementary 'core competencies' (bringing their own unique skills to the team), together they get better results than if they were operating or performing alone.

Controlling Your State and How You Feel

There are three things that control how you feel, and used together they can make great 'state shifts' instantly:

1. Physiology – the way you use and move your body.
2. Focus – what you are focusing your mind upon, both in your thoughts and within your environment.
3. Language – the way you are speaking to yourself internally and also the way you are speaking verbally.

Imagine that you're having a really bad set, you're nervous, it's all going wrong, the crowd aren't with you and you're feeling alone and wishing you were somewhere else. Really go there and imagine this experience.

When you envision this situation:
1. What would your body language be like?
2. What are you focusing on in your mind?
3. What kind of language are you using, both in your head and outwardly?

Let's do exactly the same exercise and momentarily take yourself back to a time when you felt really down, really low and defeated. Go there in your mind and notice how this feels, what your body is like, and what language is being used.

It's pretty much impossible to feel depressed whilst moving fluidly with an upright posture. On a physiological level, movement creates energy within the body which triggers endorphins. You cannot be depressed whilst smiling and uplifted in your posture and movement. How many depressed looking people do you see exercising: the two don't go hand in hand. On the contrary, think of depressed people: their movement tends to be slower, their shoulders slouched, their gaze is downward and generally it's as if there's a 'weight' burdening their body. So what? Well if you're not feeling confident at a gig or before a meeting, simply by walking tall with your shoulders back, smiling and looking upwards instantly makes you look (and more importantly feel) more confident. ACT AS IF and 'faith it until you make it'.

Use focus to your advantage. In a gig, focus your mind on having a great time. Focus on getting on well with the other DJs and the promoter, and focus on having a great set. Focus on all the good things that are happening in the room, the people who are adding to the party and hold eye contact, smile. Don't zero in on negativity (people, elements or bad mixes). You'll start enjoying yourself more, you'll feel better and people will see that, and it becomes a self-fulfilling prophecy.

Language. You've got your body posture right, you're looking confident, you're focusing on the good things, now you need to make sure your internal and external language is supporting you. Most of us would NEVER let anyone speak to us the way we often speak to ourselves in our own head. Yet many of us do it very often. Control the internal voice and start being your own biggest supporter. Talk positively inwardly and externally and notice the changes that will take place. Just catching yourself talking less than positively to yourself is the first step. Self-awareness is the key.

Every time your internal dialogue tells you bad things about yourself or tries to talk you out of the things you desire, you can consciously 'substitute' the thought for an empowering one. For example if you think to yourself that you can't play at a certain club or alongside a specific artist, substitute this with the thought that you can. Simply tell yourself 'I can, I can, I can'.

Combined together, taking control of your body (physiology), taking control of your focus (both internal and external) and taking control of your language can IMMEDIATELY shift how you feel.

Top Tip:
Our mind is only able to think one thought at any given moment in time. If you catch yourself having negative thoughts, consciously substitute the negative thought with a positive one.

Health

The music industry goes hand in hand with partying: that's what a lot of music is about. Going out, having a release, shaking off, getting lost in the music; for many that is a big part of the whole scene.

You've got to have good health if you want to be successful long term. You've got to be able to sustain a lifestyle and you should ensure that whatever you're doing is not going to seriously damage your longer-term health. I've had the great fortune to share thousands of magical moments on dancefloors and at parties all over the world, and I've partied with the best of them. But, again as I mature in my years, with hindsight, one thing I can share with you is to make sure you are in control of your escapades. Unfortunately, I've seen many people cause serious long-term damage to themselves by overindulging in habits that don't offer any long-term gain. You've got one body so if you're going to play hard you need to make sure you're striking the balance by putting a lot of goodness back into it, and balancing the play with a healthy amount of work, exercise and nutrition.

Simply drinking at least a couple of litres of water a day to help keep your system clean will also do wonders for your energy. If you've got more energy, you can get more done in a day and ultimately give off a better 'vibe' which helps you to attract more into your life.

If you have any unhealthy habits (such as drinking, substances, over-eating or cigarettes) and you'd like to change them, check out the bonus resource section where I have included some links to video tutorials demonstrating how to use Emotional Freedom Technique (EFT) to overcome them. It is an incredibly simple and powerful system that anyone can use at any time.

Tip for Dealing with Challenges

In every walk of life, we will all be faced with challenges from time to time. Rather than seeing challenges as setbacks, see them as opportunities to learn and grow.

Life throws challenges at us to see how we cope with them, and here's a very simple yet effective tool I can recommend, for dealing with awkward situations.

Step 1   Write the challenging situation down on paper, e.g. 'playing in front of 3,000 people'.

Step 2   Write down what is the worst possible outcome that could occur in this situation and accept that IF the worst-case scenario did happen, you could, and would, deal with it, e.g. fluffing the set and it not going off as you hoped.

Mentally accept that in life you always get through what comes at you: the proof is that you're here right now reading this – you're still here despite all the challenges you've encountered in the past. Simply accepting that you can and would deal with the worst-case scenario diminishes the worry and FEAR (a mnemonic for fear is False Expectations Appearing Real).

Step 3   Having realised that you can deal with the worst-case scenario IF it was to happen, think about everything that you can do in your power to avoid the scenario. What action can you take right now (no matter how small) to ensure it doesn't happen? For example, start to plan key tracks for your set, or a few mixes which work really well; or invite a couple of friends who can come and offer moral support and familiarity; see what DJ is playing before you and what kind of style they are likely to be playing, so you know roughly what you'll be taking over from.

Turn FEAR into your ally and use the adrenalin to your advantage to push your performance to heightened levels.

Preparation

Preparation is the key. If you've put in some research and work up front, then you're making your job/craft, in any walk of life, easier. And your performance will be greatly enhanced. Would you cook in a restaurant without a recipe? Would you go into an exam without doing any revision? Likewise, in DJing, preparation is essential to creating an optimal experience (and tight set).

It's much better to pre-plan and be confident in your skill. What's the opposite scenario? You turn up at a gig unprepared, you're not feeling relaxed because you're not confident in your selection, the crowd can pick up on this and you struggle a bit more with your set. The best sets are often inspired through improvisation: being in the moment and going with the flow. But you need to know your music, so you can put your hand on the right piece for the right moment.

Most leading DJs will have key parts or a section of any set pre-planned. Whether it is the introduction, the ending or some part in the middle, they will have worked certain mixes and ideas that they are confident with. Likewise you need to know the equipment in a club. It's best to get there early or ahead of the gig, or contact them in advance and ensure that you get yourself familiar with what you're playing on.

In any area of life, do your homework. Time invested upfront will pay dividends in your performance and ultimately your results.

Persistence

Nothing of value in life comes on a plate. What are you going to do when you come up against a challenge? What are you going to do when you're not feeling like showing up for a gig, or when you're tired? It's at these times that you've really got to be strong and focus on your list of 'Whys' (why you want your goal).

Take every setback and challenge as a learning experience that is essential for you to ultimately achieve your dreams. Thomas Edison, one of the greatest inventors in human history, was mocked by a probing reporter, 'But Mr Edison, you have failed over 1,000 times to make the electric light bulb', to which the scientist replied, 'Sir, I have not failed 1,000 times. I have discovered 1,000 ways NOT to make the light bulb, which makes me 1,000 times closer to finding THE way to make the light bulb.'

He went on to change human history by persisting and discovering the correct way to make the light bulb.

A lot of your success in life can be boiled down to your overall attitude towards life and your level of persistence. There's an expression 'Pleasant Persistence'. Adopt it in your life and never take the first (second, third or fourth) knock-back as final. Remember, 'Quitters never win and winners never quit'.

Adapt Your Approach Accordingly

Adapt your approach, tweak how you're doing something to get different results. After you've done something, and if you haven't got the results that you wanted, reflect on (but don't over-analyse) what you did and think about ways that you could have tweaked your performance to get the result you want.

In the analogy of a mix, dropping your mix at a different part in a track can create a totally different effect to dropping it at another. Tweak and modify until you find what works.

Moving Forward

Many people go through their whole life with a long 'would've, could've, should've' list. The truth of the matter is, once you've lived through a day, an hour, or a minute, it's done. You cannot go back. So get over it. Go forward. There is so much more for you to accomplish that you don't have time to live in the past trying to fix things that you no longer have any control over. Also things only have the meaning that you attach to them, and you have the power to make that meaning empowering or disempowering. I urge you to read the book *Man's Search for Meaning* by Viktor Frankyl (listed in my recommended reading in the bonus resources section) to illustrate someone who mastered the power of placing positive meaning on the worst possible atrocities. If you view things as 'teaching you lessons' or 'enabling you to practise your forgiveness, patience, tolerance or acceptance', I guarantee you will be in a much more positive state than if you ask yourself disempowering questions such as 'why do things always go wrong?' or 'why did that person treat me like that?'. Your mind will find answers to the questions you ask it, so move forward asking positive questions.

Decision Making

All successful people have the ability to make decisions with confidence, as opposed to people who are non-committal and change their minds as frequently as the wind changes direction.

To help you make decisions, ask yourself:

1. Do I really want this result, outcome or item?
2. Is this in line with my overall long-term goals and desires?
3. Does this fit with what I inherently know to be right?
4. Does this infringe on any other person's rights?

Decisions that are in your (and ultimately others') best long-term interests should answer YES to the first three questions above and NO to question 4. These are things that you really want to achieve, that are in line with your long-term goals, that are in alignment with what you know to be right and don't degrade, insult or defame another person.

Gratitude

So simple, yet so overlooked. Simply by taking stock of all the things in your life that you are thankful for will help shift your focus on what you don't have (or want) onto those things that you do and you are grateful for.

If you can't think of things to be grateful for, then start with the really simple things we take for granted: being alive, being healthy, having a roof over your head, having food, having clothing and running water, having friends and family, having a computer. And on, and on. Take time to be thankful for the people, experiences and blessings in your life. The Law of Attraction works on the premise that 'whatever you focus on, you get more of'. And it's true. Have you ever noticed how people without any money tend to talk constantly about 'not having enough' or 'not having any money'? Part of the problem is that they are focusing on (remember what you focus on you attract) not having enough, so sure enough 'not having enough' shows up in their life.

Contribution and the Spirit of Giving

Hand in hand with gratitude is the importance of contribution. You're obviously ambitious and want to move forward in your life, hence you're taking precious time to read material such as this to learn, grow and excel. This is commendable and an indication that you've got the drive, intention and practical sense to rapidly acquire knowledge from others.

We live in an abundant universe and your natural birthright is to tap into your innate potential and wealth, and to do it ethically without violating the rights of others, whilst helping others to do the same. It is in helping others that we generate true wealth, both monetary and spiritual.

Ask yourself each day, 'How can I enjoy contributing to the success and happiness of others?' and act upon the answers you come up with. It only works. 'The secret to living is giving.'

This book is a personal example of the spirit of giving in action. When first published on the internet it took on a life of its own, was promoted between friends online and has now been picked up by Aurum Press so that we can share the expanded and improved content as you have it now with thousands of people around the world. But it's the product of an ongoing process of feedback – of giving – so if I have missed valuable ideas, topics, insights or resources you think future readers (and versions of this book) would benefit from, please share them at: http://bit.ly/DannyRamplingBookFeedback

The Wheel of Life

What is success? Many of us will have very different opinions as to what it means to be successful. For some it will be to earn a certain amount of money. For others it will be to have a happy home and loving family. For others it may be to be healthy and to do what they love doing.

One thing that I've come to realise is that true success comes down to leading a relatively balanced life. Your life is made up of a number of different areas. For argument's sake, let's say that they are heath, physical environment, family and friends, romance, fun and recreation, business and career, finance and personal growth.

The Wheel of Life

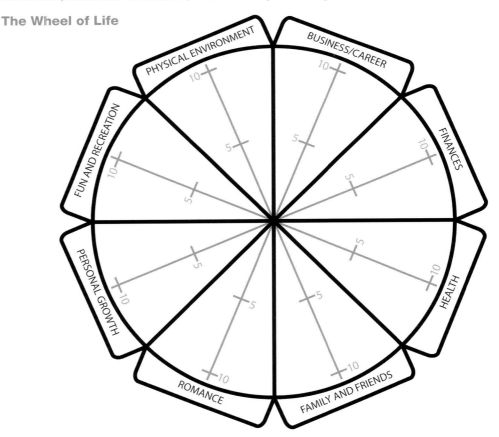

Everything You Need to Know about DJing and Success

There's an exercise you can do which will give you a good visual representation of how your life is working and what areas may need a little bit of attention. It's called the 'Wheel of Life'. On the diagram opposite, make a note of where you would rate each area of your life.

Imagine '0' in the middle would be 'awful', and '10' at the edge would be 'outstanding'. So for each area of your life mark where you currently are and then join your 'scores' so that you have a line that goes around the whole wheel. Now imagine for a moment that this line was supposed to be a 'Wheel'. How would it perform? Have you got a seriously wonky wheel like one of those crazy bikes you get at a circus? Well, the analogy holds true. How can you expect your life to run smoothly if areas of your life are totally lacking in attention and care? Imagine how much smoother your life would run if you could focus some attention on those areas to improve them and bring them closer to the scores in the other areas.

Ask yourself right now: what are 3 actions and decisions can I make in the next week to improve any of the areas?

Revisit this wheel on a regular basis and just hold the image in your head of your life as a wheel that needs to be relatively balanced for you to get the most out of it. Life can either work with you and 'flow' or you can get in the way of it and create imbalance, which inevitably leads to undue 'struggle', resistance and effort. It's much better to maintain a balance and allow life to work with you. And it's much more fun. Swim with the current of the river of life, not against it!

Help Yourself, Improve Your Self-motivation

1. **Make yourself accountable**
   If you're not accountable then it's easy to stray from your target and to make excuses. Before you know it, a week has turned into a month and a month into a year, and no real progress has been made. Make a pact with a good friend (or group of friends) to help you commit to your goals. Ensure that they are people who support your growth and have your best interests at heart. Tell them about your goals and how you plan to achieve them. You can also ask for any ideas or recommendations they have. Agree to meet or speak once a week so that you can report on your progress and tell them the key actions you will take the next week. Tell them you want to be held accountable and to give you lots of friendly yet firm support when you're flagging. If it helps and you're visually stimulated, create a graph or chart that helps you measure your achievements – be specific.

2. **Focus on the next five minutes**

   Stop looking at the final destination thinking, 'I'll never get there'. Instead just focus on what you can do right now. Five minutes is all that you need to start doing something differently. And that's the ultimate secret. If you keep on doing the same old thing, you keep on getting the same results. You will usually find that those five minutes will turn into 20; a perfect example is with exercise. However, those first five minutes allow you to break the old behaviour pattern and start creating a new habit. Focus on what you can do in the 'here and now', which helps build momentum and your motivation.

3. **Get specific about why you want what you want**

   Often we say we want X, Y & Z but ask yourself – what do you think getting X, Y & Z will actually do for you? Will it give you more respect, more love, more happiness, more freedom? Once you're clear, write down or record yourself answering the following questions: What will it be like to have more _____
   (you fill in the blank: money/freedom/love/happiness) in my life? How will I feel when I wake up in the morning/when I go to bed at night? How will I handle any future challenges feeling my new feelings? What will be different in my life? How will others react to me? How will I feel about myself? What advice will I give to others about how they can feel this way too? Read or listen to your thoughts every day. Getting to the root of what you really want in life and spelling out the actions that will get you more of that is a very motivating strategy.

4. **Promise less and set yourself up to succeed**

   If you're telling yourself that you're going to cut out all alcohol, exercise for an hour every day and start a new hobby or skill with daily practice over the next 30 days, then cut yourself some slack. Set yourself realistic goals and then lower the bar. Under promise, over deliver and you'll feel like you're actually achieving something rather than feeling you are always failing. And then you can celebrate your achievements and build rather than erode your confidence and self-reliance.

5. **Celebrate every small success**

   Don't wait until you reach the top of the mountain before you celebrate. Acknowledge yourself for the small achievements you are making every day and create a reward system. It doesn't have to be a monetary reward, just something you do for yourself that makes you feel good and reinforces your progress.

6. **Focus on how great you are**
   Low self-esteem is often at the root of lack of motivation because deep down, we don't think we can change or we don't believe we are good enough to reach our goals. To boost self-esteem, give yourself positive feedback. Write down 10 messages from 'I am a kind and thoughtful person' to 'I am wise and wonderful' or 'I am liked' and stick them on your computer, in your house, on the fridge door, or anywhere you'll see them for the next seven days. After seven days, write another 10 messages. What you focus on expands. Change your focus to support you.

7. **Change WHO you are as well as WHAT you do**
   When you change behaviour you usually just change what you're doing – if you want to be healthier, you'll stop drinking three nights a week and start going to the gym on Mondays and Wednesdays. Try a different approach and ask yourself – WHO do you want to become? (E.g. I am someone who respects my mind and body.) Then ask yourself what actions would this person take? If you want to become a person who has enormous amounts of energy – what would you eat, how would you deal with stress, how would you get up each morning? The focus is on creating a new identity for yourself versus simply trying to change what you're doing.

Become an Effective Decision Maker

Every decision carries consequences. Decisions have the power to create great rewards for your life, or they can cause negative consequences that ruin the quality of your life. You are where you are today as a direct result of the decisions that you have made in the past. Every decision that you make will affect the quality and direction of your life.

It's a sign of maturity and awareness to anticipate the consequences of your decisions in advance of actually making them. At a subconscious level your brain is constantly making three decisions:

1. What am I going to focus on?
2. What does this mean?
3. What am I going to do?

It's important to understand why many of us tend to put off making decisions, despite knowing the power that they have in our lives.

Four Reasons People Procrastinate when Making Decisions

1.   Uncertainty about what the decision is going to mean
Many of us have an illusion that decisions are based on certainty. However, there are no total certainties, thus decisions must be made based upon the greatest probability. If you wait until you're certain to make a decision, it will be too late.

2.   People have weak decision-making muscles
Decision-making is a muscle that can be developed. The way to get good at making decisions is to make more of them. Even if you make some wrong decisions, at least you acted and you can learn from the mistake to make a better judgement next time.

3.   Fear
So many people are afraid of making a wrong decision. However, the only real failure is failing to decide – putting off what you know you inevitably need to do. Making the decision is the hardest part, as once you've made your decision you can act; and if the decision is the wrong one, you can learn from it and make another, more informed decision.

4.   People feel overwhelmed
In today's age we have numerous demands on our limited time: email, voice messages, phone calls, letters, fax machines. All of these are clamouring for our attention. Very often people don't know where to start.

Four Rules for Effective Decision-making

1. Remember that almost all decisions are based upon probability. It's rare to have total certainty, thus all decision-making carries some consequence.
2. Be clear from the outset, before making your decision about what you want (your outcome) and why you want it (your purpose).
3. Make all important and difficult decisions on paper. Do not try and make big decisions which carry large repercussions in your head. Get all the pros, cons and different factors down in front of you on paper.
4. Clarify the importance of each outcome. You will often have several outcomes that you want to achieve simultaneously so make sure that you are clear about the order of importance of all of these outcomes.

The Law of Attraction

There is a piece of ancient, timeless wisdom that has recently been packaged into a more modern and palatable form for today's world. What this boils down to is the 'Law of Attraction', which describes the natural, irrefutable law that 'thoughts become things', and what you focus upon (good or bad) expands. Knowingly or unknowingly, we are always using the Law of Attraction in our life. Here are a few things you can do to produce more favorable results in your life:

1. Unlock yourself from the future
It's good to have intentions, plans and ideas for the future. However, focusing on visions of your future can be very seductive; it takes you out of the present moment and all of the gifts that come when you're in the 'here and now'. Focus on doing what is right in the present and the future will then shape itself accordingly.

2. Add value just for the joy of it
Just as we know that businesses get rewarded in return for the value they deliver to people, you can use the same principle in your personal life to advance your success. If you add value to help create more abundance and joy, with the intention of doing so just for the fun of it, your personal power and the impact of the experience grows radically.

3. Under promise, over deliver
Delivering much more than you promise in any given circumstance can be hugely rewarding. By under-promising initially, the recipient will be very appreciative when you then deliver more than is expected. Under-promising and over-delivering is a very effective tool of attraction. If you make fewer promises in your life to both yourself and others, but then deliver beyond what is expected on those promises, you will become much freer and more attractive.

4. Create a vacuum that pulls you forward
In life you have a choice to either push or pull for success. Pushing for something involves a great deal of energy and can be extremely tiring and costly. Metaphorically, think about what happens in life when you physically push into something: it either creates resistance to match your force or the object moves away from you. Pulling things to you, however, can be much less effort.

The fundamental distinction here is whether you are driven by motivation or inspiration. When inspired, you are called toward something by a deeper passion, you are drawn to something, as opposed to making an effort to achieve it.

Be conscious of what really inspires you and focus on something that is large enough to create a vacuum that pulls you forward. As you focus on your desires and how you are attracting the necessary elements to make them happen, the principles of attraction will become even more apparent.

5. Show others how to please you

In life it's important to be very clear and articulate in your communication with others. Let people know clearly how they can fulfil your needs. The clearer and more forthright you are, the more powerful the exchange, and the closer you will get to attracting your desires. This is so simple to do, yet so many of us just presume or expect that others know what pleases us. Articulate your desires and make what pleases you known.

In order to become fully present and attractive to others and yourself, it is important that you get your personal needs met. People often do not share their needs with others, thus making it difficult to even know one's needs and how they could be fulfilled. The first step in this attraction principle is to discover your needs, and secondly to ask those around you to help you fulfil those needs.

6. Become selfish

Selfish, here is defined as being a state in which you actually do what is best for you. This in turn creates a larger contribution to your family and to the world. This may be a difficult step to take, but when you do what you want in life in a responsible manner (so long as it doesn't negatively or destructively affect other people's lives), you begin to feel attractive to yourself, and consequently to those around you. We each have a special gift or personal trait that is uniquely ours. We have to take the time to be selfish in order to uncover what that gift is and how it can contribute to our lives and to society at large.

Obviously it may affect some family members or work colleagues if you change your habits, so it may be wise to inform them of your intentions and why you are doing what you are doing.

7. Get a fulfilling life, not just an impressive lifestyle

There is a distinction between gratification and fulfilment. Having a gratifying lifestyle may be nice, but it often leaves you with an emptiness that needs to be filled. Creating a fulfilling lifestyle, however, gives you a sense of completeness. Your life becomes a powerful reflection of your values, holding true to who you are at your very core.

8. Perfecting your environment

Perfecting your environment enables you to create a lifestyle for yourself that is uncluttered, organised and efficient. This, in turn, creates much less stress and anxiety in your life, allowing you to be more productive, creative and contented. You are then ultimately more attractive.

9. Have a vision

For the attraction principle to work for you it is essential to have a vision. As you articulate your vision, you will attract people into your life who have the same or similar vision.

Your vision should be beyond your own personal agenda and should take you into a larger cause for the greater good of the world. Having a vision unhooks you from the future because once you have a vision you can see clearly what is coming.

10. Simplify your life

When you simplify your life, you have a great deal more time to focus on the other principles. As a result of simplifying your life, you will find yourself much more organised, and as you organise your outer world, you will likely discover your inner world starts to follow suit.

11. Eliminate delay

Easier said than done, but when you resolve to eliminate delay in the various aspects of your life you will create an environment where there is little time lag in getting things done. This takes commitment by you and others but if applied can create huge changes. It pays to be aware of what areas or items in your life tend to have a lot of resistance or delay and to make an action plan to rid yourself of that delay.

12. Market your talents

It's important that you know what you are good at and how you can market your greatest talents effectively. This may require that you step outside of your comfort zone. You can ask people who know you best, both in personal and professional capacities, where you're delivering the most value and what they see as your key strengths.

13. Become unconditionally constructive

There are three ways in which you can work to become unconditionally constructive.

> Note that everyone is doing their best given the situation, circumstances and where they are currently at in their life.

> Never concentrate on a person's progress (past or future) but focus on their strengths in the present.

> Give up trying to fix certain aspects of yourself that are not fixable. Continuously attempting to be 'fixed' keeps you from enjoying the gifts of the present. Practising this principle gives you a greater sense of personal acceptance along with a greater unconditional acceptance of others.

Three Ways to Increase Any and Every Business

No matter what business you are in, be it manufacturing, retail, DJing, catering or construction there are essentially only three ways to increase your business:

1. Increase the number of customers
2. Increase the average transaction value of each purchase
3. Increase the frequency that customers visit and buy from you

In addition to watching costs and keeping them under tight control, these are the three core business-building strategies. Now here's the interesting part. Many businesses only seek to increase maybe one area at a time, and as a result only get incremental improvements. An example of this would be increasing the number of customers by say 10% as a result of a promotional campaign.

However, if a business owner focuses on adopting a number of tactics to increase EACH of the three areas (the number of customers, the frequency of purchase and the average transaction value) at the same time, the compounded result is an exponential increase in business turnover.

For example, if you were to simply increase:

1. the number of your customers by 10%
2. the average transaction value by 10%
3. the frequency at which those customers come back to buy your product or service by 10%

you would end up with a cumulative increase of 33%.

Strategy 1: **Increase the No. of customers**
Strategy 2: **Increase the average transaction value**
Strategy 3: **Increase the frequency of purchase**

Example 1

100 customers	£10 spent per visit	2 times per month	£2,000 per month
increase by 10%	increase by 10%	increase by 10%	
110 customers	£11 spent per visit	2.2 times per month	**£2,662 per month**

As you can see, just by increasing each factor by a mere 10% you cumulatively increase your business by 33%

Example 2

increase by 33%	increase by 25%	increase by 50%	
133 customers	£12.50 spent per visit	3 times per month	**£4987.50 per month**

In this example, increasing the customers by just 33%, the average amount spent per sale by 25% and the frequency of repurchase by 50% you significantly increase your business from £2000 to £4987.50 – an increase of 149%

Example 3

increase by 100%	increase by 50%	increase by 50%	
200 customers	£15 spent per visit	3 times per month	£9000 per month

In this final example the combined increases result in a significant turnover of £9000. An increase of £7000 (350%). **THIS IS THE POWER OF CUMULATIVE ACTION**

To implement each of the three strategies there are numerous tactics a person or business might adopt.

Some Tactics for Increasing the Number of Customers

Referral system: Ask customers to give the details of other people who may benefit from your service.

Advertising: Develop an advertising plan, with options to use many various mediums: magazines, papers, radio, internet, etc.

Direct mail: Acquiring lists and contacting potential customers directly.

Telemarketing: Using the phone as a form of direct marketing as per above.

Run special events: Put on events that will stimulate interest and desire within your target audience.

Create and emphasise your Unique Selling Point (USP): What makes your service, product or offering totally unique? Make sure that you come up with something that makes you positively and uniquely different and then shout about it.

Increase perceived value through customer education: Let people know what you can do for them and tell them how they will benefit by dealing with you.

Use public relations: Get coverage in press and media by doing something unique or with an unusual twist. Can you help the local community in any way?

Open earlier, stay open later: Give people the maximum opportunity to buy from you. Make it easy for them to do business with you.

Have a website: More and more people are turning to the internet for business. Have an online presence and if you can, sell your service over the internet.

Capitalise on internet marketing: Use social networking sites, search engines and the many tools of the internet to your advantage.

Set up joint ventures with the competition: too many people see the competition as just that. However, they also have customers interested in what you offer. Can you cross-promote or share lists in a win-win agreement?

Offer a greater array of products and services: sometimes it pays to have a very select, niche range of products. However, you want to increase your customers, in some instances it may prove beneficial to offer a broader selection.

Some Tactics for Increasing Customer Retention

Increase the selling skills of staff: Ensure that those in charge of dealing with potential customers are well versed in giving excellent customer service and understand how to sell

Educate customers about the value you provide: Too many people or businesses think about themselves and not the customer. Put yourself in your potential customer's shoes and think about what needs they have. Educate them as to the solution you can offer them.

Some Ideas for Increasing the Frequency of Purchase

Ask yourself what products or services could you offer that would complement those you already offer: Could you diversify and offer products or services that sit comfortably next to what you already offer.

Communicate frequently with customers, offering ideas and information that benefit them: Stay in your customers' minds and add value to their lives by offering information that will make their job or life easier.

Set up a series of auto-responders: Schedule a series of messages to your database of customers so that they are contacted at pre-defined points in time with offers and promotions.

Endorse other people's products or services to your customers: If it's something that may help your customers then why not support it and recommend it?

Run special events: Get customers to your event or work space by offering some kind of special event.

Help your clients use your product or service better: Ensure that your customers know how to get the most out of what you are providing them with. Don't take for granted the information and knowledge you have and don't assume that people know what to do. Share your knowledge.

Use special price inducements: Ideas include running some kind of discount scheme for different target customers or at specific times or days. Set up a 'loyalty' scheme whereby people get points as they purchase.

Ideas of How to Increase the Value of Transactions

Upsell cross sell: Give customers the opportunity to buy 'upgrades', complimentary products or more of similar products whilst they are buying. Restaurants make millions by simply asking customers if they want 'dessert', a perfect example of upselling!

Point of sale promotions: Have some kind of promotion or offer that can be offered as money is changing hands.

Package complimentary products together: Make it easy for customers to find and buy products or services that go hand in hand, by offering them packaged together.

Raise prices: If you genuinely offer a superior service, unique product and differentiate yourself by emphasising your USP, you may well be able to justify an increase in your prices.

Change the profile of your product, outlet or service to be more upmarket: Invest in your image to make your whole outfit look more professional. People will often spend more somewhere (or with someone) that appears to be superior.

Offer larger units of purchase: Offer more for a perceived good deal.

Become an Influential and Persuasive Communicator

Every day you are communicating with people on many different levels: friends, family, colleagues, partners and so on. You need to make sure that you are maximising these interactions and doing yourself justice by communicating in the most effective manner.

Here are 12 principles that can really bring this to life:

Principle 1: Be able to leverage the 7 subconscious desires.

As individuals, we all have the same basic desires, each one to varying degrees based upon our life experiences. They are:

1) Belonging
2) Respect
3) Appreciation
4) Safety
5) Success
6) Romance
7) Inspiration

In your communications you can increase your effectiveness by ensuring that you include (and pay attention to) at least three of these desires.

Principle 2: Liking

People will do things if they like you. How likeable are you? Do you smile enough? Is your brand and what you stand for likeable? Likeable people (and businesses) have more opportunities to connect and are able to bring more value to the world. It's common sense, but you'll find that more doors open for you (in the music business or any walk of life) if you have a reputation for being likeable.

Principle 3: Consistency

Make sure that you leverage consistency. People often do things because 'they've always done it that way'. They do things because they have a conditioned process. Consistency is a huge piece of the influence puzzle. People like to know (to a greater or lesser extent) what they are going to get. Do you deliver consistently? Are you a consistent character?

Principle 4: The Authority Principle

People often do things if an authoritative source tells them to. The authority principle can be evoked by quoting someone deemed an authority, for example a writer, artist or musician (or someone who's been published), or someone who's got a lot of experience in the specified area. You could interview a key influencer or opinion former, in writing, audio or on video, or you can have your photo taken with these authoritative figures, or get endorsements from them and upload the content to a website, newsletter or other publication. All of these things assist in building your authority, influence and persuasive power.

Principle 5: Rapport

Rapport is about commonalities. The more things we have in common, the more people feel that we're like them. When they feel that we're like them, we get connected. It's another important piece of the influence puzzle. Are you really concentrating on how you can build a connection; on how you can build rapport with people? To do this you need to find the commonalities. For example, in DJing this is often achieved through talking about favourite DJs, clubs, record labels, venues or genre. If you have three or four things in common you start to feel a connection, which in turn increases trust and influence.

Principle 6: Social Proof

Social proof is when people do what other people do. Someone stands in a line and everybody else stands in a line. You can leverage this principle in your communication with a couple of very simple examples. You can have really good case studies, endorsements, referrals or testimonials about your DJing, your productions, your service or whatever you're sharing. Build your portfolio of endorsements as they are powerful, and people like to hear what other people say about you.

Principle 7: The Reciprocal Principle

Do you give value upfront so that people want to give value back? Do you approach a promoter, venue or potential business client from a win-win stance – thinking about what is of value to them?

Principle 8: Anchoring

An anchor is a feeling or association you have about something, based upon something else that has happened in your life. We can walk into a club and hear a song and it can instantly make us feel a certain way. The same is true of people. You can think about (or see) a person and instantly feel happier, sadder, angrier or more at peace. This is because an association comes to mind and we are reminded (often subconsciously) of a positive or negative memory.

Look at all the great things you can do that would fire off positive associations. The people you're around, the music you play, the people you talk about, the way you talk, the way you dress. All those pieces are part of your brand, and they bring association (anchors) to both your and other people's minds.

Principle 9: How People Receive Information

For optimal influence we need to communicate with people in their preferred style, based upon their primary sense. We all have five primary senses, but the three dominant ones are audio (auditory is the way that people hear our message – our tone), kinaesthetic (physical reactions to stimulus) and visual. It's useful to know that the majority of the population likes to receive messages visually.

So what does that mean? That means that when you're communicating, you should use good visual accompaniments such as nicely designed flyers, business cards, or your website. You want to have things that you can show to people. If you've got to explain things to people then have a note pad so that you can 'illustrate' your point or connections between things you are talking about. This is why PowerPoint presentations, flip charts, whiteboards and chalk boards are so popular in the learning environment.

Make sure that you match the words you are using to communicate to the style of the person. To ascertain their preferred style, listen attentively to the language they use. Awareness and focus is key. For example, if you're talking to a venue owner who's a visual person, you don't say, 'I have the feeling that this is a good idea'. Instead you say, 'You see what I'm saying here?' 'Do you get the picture?' Perhaps physically write or draw something which illustrates your point. Similarly for an auditory person you might say, 'Do you hear where I'm coming from?'

Principle 10: The Scarcity Principle

Have you ever seen people hurry up and do things because something is going to run out? For example in promotions, you say 'limited tickets available' or 'hurry, spaces going fast'. It gets people thinking 'I'd better get one, I'd better take advantage of this now', because the scarcity principle kicks in. It's a principle that's very valuable if you want to get people to buy into your message.

Principle 11: Matching and Mirroring

One of the ways to easily build rapport is to be sure to mirror the people we want to influence. We can mirror their posture, their clothing, their music, their language or their actions. All of these things help build rapport and influence. When you get up in the morning, do you think strategically about what you're wearing? It's part of your communication. Your wardrobe is part of your brand. For maximum influence you wouldn't turn up for an underground DJ slot in a suit, just as you wouldn't turn up to DJ at a black tie function wearing a T-shirt and ripped jeans.

Principle 12: Filtering

As they are processing information, some people filter things that they want to avoid. Make sure to let these people know what they're going to be avoiding if they buy into your skills, product or service. Other people filter things that they want to move toward, the pleasure that they want to enjoy. So if you want someone to buy into what you're sharing, talk about all the benefits they're going to get, and they'll move toward you.

Tips for Personal, Business, Marketing and Sales Success

Here are 30 digestible tips to help you succeed in business, marketing and sales.

1. You are capable, so accept that fact.

2. You are better than you think, so explore your ability and make good use of it.

3. You are able to get the job done, so get the job done.

4. Persuade and convince, because it is how you get the gig, job or contract.

5. Pleasantly persist for the gig/contract, because that is how you make money.

6. Be the leader, so others will follow you.

7. Be the organiser of the event/business, so you get an organiser's rewards.

8. Say what you want and visualise what you would say, as though you were already in possession of it.

9. Expect the gigs/bookings and make them happen.

10. Succeed by making others succeed.

11. Be copy-able.

12. Have the attitude, 'I am here to make it happen and together we will succeed.'

13. Always sell the vision to your team, because the vision of what you want to achieve is a powerful motivator.

14. Don't skip 'the warm-up' process, because people generally need a little time to get to know you before they will use your services.

15. Embrace any shortcomings or mistakes you make along the way, because it is the power to improve that makes you better than you were, which marks a clear and sure path to your goals.

16. Give the service to others that you wish they would give to you.

17. The way to convince others that your opportunity is better than the thousands of others that they are being bombarded with is to show that you are more committed to their success than anyone else they know. Deliver exceptional service.

18. Assume you are liked and important, and people want and need to hear from you.

 Everything You Need to Know about DJing and Success

19. Eject the words 'I can't' from your vocabulary. Replace with: 'If I can't I must, If I must I can.'

20. Set your goals good and high, so you can 'shoot for the stars'; that way, if you only 'hit the moon,' your success will still be very high and satisfying.

21. If your existing marketing doesn't work, get feedback and try an alternative approach.

22. Leadership is learned, not in-born, so act like a leader and you'll be one.

23. Nothing sells like sincerity, so the best selling sincerity is the truly sincere kind. Be sincere for real.

24. You are responsible for your own self-image, so craft your self-image responsibly.

25. Don't let your emails, newsletters, flyers, stickers, tickets or website go without a spell-check, because mis-spelled words are presumed to be a sign of ignorance, and people will do more business with those they respect than those they look down upon.

26. Accept your future as successful, so you can get on with the business of making it happen.

27. You've got to be in the game. No matter how you are feeling, 'Get Up, Dress Up, Show Up'.

28. Timid doesn't get you business, so get daring. Step out of your comfort zone.

29. It's not a matter of whether you can have success, it's a matter of how long you'll waste your time wondering if you can.

30. It's always today tomorrow, so do it today, not tomorrow.

Use the Power and Leverage of the Internet

Using the internet means more than just creating a website and waiting for people to find it. There are billions and billions of pages on the internet and millions added every day. That does not mean that standing out is impossible, but like anything else, it requires a little planning and creativity to carve out your own little piece of the global internet market.

Remember always to focus on your target audience or customer and not just on what you are selling. Updated information along with valuable, fun and fresh ideas will keep your visitors coming back to your site. Not all of the items in the following list may pertain to you, but you should be able to think of dozens more as you read it.

Marketing Ideas to Promote Your Website

1. Tell at least one new person a day your URL.

2. Carry business cards at all times.

3. Be sure your email address contains your website and create a signature at the bottom of your emails which contains your URL.

4. Wear a name tag or neck tie with your website on it when at trade events.

5. Join an internet chat group and post responses or questions and include your URL.

6. Place your website on anything you 'put out' – records, flyers, marketing materials.

7. Place your URL on your invoice, postage and shipping labels.

8. Publish an e-newsletter with links to the website.

9. Include your website on your envelopes and letterhead.

10. Have your URL on any banners you display at sponsored events, gigs, etc.

11. Make your URL memorable and distinctive.

12. Put your website on your faxes, cheques, receipts and all business literature.

13. Place your URL on your press releases and articles.

14. Circulate articles you like…and mention your URL.

15. If you ever guest DJ or advertise on radio, mention your URL. Post your URL prominently in any newspaper ads.

16. Have your URL designed onto a 'Gobo' lighting effect.

17. Have publicity photos taken with your URL banner prominently visible.

18. If you're getting merchandise made up, place your website on your pens, pads and other give-aways.

19. Ensure all of your CDs have sleeve inserts with your URL.

20. Donate to your favourite charity auction your product and something featuring your URL.

21. Include your URL on all communications with your lawyer, accountant, agent, clients or bank.

22. Use search engine optimisation for your website so your URL will rank highly in searches.

Everything You Need to Know about DJing and Success

23. Utilise Pay Per Click techniques to post your URL on key phrases for you.

24. Link to your website from other websites (exchange links).

25. Trade/buy banner space featuring your URL.

26. Call your clients and ask them to visit your updated website.

27. Buy mis-spelled versions of your URL and redirect them to your site.

28. Rent appropriate email lists to post to with your URL.

29. Exchange services with businesses, promoters and publications who will post your URL in their publications or on their websites.

30. Keep your website information fresh and interesting so people will want to come back.

Additional Advice

> Study your website traffic patterns regularly.

> Compare your marketing efforts with the traffic patterns.

> Understand where unique visitors may have come from.

> Repeat the efforts which create positive responses.

> Drop the efforts that provide no response or redeploy them with new ideas or new locations.

> Document your marketing efforts.

> Do not give up. Not everything works for everyone every time.

> Changes in one word can change responses dramatically. Change one variable at a time in your online marketing efforts, so that you know what it is that is responsible for your results. If you change two or more things at once, you don't know which the results are attributable to.

> Keep your message positive.

Embrace Affiliate Marketing

In the 21st century many people are entering a new way of business that is sweeping the world and is set to become a standard way of doing business, based on a 100% win-win model.

In a nutshell, affiliate marketing is a marketing practice in which a business rewards the affiliate partner for each customer brought about by the affiliate's marketing efforts.

How many times in your life have you recommended a friend, colleague or family member to go and see a film or to eat at a good restaurant? You never get rewarded for pointing those people in the direction of the product or service that you believe in. Imagine if you got paid simply for helping people fulfil their needs: this is the premise of affiliate marketing.

Amazon was one of the first companies to set up an affiliate programme and it has been key to the business's success. They knew it made sense to have other businesses and individuals 'sell' their product, and to reward them for doing so. The beauty of affiliate marketing is that it is a 'pay for performance' model, meaning that you only get paid if you actually create sales, and similarly the affiliate merchant doesn't pay for marketing (your efforts) unless they are effective. So it's a zero cost, zero risk model for both parties: win-win.

So for example, many online businesses will award anything from 5% up to 60% of a sale price to an affiliate partner for helping bring new business to them. Taking the example of an online business, you might earn your commission by:

1. Emailing your database with a review of the product and putting your own unique link to the product at the bottom of the review

2. Putting active banners or links on your site (or sites you have access to), for people to click through and buy on

3. Sending the link to your database recommending that your members check out what is on offer

4. If you're not a business and don't have a huge list, then think about who you know who could benefit from the product you're promoting and email them your affiliate link (sometimes being more targeted can deliver higher results, especially if someone thinks you've been thinking of them.)

5. Set up your own site especially to promote the product and use online search engine optimisation techniques such as 'Google Adwords' to drive traffic there.

In the 21st century, business really is about working smarter, not harder. You want to get more reward for the energy and time you expend, and the affiliate marketing model helps you do this.

Welcome to the wonderful, exciting, mutually beneficial world of affiliate marketing. If you'd like to find out more about affiliate marketing then check out ClickBank or Commission Junction, the leading online retail outlets for over 20,000 digital product publishers. I also run an affiliate scheme on my website at www.learnhowtobeadj.com if you want to support the information shared in this book.

Danny's Top Ten Tips for Success

1. Confidence
You must be confident in everything that you do. You must believe that you will succeed if you take all-out action. And if you don't feel confident at first, then 'Act as if' and 'Faith it until you make it', and the confidence will come.

2. Focus
Narrow your focus to your task at hand, and get 'in the zone'. Fears about the outcome, and regret about the past, cannot exist.

3. Control your state
Learn to be aware of your language, focus and physiology to be able to control how you feel in an instant.

4. Visualisation
Begin with the end in mind and have a clear picture in your head of what you want to achieve. The bigger, brighter and clearer the image the better. Keep this image in mind to help you 'stay in the zone'.

5. Relaxation
Always remember that whatever happens, you can and will handle it. Fear tends to take you out of the zone and dissipates otherwise productive energy. If you have nerves in a situation, rather than letting them take control over you, take control over them and realise that they present you with an opportunity to use the energy to deliver a superior

performance. All performers get nervous from time to time, but the best have mastered how to use this emotion productively rather than let the emotion use them.

6. Excitement
Some tension can help performance but too much intensity will create undue stress. Remaining excited about what you are doing can ease that tension.

7. Preparation
All top-level professionals practise dealing with pressure. Take any sportsman in a high-level game or match, with a key point to score and millions of people watching them. They will hit key shots under pressure because they have practised ahead of time. In the same way certain mixes or 'set-pieces' can be pre-arranged, so that when you're under pressure they become automatic and thus increase your confidence. You must do the same: spend time preparing and practising, so that you can develop the skills you need to 'succeed in the zone'.

8. Model
Don't reinvent the wheel. Be smart and find people who are already getting the kind of results you want. Find out what they are doing (if need be, approach them sincerely and ask them) and start emulating aspects to get similar results. ALL successful people learn from others. Life's too short to figure it all out yourself.

9. Balance
Take precautions to ensure that your health doesn't suffer: without your health you have nothing to function upon. Balance work and play so you can sustain and develop your success and achievements over a prolonged period of time. Imagine the 'wheel of life' and be mindful of balancing the different areas of your life.

10. Pleasure
Make what you do fun. Those who view what they do as work will always struggle. Even if an individual task is challenging, think about how you can make it rewarding or more pleasurable. Those who love what they do emanate a different frequency to the person

who resists and ultimately the happier of the two will always find that opportunities present themselves more frequently and easily. Don't approach life in a 'Have-Do-Be' fashion ('When I have this and do that, then I'll be . . .'). The true way is to 'Be-Do-Have'; be happy: the rest will follow.

I'm sharing a huge wealth of bonus resources with you in the following section. There are lists, links, tips and contacts that have taken me years to compile, so please be sure to use them and let me know of your successes. Please help me to keep the lists as up-to-date as possible by recommending links at http://bit.ly/DannyRamplingBookfeedback.

Everything
You Need to Know
About DJing and Success
© 2010 Copyright
Danny Rampling
04081

Section 3:
Bonus Resources

Bonus Resource 1: DJ Tuition and Courses

This is not an exhaustive list. For up to date listings, search on the internet under 'DJ Courses' and 'DJ Tuition'. This is, however, a very good starting point for some very helpful resources.

UK listings

Rampling's Recommended Reading
http://bit.ly/RamplingMusicReadRecommendations
Anyone serious about their profession always learns and schools themselves to grow, expand and understand their heritage and craft. This address is to some of my suggested reading.

Danny Rampling and The Learn How To Be A DJ Team
www.learnhowtobeadj.com
Andy 'Touchfingers' Baddaley is an expert tutor and master teacher who's also a fully qualified and experienced musician, band leader, producer and DJ, you can contact him via info@learnhowtobeadj.com, or you can check the availability of myself and my team for DJ coaching, motivation or internet business coaching sessions and talks.

Sean Gallagher's Online Training Resources
Sean has fully embraced the internet as a training medium and has created a series of superb tutorials that you can watch in the privacy of your own home, as and when you want. They are extremely insightful and well presented. You can access them at the following addresses:
www.bit.ly/Free DJTrainingVideos0
www.bit.ly/EssentialFreeDJTrainingVideos1
www.bit.ly/Pro DJMixingQuicknEasy3

DJ Academy
www.djacademy.org.uk
The Academy specialises in all aspects of a DJ's career. It is a hands-on course operated by award winning professional DJs with many years of experience at the very highest level within the nightclub industry.

Point Blank London
www.pointblanklondon.com
Probably one of the best-known and most authoritative DJ and music production audio courses in the UK. Wide range of courses from beginner upwards, short- and long-term. They say: 'Whether you want to make music or spin tunes, you've come to the right place.'

Ministry of Sound DJ Academy
www.ministryofsound.com/djacademy
From absolute beginners to advanced DJs, the Ministry of Sound DJ Academy has a range of courses that aim to develop DJ performance at any level.

Global Music Entertainment Group
www.globalmusicplacements.co.uk/www.globalmusicentertainments.co.uk
Run by one of the UK's most experienced and respected DJs/music tutors Jim Jomoa, who also helped to set up the Ministry of Sound DJ Academy.

SAE: School of Audio Engineering
www.sae.edu/www.saeuk.com
SAE Institute is the largest worldwide private college for Audio Engineering, Creative Media and Digital Film training. SAE provides practical training courses, as well as academic degree programmes and has over 50 locations worldwide.

Subbass DJ
www.subbassdj.com
Subbass DJ Academy offers a full range of courses to suit everyone from the beginner to those looking to refine and broaden their skills, whether you want to play for your own enjoyment or to make a career as a DJ or producer.

DJ Radio School
www.djradioschool.co.uk
The DJ Radio School runs one-to-one radio DJ courses in both radio presentation and production techniques. Their courses are used by both newcomers and established DJs of all kinds where they will assist you in learning presentation styles, techniques, and production values. They welcome students of all ages and nationalities.

Manchester Midi School
www.midischool.com
Renowned for delivering some of the UK's finest music production and DJ courses, alongside live sound engineering training and individual private tuition.

DJ Academy
www.s-s-r.com
SSR Manchester, Audio Engineering courses, training for the music and media industries.

DJ Academy
www.djacademy.org.uk
DJ Academy train real DJs to reach the highest standards, leading to genuine job opportunities. The academy specialises in all aspects of a career in DJing. Courses are operated by award-winning pro DJs with many years of experience at the very highest standards within the nightclub industry.

London School of Sound
www.londonschoolofsound.co.uk
London School of Sound means advanced training in music production, audio engineering, industry support, music business and unique course content. The best students from all over the world choose LSS for its combination of unique location, extraordinary teachers, facilities, hands-on training, industry support, and unique course content.

Radio School

www.radioschool.co.uk

The Radio School provides one-to-one Radio Presenter Training and Radio DJ Training courses for the presentation and production of professional radio.

Music Fusion

www.musicfusion.org.uk/category.asp?p=music:+SKILLS

Music Fusion is a music project for young people aged 0–18 in Fareham, Gosport, Havant, Portsmouth and Hampshire in England. They offer everything from DJ skills to World Music, Classical to Music Technology. They can put you in touch with other music projects, point you in the direction of advice about a career in music, information about training and work experience and a whole range of other musical connections. Music Fusion activities are absolutely free, thanks to the support of their partners.

Liberty Hall Studios

www.libertyhallstudios.com

Fantastic music and recording studios based in London.

Deep Blue Sound

www.deepbluesound.co.uk

Specialists in sound and music technology education. They have a mission to provide an inspirational educational experience in a top class professional recording studio facility competing with the best in the country.

The Midi Music Company

www.themidimusiccompany.co.uk

The Midi Music Company offers a whole range of musical options.

Online Studios

www.onlinestudios.co.uk

They offer tailored tuition and short courses; all taught in a practical, hands-on way.

DJ Radio School

www.djradioschool.com

National Broadcasting School UK offers varied one-to-one radio presenter and production training courses for the presentation and production of professional British radio.

Music Everything

www.musiceverything.com

Music Everything, studio and music school for music production, music courses and sound engineering offering hands-on, individual tuition.

Gold Seal Recordings

www.goldsealproject.com/courses.html

Gold Seal Recordings offer an excellent DJ course for those aspiring to reach a professional level in DJing.

Everything You Need to Know about DJing and Success

Hot Courses
www.hotcourses.com
The UK's largest course finder. Search over a million courses and thousands of student reviews.

Sonic Academy
www.sonicacademy.com
Excellent online training resource with video tutorials covering music production, sound recording and DJing.

Mac Video Tutorials
www.macprovideotutorials.com
Superb range of in-depth online training videos covering all the key Apple Mac music and production software.

QBert's Scratch University
www.qbertskratchuniversity.com
The online training resource from one of the world's leading turntablists.

Red Bull Music Academy
www.redbullmusicacademy.com
The Red Bull Music Academy brings together DJs and music producers from diverse musical and cultural backgrounds to exchange their ideas about music and their knowledge of how life in the music industry works. The two-week term schedules aim to cover all major aspects of DJ culture, including music history, technology and production, business and skills. They invite a variety of accomplished international guests – from industry movers and shakers to pirate radio station operators, from turntablists to sonic theorists – to meet their students and tell their own stories in their own words. Their website archives these superb interviews and provide a great education in themselves.

United States

XMix University
www.xmix.com
Highly intensive, hands-on, six-day course that teaches many aspects of production, planning, audio extraction, tempo mapping, beat loop generation, use of MIDI, plugins, and much more. You will leave having had hands-on experience, working on your own remix starting with only a vocal track.

DJ Mix Academy
www.djmixacademy.com
DJ Mix Academy is a DJ training centre catering to the non-DJ and DJ alike. They've assembled some of the industry's premier talent and developed a strong course curriculum. Whether you're

interested in becoming a DJ, already working in the industry or merely looking for a unique and exciting extracurricular activity after school or work, DJ Mix Academy has a course designed for you. Courses are held in their state-of-the-art facility and a strong emphasis is placed on maintaining a professional, fun and non-intimidating atmosphere for all participants.

Scratch DJ Academy
www.scratch.com
A world leader in DJ and music production and education. Whether you want to DJ, produce music, mix or scratch, or explore Serato or Traktor, Scratch DJ Academy has course options appropriate for people of all skill levels, and their instructors cover all genres of music, from House to Funk, Hip-Hop to Dub, Electronic to Soul, and beyond.

Skills DJ Workshop
www.skillsdjworkshop.com
Fantastic San Francisco-based music production course.

Australia

DJ Boot Camp
www.djbootcamp.com.au
The DJ/MC BootCamp launched its first training course in 1997. The concept behind the BootCamp was to bring together retailers, distributors and professionally trained students across 14 sites in Australia.

DJs United
www.djsunited.com.au
The course is taught with their renowned step-by-step technique which has been the foundation to thousands of working DJ graduates across Australia.

Bonus Resource 2: Learn How to Scratch – Tutorials and Instruction

QBert's Scratch University Site – get free sample lessons or enrol
www.qbertskratchuniversity.com

DJ QBert – Tip Scratching
www.youtube.com/watch?v=E2oFG7P-lOg

Ministry of Sound Scratch DJ Tutor J-Me teaching to scratch on CDJ1000
http://www.youtube.com/watch?v=tUCjS0K57es

Top UK Scratch DJ J-Me (Jamie Griffiths) Personal DJ Scratch Tuition and Instruction
j-me@synthetikvoices.com

DJ Shortee – Dropping Out
www.youtube.com/watch?v=Wpv5PomYSA4

DJ tutorial videos at the 'howtodj' Channel
www.youtube.com/user/how2dj

A world leader in DJ and music production education
www.scratch.com

Multiple videos from one of the most popular online DJ training resources – from DJ tutor 'Ella Skins' covering all aspects of DJing – mobile and club.
www.youtube.com/watch?v=8T7Lmkfil3I
www.djtutor.com/scratching

DJ Vibe's guide to Scratching
www.djvibe.com/learn/mix/scratch.php

Lessons in Scratching from DJ Tutorial.com
www.djtutorial.com/free_dj_lessons.htm

DJ Angelo's popular Scratch tutorial video channel
www.youtube.com/user/DJAngeloUK
www.myspace.com/djangelouk

DJ Spinbad's how to Scratch 101
www.youtube.com/watch?v=7AkZq82HX9g

Scratch flares
www.youtube.com/watch?v=qZhohdE3Y14

Scratch tears flares and orbits
www.youtube.com/watch?v=7LlnLjZOqVI&feature=channel

Scratch complete orbit
www.youtube.com/watch?v=sja_oW3kzHU&feature=channel

Ehow's videos on scratching
www.ehow.com/video_4953693_dj-scratching-techniques-forearm-position.html

Wonder How To's guide to scratching
www.wonderhowto.com/how-to-scratch-record-176118/

5 Min Videos – tips on scratching techniques
www.5min.com/Video/Learn-to-Combine-Scratch-Styles-5192

Turntablists QBert and Rafik scratch drumming
oldschoolscholar.com/dj-qbert-and-dj-rafik-experiment-with-scratch-drumming/
www.youtube.com/watch?v=pNZPsGTVgBY

DVD Resources

'Built to Scratch' is a step-by-step tutorial from the renowned X-ecutioners, designed to teach novices everything they need to know to become masters of the turntable.
www.amazon.com/X-ecutioners-Built-Scratch-X-Ecutioners/dp/B000127Z8C

Respected as one of the world's very best Scratch DJ teachers, in this DVD, Qbert gives a very good introduction to all the basic scratching techniques
www.amazon.com/Qberts-complete-YOURSELF-Vol-Skratching/dp/B000096JHI/ref=pd_sim_d_1

The scratch techniques are taken a step deeper in this second instalment from DJ Qbert.
www.amazon.com/DJ-Qberts-Complete-Yourself-Vol/dp/B0000CAPVP/ref=pd_bxgy_d_img_b

Learn turntable technique with a professor from the esteemed Berkeley College of Music
www.amazon.com/Turntable-Technique-Art-Stephen-Webber/dp/B00008G90U/ref=pd_bxgy_d_img_c

Bonus Resource 3: Essential Music Links – Forums, Events, Suppliers, Downloads and Radio Links

I want you to be able to get right to the heart of whatever scene you're into, so I've collated a selection of sites that will really help you learn more. Most forums are frequented by extremely knowledgeable people. Get involved, look at the threads and posts on the forums and ask any questions you may have. Many of these will prove to be the best sources of up-to-date information for you.

The following lists, if utilised properly, will prove to be an extremely powerful aid to your advancement.

www.bit.ly/MusicBusinessRecommendations & www.astore.amazon.co.uk/djbookresources-21?_encoding=UTF8&node=1 – A range of personally recommended books and music.

Dance Music Download Sites (see also dedicated Download Stores Resource)

www.traxsource.com – Leading site for Soulful Underground House MP3 and WAVs.

www.djdownload.com – Specialists in dance music MP3 downloads, from the team behind DJ Magazine.

www.juno.co.uk – The world's largest range of dance music vinyl, CD and downloads, with over 1,000,000 tracks available.

www.beatport.com – Beatport is the recognised leader in electronic dance music downloads for DJs and club music enthusiasts.

www.stompy.com – House music downloads.

www.trackitdown.net – Leading dance music download store with high quality MP3 and WAVs.

www.imesh.com – Free iPod music downloads. Get playlists and albums of all the new artists.

www.dublab.com – Excellent WIFI internet radio station.

www.mixriot.com – Excellent membership site for mix downloads.

www.tribalmixes.com – Great source for live DJ mixes and DJ sets.

www.piratebay.com – Get instant access to the largest P2P networks.

www.junodownload.com – Dance MP3 download store with over one million MP3 and wav tracks available.

www.dancetracksdigital.com – Digital musical store from one of New York's most respected shops.

www.itunes.com – The world's largest digital music player. Download music, movies, TV shows, apps, and more to your Mac, PC, iPod, and iPhone.

www.spotify.com – Great for evaluating new and old music before purchasing. It's also connected to a record store that sells DRM-free music.

DJ Tutorial Sites (Please also see dedicated Scratch DJ Tutorial Resources)

http://bit.ly/RamplingRecommendedDJMusicBusinessReading – Many highly recommended resources for deepening your understanding of the music and DJ business.

www.vinspired.com – Volunteer opportunities for the youth.

www.dj-tips-and-tricks.com – How to use DJ mixers and turntables like top international DJs. Introduction to what DJ equipment a novice DJ should get.

www.sonicacademy.com – Music production courses, DJ courses, live recording courses.

www.youtube.com/user/SFLogicNinja – Great online Logic Pro tutorials.

www.pointblankonline.net – Online music production school, online music school, audio production school.

www.musictechtutorials.com – Great site for all of your music tech tutorial needs.

www.recess.co.uk – Learn how to become a DJ from the author of *DJing for Dummies*. DJ advice on how to be a DJ, videos, tips and help on mixing techniques and equipment.

www.idjondemand.com – Learn how to DJ from over 7 hours of DJ videos.

www.djtutor.com – Free online video DJ tutorials, demos of DJ Gear, DJ competitions, and a growing community of new and experienced DJs worldwide.

www.qbertskratchuniversity.com – Learn how to scratch online at Qbert Skratch University founded by DJ Qbert, who teaches scratching online through personal video exchange lessons with students. Learn to scratch, beat juggle and digital scratch with DJ Qbert.

www.buzzsonic.dj/detail.php?linkid=3688 – Great source for course information and detailed links.

www.hotcourses.com – Thousands of courses listed.

www.dj-academy.com – SSR Manchester, audio engineering courses, training for the music and media industries.

www.musiceverything.com – Music Everything, studio and music school for music production, music courses and sound engineering, offering hands-on, individual tuition in a friendly recording studio environment.

www.djacademy.org.uk – DJ tuition website to definitely visit.

www.howtodjfast.com – Good resource to learn all aspects of DJing.

www.londonschoolofsound.co.uk – Record, mix and practice in Pink Floyd's original studio. Music production and sound engineering courses in central London.

www.deepbluesound.co.uk – Professional recording studio facility providing nationally recognised sound engineering courses, music technology courses and music production courses up to degree level.

www.xmix.com/xu/index.html – One of America's best remix and production schools.

www.djradioschool.com – Provides quality radio presenter production training.

www.scratch.com – A world leader in DJ and music production education.

www.radioschool.co.uk – One-to-one radio presenter and DJ training courses in both radio presentation and production techniques.

www.libertyhallstudios.com – Live music venue and recording venue with training.

www.themidimusiccompany.co.uk – The Midi Music Company is a charity in Deptford, South London set up as a space for all children and young people to be inspired and get into music and the creative industries.

www.musiceverything.com – Studio and music school for music production, music courses and sound engineering offering hands-on, individual tuition in a friendly recording studio environment.

www.onlinestudios.co.uk – Leaders in audio recording and mastering.

Music Tool Sites

www.platinumnotes.com – Download software that improves the pitch and volume of your MP3s using studio filters, helping to improve your sound.

www.buymixedinkey.com – Download software that enables you to mix harmonically in minutes.

www.soundcloud.com – A music platform that takes the daily hassle out of receiving, sending and distributing music for artists, record labels and other music professionals.

www.4shared.com – Online file sharing and storage – 10 GB free web space. Easy registration. File upload progressor. Multiple file transfer. Fast download.

www.djmix.net – Download and upload your mixes.

www.musictechtutorials.com – Very handy site for all of your music tech tutorial needs.

www.ableton.com – The home of Ableton Live with tutorials, updates and useful information.

www.musictechmag.co.uk – Good tutorials and lessons.

www.computermusic.co.uk – Interviews, reviews and tutorials.

www.funknaughty.com – Excellent digital DJing coaching and tuition.

www.forum.ableton.com – The place to learn about Ableton from users worldwide.

www.native-instruments.com/forum – Learn the latest and get the inside tips from Traktor users globally.

www.serato.com/forum – The place to learn anything and everything about Serato.

www.macprovideotutorials.com – Training on all the main Apple Mac software programs.

www.numark.com/content1417.html – Numark Digital DJing.

www.virtualdj.com/download/trial.html – Free trial version of Numark Virtual DJ.

www.deckadance.image-line.com/downloads.html – Download digital DJ software.

www.mixmeister.com/download.html – Digital DJing software download.

www.mixvibes.com/site/pageeng/page.php?x=demos – Digital DJing software.

www.native-instruments.com/#/en/products/dj/traktor-pro – Download Traktor Pro.

www.native-instruments.com/index.php?id=tprodemoversion – Free Demo Version of Traktor.

www.serato.com – Download Serato Digital DJ software.

www.serato.com/downloads/itch – Free Demo Version.

www.ableton.com – Home of all things Ableton.

www.ableton.com/downloads – Free Demo Version.

www.gearslutz.com – Online forum discussing music gear and technology.

www.torq-dj.com/forum/viewtopic.php?f=8&t=1521 – Forum for the Torq digital DJ products.

www.virtualdj.com/download/trial.html – Free download trial of Virtual DJ.

www.brothersoft.com/deckadance-62322.html – DJ mixing tools that work either as a standalone program OR as a VSTi plugin.

www.mixmeister.com/download.html – Excellent Digital DJ tools.

www.mixvibes.com/site/pageeng/page.php?x=demos – Mix video like music. Powerful cutting edge software and hardware.

www.loopmasters.com – The place to get your loops, samples and royalty-free music.

www.findremix.com – Lists the best electronic, house remix competitions and remix contests as well as music production tips, tutorials and samples. Also free remix packs and stems.

www.zippyshare.com – Free File Hosting.

www.yousendit.com – The most popular online file sharing software that provides secure file transfer and allows you to easily send large files and large email attachments.

www.keepandshare.com Share online: share calendars, files and photos online for free. Secure private sharing – you always control who sees what.

www.4shared.com – Online file sharing and storage with 10 GB of free web space. Easy registration. File upload progressor. Multiple file transfer. Fast download.

www.mediafire.com – A very simple, free file hosting service for businesses, professionals, and individuals to share files and images with others.

www.sendspace.com – Free file hosting for emailing large files.

www.filestube.com – Enables you to search for shared files from various file hosting sites such as Rapidshare, Megaupload, Hotfile, Mediafire, 4shared and Netload.

www.tunecore.com – Get your music up on iTunes™ with Tunecore.

www.transmissionfm.com – DJ promotion network with free mix hosting, user profiles, mixes for download, on demand and live online streaming radio.

www.widgets.yahoo.com/widgets/itunes-companion – iTunes Companion is a free widget that helps find all the cover artwork for your iTunes library, meaning you can put an image to the music and search it more easily.

General Music Community Sites

www.mim.dj – Excellent guide to music-related service providers covering all aspects.

www.djhistory.com – Knowledgeable and full of essential content. Dance music's basement.

www.residentadvisor.net – Highly respected electronic music magazine.

www.faithfanzine.com – One of the world's most active and dedicated House music forums.

www.offthemeters.com – Underground news on all things deep and soulful.

www.livingelectro.com – Providing you the best electro, house and trance songs 24/7.

www.djmagitalia.com – Living and breathing Dance music.

www.southportweekender.co.uk/chat.php – Home of the world's leading Soulful House event with active community forum.

www.en.wikipedia.org/wiki/Music_festival – List of all the key music festivals around the world. Often a fun and informal place to network.

www.hypem.com – MP3 and music blog aggregator – the best songs and blog posts of music on the web.

www.wigidsoundwaves.blogspot.com – Excellent House music blog.

www.theacidhouse.wordpress.com – The Acid House blog.

www.kick106.co.uk – Beats, banter, radio, house music, underground, progressive, tech house, electro, fidget, funky house.

www.djmag.com – Living and Breathing Dance Music considered the DJ Bible.

www.corkdjs.com – Active DJ forum.

www.djtechtools.com – Superb blog for digital DJing.

www.trugroovez.com/forums – Providing a comprehensive listing of exclusive DJ web sites and electronic dance music industry-related resources.

www.djpassion.co.uk/forums – DJ and dance music discussion forums for electronic music DJs, producers and music fans.

www.systemsbyshorty.com – PA systems carrying the heritage of Richard Long Associates (RLA) as heard at the Paradise Garage. NYC style.

www.deephousemix.com – Great online deep house mix website.

www.mpiii.com – Electronic music community inside a big orange box.

www.MediaNightlife.com – New York underground nightlife.

www.thedjlist.com – The world's largest DJ directory and Dance music resource.

www.soundonsound.com/sos/sep07/articles/recordlabel.htm – News from the world's most famous club, Ministry of Sound.

www.housemusicchannel.net – Handy resource for House music lovers.

www.remixmag.com – Articles and tutorials on music production and performance for urban, electronic and hip-hop artists.

www.DJTimes.com – DJ Times magazine is for the professional, mobile and club DJ.

www.fabriclondon.com – Undoubtedly one of the world's very best nightclubs supporting and promoting the best in underground talent.

www.BPMMagazine.net – Great fashion and music website.

www.breakbeat.co.uk – Excellent UK breakbeat website.

www.mixmatters.com – Site dedicated to working DJs and DJ community: news, new music, charts, reviews, DJ search, mixes, record pools, interviews, record promotion, featured artists, records and DJs.

www.entertainas.com – Europe's leading entertainment booking service.

www.ticketweb.com – Full service ticket distribution company to help you sell your tickets on the internet.

www.ticketmaster.com – Sell tickets for your event professionally, online.

www.dj-links.net – The biggest online DJ directory with many links.

www.deejaylink.com – New songs, links archive and music charts.

www.djsounds.com – Online portal with DJ videos, interviews and product reviews.

www.beatburguer.com/home – Spanish site of all things Dance.

www.boomkat.com – Electronic music from the USA.

www.clubbingspain.com – Spanish clubbing directory.

www.acidcow.com – Humour site featuring entertaining content from all over the world.

www.back2basics.biz – A wonderful forum of diverse musical topics.

www.muzicforums.com – Discuss music and lyrics, including musical instruments, upcoming music and different kinds of music and lyrics.

www.musicforte.com/forums – Discuss music issues.

www.digitalspy.co.uk/forums – Entertainment, showbiz and digital TV discussions on the Digital Spy Forums.

www.requestlyrics.com – Find your favourite lyrics online here.

www.futureproducers.com – Helpful forum for producers.

www.forum.djpages.com – DMC World DJ Forums: insights, tips and advice from around the world.

www.denondjforums.com/ – Active DJ forum.

www.forums.pioneerdj.com – Forum for DJs who use Pioneer DJ equipment.

www.djforums.com – Share with DJs around the world – the latest news and information from the dance world.

www.staticsystemmusic.com – House music resource.

www.defected.com – For the last 10 years Defected have been releasing tunes that have defined the scene.

www.defmix.com – House music label, home of David Morales, Frankie Knuckles, and Hector Romero.

www.clone.nl – Dutch record label and shop specialising in experimental/underground electronic dance music.

www.house-mixes.com/forum – Download house music mixes and chat.

www.notstrictlydubstep.com – Dubstep music and sharing portal.

www.onlyoldskool.com – Popular free old skool music forum with 1000s of old skool DJ sets from all the big old skool/rave events including Fantazia, Amnesia, Dreamscape, Universe and many more.

www.livingelectro.com – Providing the best electro, house and trance songs 24/7.

www.houseplanet.dj – Unique house music news portal.

www.vinyl-junkies.com – One of London and the world's best vinyl music shops.

www.americanmusical.com – DJ equipment and musical instruments.

www.dolphinmusic.co.uk – All DJ and musical instruments including, guitars, amps and studio equipment.

www.discogs.com – Buy rare and hard to find music on vinyl records and used CDs from thousands of online record stores. Manage your music collection with a detailed discography on rock, electronic, hip hop, classical and other popular and obscure music genres.

www.chemical-records.co.uk – Worldwide mail order service for vinyl, CDs, MP3s, clothing and DJ/Home audio equipment.

www.htfr.co.uk – Hard to Find Records specialises in supplying new, deleted and rare dance music vinyl.

www.craigslist.com – Amazing global portal to advertise and source skills, services and products.

www.gumtree.co.uk – Powerful platform to advertise and locate services or products.

Book-keeping and Accounts for the Music Industry

www.yearendaccounting.co.uk – Friendly specialist financial advice and support, specifically for those in the music, entertainment and leisure industries.

Protect Your Hearing: Essential Tips

www.dontlosethemusic.com – Excellent site dedicated to hearing protection with links to the best online stores for ear protectors, tips on protecting your ears and technical advice.

www.etymotic.com – An additional resource for professional ear plugs which enable you to mix in your studio or live whilst saving your hearing.

www.hyperacusis.net – A very useful site dedicated to all who have sensitive hearing with a wealth of insight, resources and information.

www.tinnitus-pjj.com – This is the site of hearing expert Dr Jastreboff, the pioneer who created TRT retraining therapy for tinnitus and hyperacusis patients.

Sites for Sourcing and Uncovering Samples Used in Records

If you'd like to find the corresponding sampled or sampling tune then here's a great couple of links. For example on www.inlounge.de you can search by House tune or by original tune. It's a great way to learn about your music and will help you surprise people in a set by being able to pull out either the original or sampling, contemporary version of a track.
www.inlounge.de/e107_plugins/house_originals/guide.php
www.the-breaks.com

DJ Mix Sites and Online Radio Stations

Here is a small selection of musical resources for you to enjoy. You can also find hundreds of great podcasts online – simply type in the style of music you're after or the DJ name into your search engine and see what comes up. Every day, more great sites are springing up.

www.redbullmusicacademyradio.com – Red Bull Music Academy Radio offers endless shows for your ear port, recorded in the sharpest studios and deepest dancefloors worldwide. The entire archive streams on demand – just match the mix to the mood and explore the spectrum.

www.last.fm – The world's largest online music catalogue, with music streaming, videos, pictures, charts, artist biographies, concerts and internet radio.

www.samurai.fm – New music radio from Japan. Transcending national boundaries, providing the best of international electronic music with many exclusive shows archived from the world's pioneering musicians and DJs.

www.soundcloud.com – Superb source for hosting and listening to mixes from many of the world's best DJs and producers.

www.mixcloud.com – Mixcloud is rethinking radio. Listen to great radio shows, podcasts and DJ mix sets on-demand. Upload and promote your own cloudcast for free.

www.podomatic.com – PodOmatic is a great place to create and listen to free podcasts. Browse large selection of music podcasts, news podcasts, educational podcasts, religious podcasts, political podcasts and comedy podcasts in the world.

www.digitallyImported.com – Enjoy free radio channels featuring world renowned Artists, DJs, and hot exclusive shows.

www.bbc.co.uk/iplayer – catch up on the last 7 days' broadcasting from the BBC, including some of the best radio shows from the likes of Gilles Peterson, Benji B, Fabio and Grooverider.

www.bbc.co.uk/1xtra – The BBC's black music network, showcasing some of the world's finest talent.

www.Grooveradio.com – Tune in to the rhythm of the future.

www.downtownsoul.co.uk – The very best in upfront Deep and Soulful House.

www.friskyradio.com – Broadcasting Trance, Progressive, House, Breaks, Techno, Electronica, Ambient, Chill Out along with mix downloads.

www.perfectbeat.com – A one-stop source for Dance music.

www.alldj.org – Download fresh DJs mixes and live sets, spanning Trance, Techno, House, Electro, Progressive and other styles.

www.piraterevival.co.uk/forum/cmps_index.php – Old skool internet radio: Dance, Techno, House, Electro, Hardcore.

www.housefreaks.co.uk – House music radio station – Deep House, Soulful House.

www.media2radio.com – over 1000 radio stations worldwide playing House.

www.boost.fm – Playing the best live House, Techno, Dance, Breaks and Electronic dance music from around the world by our international resident and special guest DJs.

www.inthemix.com.au – Australia's most popular dance music website: music news, reviews, photos, forums and club guides for every city in Australia.

www.ibizaglobalradio.com – 24-hour Electronic Dance music online from Ibiza.

www.locafm.com – Spanish house music radio.

www.Phatbeats.net – Internet online radio featuring 4 studios with webcams and live DJs playing 24/7.

www.unityradio.fm – Great radio station from Manchester.

www.resonantvibes.com – Download dance music and free DJ mixes covering the best in Deep House, Techno, Trance, Electronica and more.

www.audiojelly.com – An online music label and store with exclusive Dance, Trance, House and Chill Out tracks.

www.libsyn.com – Podcasting and iPhone apps.

www.deepershades.net – Home to Deep House maestro Lars Behrenroth and his weekly shows.

www.freerangerecords.podomatic.com/entry/2010-06-14T08_29_58_07_00 – Freerange Records Podcast.

www.apple.com/itunes/podcasts/specs.html – Thousands of podcasts from around the world covering all genres and subjects. Simply search for the style you want.

www.rcrdlbl.com – Free MP3 Download Site.

www.elbo.ws – Most comprehensive music blog aggregator – search and browse hundreds of thousands of music posts and music videos.

www.ibizasonica.com – Radio born out of love and passion for music and spreading the musical culture of Ibiza.

www.djhistory.com – Amazingly clued up site with lots of valuable content.

www.deephousepage.com – Over fifteen-hundred mixes from House music legends, spanning three decades.

www.bbc.co.uk/radio – Home to some fantastic specialist shows covering Drum & Bass, House, Jazz, Soul and more.

www.cyberjamz.com – Deep House mixes archived daily.

www.alldj.org – Numerous mixes covering hundreds of artists.

www.deephousemafia.org – Deep House mixes and interviews.

www.milliondollardisco.com – Some classic mixes from respected DJs.

www.pushfm.com – One of London's most respected pirate radio stations, now online.

www.samurai.fm/home – Huge range of mixes available from a large roster of artists.

www.ministryofsound.com/radio – Radio from the world's most famous club.

www.thefreshpage.com/housemusicforum – House music forum with DJ mixes, mixing, dance events, Electronic and Dance music forums.

Rare Groove, Soul and Funk

www.normanjay.com – Norman Jay OBE's music site with top forum.

www.surefunk.com – Funk music and Hip-hop music resources including Soul, Roots and Jazz plus information and guides on funk clubs, Hip-hop venues, UK gig guide and funk MP3 music podcasts.

www.afrofunkforum.com – Daily news, music reviews and commentary on Afrobeat and related music from Africa, The Caribbean and The Americas.

www.amazon.com/tag/funk%20music/forum – Funk music customer discussion board at Amazon. com. Ask the experts on this forum for their advice and share your own views.

http://towerofpower.yuku.com/forums/71/t/WHAT-IS-HIP-Other-Soul-and-Funk-Music-Of-Interest.html – The Official Tower of Power Message Board.

www.electrofunkroots.co.uk – Greg Wilson's infamous site.

Jazz

www.vancouverjazz.com/forums – The complete guide to Jazz in Vancouver.

www.topix.com/forum/music/jazz – Forums and message boards for Jazz.

www.jazz.about.com – The place to learn about Jazz. Read about its history and the musicians who shaped it throughout its development. Find album reviews of new releases as well as the classics. Also, catch up on what's new in the Jazz world.

www.nojazzfest.com – The official site for the New Orleans Jazz Heritage Festival.

D&B and Breaks

www.dogsonacid.com – The world's largest drum and bass/jungle message board with news, interviews and dubplates.

www.breakbeat.co.uk (D&B Arena) – The biggest D&B website. Audio, video, downloads, podcasts, discussions and more.

www.ravelinks.com/forums – Covering all things Breakbeat and Rave.

www.nuskoolbreaks.co.uk – The world's biggest and award-winning online breaks music community, with news, features, reviews, Breakbeat radio and more.

www.unitedbreaks.fm – Broadcasts Domestic Breakbeats, Club Breakbeats, US Breakbeats, Electro and Old School.

www.rolldabeats.com – Online dance music discography resource specialising in Hardcore, Jungle, Drum & Amp, Bass and related musical styles.

Hardcore

www.happyhardcore.com – Your central station for Happy Hardcore music, news, tunes and information.

www.hardcorewillneverdie.com – Dedicated to the Hardcore scene.

Soul Music

www.soul-source.co.uk – A rare Northern Soul source online magazine – current news, events, forum, music and many rare and Northern Soul music related features.

www.northernsoulmusic.co.uk – Northern Soul Music is one of the original sites with many pages of information, sounds, future events, a forum with 3,000 + members and regular updates.

www.surefunk.com – Funk music and Hip-Hop music resources including Soul, Roots and Jazz plus information and guides on Funk clubs, Hip-Hop venues, UK gig guide and Funk MP3 music podcasts.

www.buzzjack.com – Music entertainment discussion.

www.northernsoul.proboards37.com – Respected Northern Soul forum.

www.digitalspy.co.uk/forums/showthread.php?p=5034210 – A fantastic resource for Northern Soul lovers.

www.soul-source.co.uk – A rare Northern Soul source online magazine – current news, events, forum, music and many rare and Northern Soul music related features.

www.back2basics.biz – A wonderful forum on diverse musical topics.

R&B

www.RnBforums.com – R&B music discussion forum.

www.RnBmusicblog.com – Latest R&B music news, music, videos, gossip, rumours.

www.realRnB.com/forum – Your source for R&B, Soul and Urban music.

www.RnBmusic.info/forums – For lovers of Soul and R&B, this great forum is for you.

www.tjsdjs.com/forums – Forum for all things Rap, Hip Hop, Reggaeton and R&B.

Bonus Resource 4:
Record Stores

UK STORES

Due to the increase in sales of downloadable music files, independent record stores are struggling to compete in the marketplace. There are, fortunately, some key outlets still in business located in most major cities in the UK as well as numerous online vinyl warehouses. Phonica, BM Soho, Piccadilly Records and 3 Beat Records are four particularly strong shops worthy of note for their contributions to the scene. For a totally up-to-date and comprehensive list, search for record stores online.

2FUNKY
62 Belgrave Gate,
Leicester LE1 3GQ
Tel: +44 (0)1162 990 700
Fax: +44 (0)1162 990 077
Email: shop@2-funky.co.uk
www.2-funky.co.uk

3BEAT RECORDS
5 Slater Street,
Liverpool L1 4BW
Tel: +44 (0)151 709 3355
Fax: +44 (0)151 709 3707
Email: sales@threebeatrecords.co.uk
www.threebeatrecords.co.uk

AREA 51 RECORDS
63-65 South Street, Braintree,
Essex CM7 3QD
Tel: +44 (0)1376 331 701
Fax: +44 (0)1376 331 701
Email: area51records@btconnect.com
www.area51-records.co.uk

BANGING TUNES
PO Box 2136, Seaford,
East Sussex BN25 9BP
Tel: +44 (0)1323 872 100
www.bangingtunes.com

BASE RECORDS
Tel: +44 (0)870 787 0399
Fax: +44 (0)870 787 0399
Email: info@baserecords.com
www.baserecords.com

BASS DIVISION (Formerly Mixmaster) RECORDS
31 Queen Street, Belfast,
County Antrim, Northern Ireland BT1 6EA
Tel: +44 (0)289 043 9159
Fax: +44 (0)289 043 9159
Email: info@bassdivision.com
www.bassdivision.com

BEATIN' RHYTHM
42 Tib Street,
Manchester M4 1LA
Tel: +44 (0)161 834 7783
www.beatinrhythm.com

BM SOHO (Black Market) RECORDS
25 D'Arblay Street, Soho,
London W1F 8EJ
Tel: +44 (0)207 437 0478
Fax: +44 (0)207 494 1303
Email: mailorder@bm-soho.com
www.bm-soho.com

BOOMKAT LIMITED
Unit 101, Ducie House, 37 Ducie Street,
Manchester M1 2JW
Tel: +44 (0)161 236 4792
www.boomkat.com

BOSS TUNES
28 Morley Street, Swindon,
Wiltshire SN1 1SG
Email: sales@bosstunes.co.uk
www.bosstunes.co.uk

CAPITOL VINYL
PO Box 4090
Cardiff CF14 3XD
Tel: +44 (0)292 040 4421
Fax: +44 (0)292 040 4421
Email: sales@capitolvinyl.com
www.capitalvinyl.com

CATAPULT RECORDS
22, High Street Arcade, Cardiff,
South Glamorgan, Wales CF10 1BB
Tel: +44 (0)292 022 8990
Fax: +44 (0)292 023 1690
Email: enquiries@catapult.co.uk
www.catapult.co.uk

CHEMICAL LIMITED
Unit C2, St. Vincents Trading Est.,
Feeder Road, Bristol BS2 0UY
Tel: +44 (0)1179 714 924
www.chemical-records.co.uk

CHOICE RECORDS
PO Box 411,
Manchester M14 0AE
Tel: +44 (0)161 445 0857
www.choicerecords.co.uk

CRASH RECORDS
35, The Headrow, Leeds,
West Yorkshire LS1 6PU
Tel: +44 (0)113 243 6743
Fax: +44 (0)113 234 0421
Email: sales@crashrecords.co.uk
www.crashrecords.co.uk

CRAZY BEAT
87 Corbets Tey Road, Upminster,
Essex RM14 2AH
Tel: +44 (0)1708 228 678
Fax: +44 (0)1708 640 946
Email: sales@crazybeat.co.uk
www.crazybeat.co.uk

DNR VINYL
18 Lower Addiscombe Road,
Croydon CR0 6AA
Tel: +44 (0)208 406 9905
www.dnrvinyl.co.uk

EASTERN BLOC RECORDS
Unit 5/6, Central Buildings, Oldham Street,
Manchester M1 1JQ
Tel: +44 (0)161 228 6432
Fax: +44 (0)161 228 6432
Email: easternbloc1985@hotmail.co.uk

ENERGY FLASH RECORDS
486 Palmer Road, Brighton
East Sussex BN2 6LH
Tel: +44 (0)127 330 6692
Email: info@energyflash.co.uk
www.energyflash.co.uk

FAT CITY RECORDS
20 Oldham Street, Northern Quarter
Manchester M1 1JN
Tel: +44 (0)161 237 1181
Email: mailorder@fatcity.co.uk
www.fatcity.co.uk/sales/shop.aspx

FIRST RHYTHM RECORDS
Tel: +44 (0)161 408 1377
Email: sales@firstrhythm.co.uk
www.firstrhythm.co.uk

FLASHBACK RECORDS
50 Essex Road,
London N1 8LR
Tel: +44 (0)207 354 9356
Fax: +44 (0)207 354 9358
Email: mark@flashback.co.uk
www.flashback.co.uk

GLOBAL GROOVE RECORDS
Global House 13, Bucknall New Road,
Stoke-On-Trent, Staffordshire ST1 2BA
Tel: +44 (0)1782 215 554
Fax: +44 (0)1782 201 698
Email: mail@globalgroove.co.uk
www.globalgroove.co.uk

HAGGLE VINYL
114-116 Essex Road, Islington,
London N1 8LX
Tel: +44 (0)207 704 3101
Email: lyn@haggle.freeserve.co.uk
www.hagglevinyl.com

HAIRY RECORDS
124 Bold Street
Liverpool L1 4JA
Tel: +44 (0)151 709 3121

HARD TO FIND RECORDS
Vinyl House, 10 Upper Gough Street,
Birmingham, West Midlands B1 1JG
Tel: +44 (0)121 687 7774
Fax: +44 (0)121 687 7774
Email: jk@htfr.com
www.htfr.com

HONEST JON'S
278, Portobello Road,
London W10 5TE
Tel: +44(0)208 969 9822
Email: mail@honestjons.com
www.honestjons.com/shop.php

IF MUSIC
2nd Floor, Victory House,
99-101 Regent Street, London W1B 4EZ
Tel: +44 (0)207 437 4799
www.ifmusic.co.uk

JUNO RECORDS
PO Box 45557,
London NW1 0UT
Tel: +44 (0)207 424 2800
Email: admin@juno.co.uk
www.juno.co.uk

KING BEE RECORDS
519 Wilbraham Road, Chorlton,
Manchester M21 0UF
Tel: +44 (0)161 860 4762
www.kingbeerecords.co.uk

MIXED UP RECORDS
18 Otago Lane,
Glasgow G12 8PB
Tel: +44(0)141 357 5737
Email: mixedup98@gmail.com
www.mixeduprecords.com

PHONICA RECORDS
51 Poland Street, Soho,
London W1
Tel: +44 (0)207 026 6070
Email: customerservice@phonicarecords.co.uk
www.phonicarecords.co.uk

PICCADILLY RECORDS
53, Oldham Street,
Manchester M1 1JR
Tel: +44 (0)161 839 8008
Fax: +44 (0)161 839 6561
Email: mail@piccadillyrecords.com
www.piccadillyrecords.com

POWER RECORDS
4 Bishopsgate, Wigan
Lancashire WN1 1NL
Tel: +44 (0)1942 518 552
www.powerrecords.co.uk

PROBE RECORDS
9 Slater Street
Liverpool L1 4BW
Tel: +44 (0)151 708 8815
Email: probe-records@btconnect.com
www.probe-records.com

PURE GROOVE
6-7 West Smithfield,
London EC1A 9JX
Tel: +44 (0)207 778 9278
www.puregroove.co.uk

REFORM RECORDS
121 Fore Street, Exeter
Devon EX4 3JQ
Tel: +44 (0)1392 435 577
Fax: +44 (0)1392 435 577
Email: sales@reform-records.co.uk
www.reform-records.co.uk

ROUGH TRADE
Tel: +44 (0)207 392 7790
Email: webmaster@roughtrade.com
www.roughtrade.com

RUBADUB RECORDS
35 Howard Street, Glasgow G1 4BA
Tel +44 (0)141 221 9657
Email: info@rubadub.co.uk
www.rubadub.co.uk

SOUL BROTHER RECORDS
1 Keswick Road, East Putney,
London SW15 2HL
Tel: +44 (0)208 875 1018
Tel: +44 (0)208 871 0181
Email: soulbrothers@soulbrother.com
www.soulbrother.com

SOUNDS OF THE UNIVERSE (Soul Jazz)
7 Broadwick Street, Soho,
London W1F 0DA
Tel: +44 (0)207 734 3430
Fax: +44 (0)207 494 1035
Email: info@soundsoftheuniverse.com
www.soundsoftheuniverse.com

STREETWISE MUSIC LTD
20A High Street, Tuddenham,
Suffolk IP28 6SA
Tel: +44 (0)1638 714 319
Fax: +44 (0)1638 714 319
Email: will@streetwisemusic.co.uk
www.streetwisemusic.co.uk

SWAG RECORDS
42 Station Road,
Croydon CR0 2RB
Tel: +44 (0)208 667 0410
Fax: +44 (0)208 681 2879
Email shop@swagrecords.com
www.swagrecords.com

TEMPEST RECORDS
83 Bull Street,
Birmingham B4 6AB
Tel: +44(0)121 236 9170
Fax: +44(0)121 236 9279
Email: info@tempestrecords.co.uk
www.tempestrecords.co.uk

THE DISC
118 Sunbridge Road, Bradford,
West Yorkshire BD1 2NE
Tel: +44 (0)1274 394 730
Fax: +44 (0)127 477 4999
Email: sales@thediscrecords.co.uk
www.thedisc.net

TRIBE RECORDS
7, Call Lane,
Leeds, West Yorkshire LS1 7DH
Tel: +44(0)113 243

UK DANCE
Tel: +44 (0)7968 737 085
Email: sales@ukdancerecords.com
www.ukdancerecords.com

UNDERGROUND SOLUSHN
9 Coburn Street,
Edinburgh EH1 1BH
Tel: +44 (0)1312 262242
Email: gav@undergroundsolushn.com
www.undergroundsolushn.com

URBAN GROOVEZ
Unit 9, Rivermead Industrial Estate,
Pipersway, Thatcham, Berkshire RG19 4EP
Tel: +44 (0)1635 587 896
Fax: +44 (0)1635 292 314
Email: shop@urbangroovez.co.uk
www.urbangroovez.co.uk

VINYL JUNKIES
94 Berwick Street, Soho,
London W1F 0QD
Tel: +44 (0)207 439 2923/2775
Email: vjunkies@vinyl-junkies.co.uk
www.vinyl-junkies.com

VINYL REVIVAL RECORDS
5 Hilton Street,
Manchester M4 1LP
Tel: +44 (0)161 661 6393
Email: vinylrevival@btinternet.com
www.vinylrevivalmcr.com

In addition to these stores, which
specialise for the most part in upfront
dance music, there are also numerous
secondhand vinyl stores across the
country. Included in this list are a few of
the global internet marketplaces where you
can buy, sell and trade vinyl and CDs.

AMAZON
www.amazon.co.uk

DISCOGS
www.discogs.com

EBAY
www.ebay.com

GEMM
www.gemm.com

MUSIC & VIDEO EXCHANGE
Tel: +44 (0)8456 441 442
www.mveshops.co.uk

INTERNATIONAL RECORD STORES

AUSTRALIA

618 RECORDS
Tel: +61 8 8211 9933
Email: info@618records.com
www.618records.com

ACETATE RECORDS
Tel: +61 2 9331 8900
Email: acetate@dot.net.au
www.acetate.com

BLOWFLY RECORDS
Tel: +61 9 4211227

BPM RECORDS AND CLOTHING
Tel: + 61 2 9380 8223
www.recordjunkie.com

BUTTER BEATS
Tel: +61 7 3257 3257
www.butterbeatsrecordstore.com

CENTRAL STATION
Tel: +61 8 8377-5300
Email: csrmarion@sesent.com.au
www.centralstationrec.com

CHAOS MUSIC
Tel: +61 3 8662 4220
Email: info@chaosmusic.com
www.chaosmusic.com

CHECKOUT WAX
Tel: +61 7 3262 5878
Email: info@checkoutwax.com
www.checkoutwax.com

DOWNBEAT MUSIC
Tel: +61 2 9389 1683
Email: blake@downbeat.com.au
www.downbeatmusic.com

GOOD GROOVE
Tel: +61 2 9331 2942

IDEAL RECORDS
Tel: +61 2 4732 6070
idealrecordsinfo@telstra.com

ONE STOP DEE JAY
Tel: +61 3 9533 6434
Email: recordsmelb@onestopdeejay.com.au
www.onestopdeejay.com.au

RARE DANCE VINYL
Tel: +61 4 1030 8089
Email: info@raredancevinyl.com.au
www.raredancevinyl.com.au

REACHIN RECORDS
Tel: +61 2 9380 5371
Email: reachin@reachin.com.au

RED EYE RECORDS
Tel: +61 2 9299 4233
www.redeye.com.au

RHYTHM & SOUL
Tel: +613 9662 4322
Email: enquiries@rhythmandsoul.com.au
www.rhythmandsoul.com.au

SANITY MUSIC
Tel: +61 3 9320 9980
Email: sanityinfo@wishlist.com.au
www.sanity.com.au

ARGENTINA

AF MUSIC SRL
Tel: +54 11 4582 3633
www.afmusic.com.ar

DBN SRL
Tel: +54 11 4555 6100

BELGIUM

ARLEQUIN
Tel: +32 2 514 54 28

ARLEQUIN DANCE DEVISION
Tel: +32 2 512 42 59

DIGITAL ELEMENTS
Tel: +32 37809720
Email: info@digitalelements.be
www.digitalelements.be

MUSICMAN/DANCE SOLUTION
Tel: +32 9 2251165
Email: musicman@musicman.be
www.musicman.be

STEREOPHONIC RECORDS
Tel: +32 3 232 9870
Email: Stereophonic.mailorder@pandora.be

TABOO RECORDS
Tel: +32 3 233 39 73
Email: aorta@tabooproductions.com
www.tabooproductions.com

BRAZIL

B SIDE
Tel: +55 11 3224 0150
Email: bside@bside.com.br
www.bside.com.br

CANADA

ALCHEMY RECORDS
Tel: +1 204 957 8756
Email: Steve@Alchemyrecords.mb.ca
www.alchemyrecords.com

AREA 51
Tel: +1 250 746 8869
www.seaside.net

ATOM HEART
Tel: +1 514 843 8484
Email: info@atomheart.ca
www.atomheart.ca

BEAT STREET
Email: soundscientists@hotmail.com
www.beatstreet.ca/store_details.php

BASSIX
Tel: +1 604 689 7734

BOOMTOWN IMPORT, RECORDS & CDS
Tel: +1 250 380 5090

BOWGGY RECORDS
Tel: +1 613 562 1521

DISQUIVEL
Tel: +1 514 842 1607

DJ MONTREAL RECORDS
Email: feedback@djmr.com
www.djmr.com

DNA
Tel: +1 514 284 7434
www.dnarecords.com

DOLLAR BILL RECORDS
Tel: +1 514 614 7230
Email: sales@dollarbillrecords.ca
www.dollarbillrecords.ca

EASTERN BLOC RECORDS
Tel: +1 416 593 4355

FEROSHUS
Tel: +1 0 403 617 9700
Email: feroshusrecords@hotmail.com
www.feroshus.com

FEROSHUS.2
Tel: +1 780 491 0436
Email: feroshus@telusplanet.net
www.feroshus.com

FOOSH CLOTHING/RECORDS
Tel: +1 780 491 6980
Email: info@foosh-inc.com
www.foosh.ca

FUNKY TANGS
Tel: +1 345 949 0998

FUTURISTIC FLAVOUR
Email: flavour@van.cybersurf.net

HMV ROBSON
Tel: +1 604 685 9203

HOMEBASS
Tel: +1 514 522 2066
Email: communications@homebass.com
www.homebass.com

HOOKED ON WAX INC.
Tel: +1 416 504 8669
Email: hookedon@netcom.ca

IN YER EAR
Tel: +1 905 777 8898

INSIDE RECORDS
Tel: +1 514 844 8519
Email: info@insiderecords.com
www.inside-records.be

MEKANIX MUSIC INC.
Tel: +1 604 899 5432
Email: CDWong@creo.com

ORGANISED SOUND
Email: discreets@aol.com

OTIS USED RECORDS
Tel: +1 604 669 5414

PIT & TRANCEATLANTIC MUSIC CANADA
Tel: +1 416 979 9415
www.thepitrecords.com

PLAY DE RECORD
Tel: +1 416 586 0380
Email: info@playderecord.com
www.playderecord.com

PLAYHOUSE RECORDS
Tel: +1 306 242 1710
Email: djsugar77@hotmail.com
www.playhouse.8k.com

PUT IT ON WAX
Tel: +1 506 642 8953
Email: tlsnow@nbnet.nb.ca
www.putitonwax.ca

ROTATE
www.rotate.com

ROTATE THIS
Email: rotate@rotate.com

ROTATION
Tel: +1 514 848 9562

**S4, SUPERSONIC SOUNDSCAPES/
GALAXY LOUNGE**
Tel: +1 306 789 2129

SPEED
Tel: +1 519 576 4041
Email: speed@techno.ca

SPINNABLES
Tel: +1 613 241 1011
Email: trackstaar@home.com

T426
Tel: +1 416 703 4081

**TABOU BEATSTREET INTERNATIONAL DJ
SHOP**
Tel: +1 514 288 5609
Email: eatstreet@videotron.ca

TEMPO
Tel: +1 604 685 7966

TRAXX
Tel: +1 416 977 4888

ZULU
Tel: +1 604 738 3232

DENMARK

BLACKOUT
Tel: +45 33141495
Email: info@blackoutshop.dk
www.blackoutshop.it

GOASHOPPEN
Tel: +45 96264465
Email: strou@mail.tele.dk
www.goashoppen.dk

LOUD
Tel: +45 33112316
Email: loud@get2net.dk
www.loudmusic.dk

ONE STOP IMPORT
Tel: +45 23 82 35 50
www.onestopimport.dk

STREET DANCE RECORDS
Vestergade, Copenhagen, Denmark

FRANCE

10000 FRENCH VINYL RECORDS
Email: jackruet@aol.com
www.ruet.com

12 INCH
Tel: +33 1 4013 9000
Email: 12inch@12inc.fr
www.12inch.fr

ABSOLUT SHOP SYSTEM
Tel: +33 4 94 14 10 70
Email: absolutshop@wanadoo.fr
http:///absolutshop.free.fr

ARMADILLO
Tel: +33 05 62 26 28 57

BELLOT RECORDS THREE
Tel: +331 44 75 87 40

CAPITALE RECORDS
Tel: +33 1 42 85 09 72

DAILY MUSIC
Tel: +33 1 48 02 20 20
www.dailymusic.fr

LUCKY RECORDS
Tel: +33 01 42 72 74 13

PLUS DE BRUIT
Tel: +33 1 49 70 08 70

SAMAD RECORD
Tel: +33 1 48 87 30 01

GERMANY

FORCE INC
Tel: +49 69 239 918
Email: ac@force-inc.com
www.force-inc.com

ITALY

ALPHAVILLE
Tel: +39 0523/337157

BOOTLEG
Tel: +39 0874/69670
Emalil: bootleg@sannio.com

CAIROLI MUSICA & DISCHI
Tel: +39 010/2461659
Emalil: maxmusic@mclink.it

DIMAR DISCHI
Tel: +39 054 178 6292
Email: djmar@rimini.com
www.dimardischimusica.it

DISCO STORY
Tel: +39 0364/533207
Email: discostory@libero.it

FUORITEMPO
Tel: +39 099/4593921
Email: ftempo@katamail.com

GROOVE DJ POINT
Tel: +39 059 239916
Email: info@groovedjpoint.com
www.groovedjpoint.com

IL DISCO
Tel: +39 0165/32853

LALLEGRETTO
Tel: +39 06/3613284

MELLUSO SALVATORE
Tel: +39 090/718596

JAPAN

FUTURAMA CO. Ltd/JET SET
Tel: +81 81 75 253 3530
www.jetsetrecords.net

TOWER RECORDS JAPAN INC
Tel: +81 3 5479 8620
www.towerrecords.co.jp

NETHERLANDS

BLACK RHYTHM RECORDS
Tel: +31 318 48 2399
Email: info@blackrhythm.com
www.blackrhythm.com

BOOM RECORDS
Tel: + 31 50 571 45 37
Email: boom@boomrecords.com
www.boomrecords.com

DANCE GROOVES
Tel: +31 71 542 3676
Email: info@dancegrooves.com
www.dancegrooves.com

FORBIDDEN PLANET
Tel: +31 71 512 1546

RECORD MANIA
Tel: +31 20 620 9912
Email: shop@recordmania.nl
www.recordmania.nl

ROCKHOUSE RECORDS
Tel: +31 29 446 0548
Email: info@cdexpress.com
www.cdexpress.com

RUSH HOUR MUSIC
Tel: +31 20 427 4505
Email: info@rushhour.nl
www.rushhour.nl

NEW ZEALAND

BEAT MERCHANTS
Tel: +64 9 302 2328
Email: beatmerchants@beatmerchants.co.nz
www.beatmerchants.co.nz

PORTUGAL

ABILIO SILVA & SEMANAS LDA
Tel: +351 22 948 1393

LINK VIDEO SA
Tel: +351 21 392 9750

MODELO CONTINENTE HIPERMERCADOS SA
Tel: +351 21 472 1300
www.continente.pt

X-CLUB
Tel: +351 13 17 25 90
Email: x-club@djagency.com
http:///x-club.djagency.com/id.htm

SINGAPORE

SEMBAWANG MUSIC CENTRE PTE
Tel: +65 6454 3088

SOUTH AFRICA

TECHNICS DJ MIX CLUB
Tel: +27 011 886 – 9113
Email: info@vaultage.com

SPAIN

100% PROFESIONAL
Tel: +34 958 292241
www.jet.es/100profesional

ATLAS
Tel: +34 91 448 17 17
www.atlas-records.com

CYBERTECH MUSIC SL
Tel: +34 0 94 479 23 26
Email: cybertech@cybertechmusic.com
www.cybertechmusic.com

FAMILY RECORDS
Tel: +34 91 308 55 58

INDUSTRIA ELECTRONIC SHOP
Tel: +34 942 227 617
Email: pablo@laindustriashop.com
www.laindustriashop.com

MUSKARIA TRANCE SHOP
Tel: +34 93 302 7698
www.muskaria.com

NUCLE RECORDS
Tel: +34 957 078 684
www.nuclerecords.com

STRESS RECORDS
Tel: +34 976 30 63 77
Email: Info@stressrecords.com
www.stressrecords.com

ULTRASOUND MUSIC
Tel: +34 96 382 5556
Email: usm@ultrasoundmusic.com
www.ultrasoundmusic.com

SWEDEN

EXPERT MARKNAD AB
Tel: +46 13 28 86 13

RECORDMANIA
Tel: +46 8 7442494
Email: recordmania@swipnet.se
www.recordmania.net

YELL RECORDS
Email: info@yell.nu
www.yellrecords.com

Bonus Resource 5: Digital Download Stores

UK STORES

There is an ever-growing demand for downloadable digital music. There are simply thousands of sites where you can buy music online in either MP3 or WAV format.

For a more comprehensive list (and for outside of the UK) you can simply search for downloadable music online via your internet browser, or check your favourite record labels who may offer downloads direct.

ANJUNA BEATS
www.anjunabeats.com

AUDIOJELLY LTD
Email: info@audiojelly.com
www.audiojelly.com

BEATPORT
www.beatport.com

BLEEP.COM
Email: info@bleep.com
www.bleep.com

CRITICAL RHYTHM
Email: info@criticalrhythm.co.uk
www.criticalrhythm.co.uk

DANCE TUNES
www.dance-tunes.com

DIGIBAG.COM
Email: info@digibag.com
www.digibag.com

DJDOWNLOAD.COM
Email: guy@djdownload.com
www.djdownload.com

EASYMUSIC
www.easymusic.com

EMUSIC
www.emusic.com

ENTERTAINMENT, INC
Email: info@playittonight.com

ESSENTIAL DIRECT
www.essentialdirect.com

FRESHMUSIC
Email: info@freshmusic.co.uk
www.freshmusic.co.uk

IMO DISTRIBUTION
www.imodownload.com

INDEPENDENT DANCE
Email: kontakt@independentdance.com
www.independentdance.com

ITUNES™
www.apple.com/itunes/store

JUNO RECORDS:
Email: admin@juno.co.uk
www.juno.co.uk

MIXALBUM COM
Email: info@mixalbum.com
www.mixalbum.com

MP3DOWNLOADHQ
www.MP3downloadhq.com

NAPSTER UK
www.napster.co.uk

NET SOUND MUSIC.COM
www.netsoundsmusic.com

PEOPLESOUND
www.peoplesound.com

PLAY IT TONIGHT
www.playittonight.com

RAFT
Email: vrlpress@vmg.co.uk
www.the-raft.com

SQUARE MUSIC
Email: info@squaremusic.com
www.squaremusic.com

TRACK IT DOWN
Email: info@trackitdown.net
www.trackitdown.net

TRAX2BURN.COM
Email: info@trax2burn.com
www.trax2burn.com

TRAXSOURCE.COM
Email: support@traxsource.com
www.traxsource.com

TRUE LOVE LABEL COLLECTIVE
Email: broach@truelove.co.uk
www.truelove.co.uk

TUNETRIBE
Email: info@tunetribe.com
www.tunetribe.com

VIDZONE
www.vidzone.tv/IndexAction.do

VIRGIN DIGITAL
www.virgin.com/music

XCHANGEMUSIC.COM
www.xchangemusic.com

INTERNATIONAL DOWNLOAD STORES

Here is a non-exhaustive list of online music stores from around the world that offer music for sale as a download or stream, listed by country.

EUROPE

Austria & Denmark

A & M Weltbild	www.weltbild.at
Aon Music Download	www.aonmusiconline.com
Axelmusic	www.axelmusic.com
Libro	www.libro.ca
B.T. Musik	www.btmusic.com
Austria CD Skiven	www.cdskiven.dk
CDON.com Denmark	www.cdon.com
Preiser	www.preiser.com
Soulseduction	www.soulseduction.com
Media Milkshake Denmark	www.mediamilkshake.dk

Belgium

Merlin	www.merlinprojects.com
Belgian Music Online	www.belgianmusiconline.be
MTV	www.mtvnetworks.be
Musikhylden	www.musikhylden.dk
Prefueled	www.prefueled.com
Free Record Shop Belgium	www.freerecordshop.be
Saxo	www.saxobank.com
TDC Online	www.tdc-online.co.uk
MSN Music	music.msn.com
Club Belgium	www.clubzone.com
Urban Payload	www.urbandictionary.com
Q-Music Downloadshop	www.q-music.nl
TempoMusic	www.tempomusic.be

Estonia

Allthenoise	www.allnoisecontrol.com

Croatia

Elisa Jukeboksi	www.elisa.fi
iTunes Finland	www.apple.com/fi/itunes

Cyprus

Go MP3	www.goMP3.gr

Czech Republic

All Music	www.allmusic.com
mpGreek	www.mpgreek.com
i-legalne	www.i-legalne.cz
Sony BMG Music Store Greece	www.sonymusic.gr
StarZone	www.starzone.co.nz
Tellas Music	www.music.tellas.gr
Media Milkshake Finland	www.mediamilkshake.com
Virgin Mega Downloads	www.virginmega.gr
MTV Music Shop	www.mtv.com
Nokia Musiikkikauppa	www.nokia.fi

Hungary

Phnet musiikki Songo	www.phnetmusiikki.fi
Poimuri Track	www.poimuri.fi
Pop City	www.popcitymedia.com
Saunalahti Musakauppa	palsta.saunalahti.fi

Iceland

Tonlist.is	www.tonlist.is

France

121 MusicStore	www.121musicstore.eu
Airtist Bleep.com	www.airtist.com
Alapage.com	www.alapage.com
E-Compil	www.ecompil.fr

Ireland

4deejays.com	www.4deejays.com
7digital	www.7digital.com
Downloadmusic	www.downloadhindiMP3s.com
Cultura.com	www.cultura.com
MusicBrigade	www.musicbrigade.com

Italy

musicMe	www.musicme.com
MTV	www.mtv.it
M2O Store	www.m2o.it
Orange Music	www.orangemusicnet.com
Packard Bell	www.packardbell.com
Nokia Store	www.nokia.com
Qobuz Radio Deejay Music Store	www.qobuz.com
Starzik	www.starzik.com
TVSorrisie	www.sorrisi.com

Germany

AOL Musik Downloads	www.musikdownloads.aol.de

Lithuania

Freenet	www.freenet.com
Hotvision	www.hotvision.pl

Luxembourg

Jamba	www.jamba.net
iTunes Luxembourg	www.luxembourgforict.lu
Kontor	www.kontor.cc
TuneTribe	www.tunetribe.com
Magix Music Shop	www.magixmusic.de
Mediamarkt	www.mediamarkt.de

Monaco

Musicload	www.musicload.de

Netherlands

Saturn Dance Tunes	www.dance-tunes.com
Vodafone Glandigo Music	www.vodafonemusic.co.uk
Weltbild	www.weltbild.de

Norway

Bulls Press	www.bullspress.com
DJuice	www.djuice.com.bd
Mediagigant Expert	www.mediagigant.nl
Mega-Media	www.megamedia.com.sg
MP3downloaden	www.downloads.nl
Mediamilkshake	www.mediamilkshake.com
Music Minutes	www.musicminutes.hu
MusicNow	www.musicnow.co.uk
Music Store Musikkonline	www.mfn.musiconline.no
Toost Tunes	www.toost.com
TuneTribe	www.tunetribe.com
vanLeest	www.vanleest.nl
YouMakeMusic	www.youmakemusic.com
ZoekMuziek	www.zoekmuziek.com

USA, CANADA & SOUTH AMERICA

AmazonMP3	www.amazon.com
Beatport	www.beatport.com
10musica	www.10musica.com
BuyMusic	www.buy.com
Farolatino	www.farolatino.com
Clear Channel	www.clearchannel.com
Zapmusic	www.zapmusic.co.uk
eMusic	www.eMusic.com
Fox Music	www.foxmusic.com
Baixa Hits	www.baixafilmesdublados.com
FYE Download	www.fye.com
lifewaystores	www.lifewaystores.com
MusicRebellion.com	www.musicrebellion.com
Napster	www.napster.com
National Geographic World Music	www.nationalgeographic.com
iMusica	www.imusica.com.br
Philadelphia Orchestra	www.philorch.org
Net Music	www.netmusic.com
RealPlayer Music Store	www.real.com
Rhapsody	www.rhapsody.com
MSN Music Store	music.msn.com
Tower Records	www.tower.com
Som Livre	www.somlivre.com
Submarino	www.submarino.com.br
TIM Music Store	www.timmusicstore.com.br
UOL Megastore	megastore.uol.com.br
Warner Music Store	www.warnermusicstore.com.br
Archambault	www.archambault.ca
eMusic	www.emusic.com
Vineyard Music	www.vineyardmusic.com
iMesh	www.imesh.com
iTunes Canada	www.apple.com
Yahoo. Music	new.music.yahoo.com
MuchMusic	www.muchmusic.com
Napster Canada	www.napster.ca
Sympatico	www.sympatico.ca
Puretracks	www.puretracks.com
Yahoo. Music	new.music.yahoo.com
Beon	www.beon.com

ASIA

Hong Kong
Naver	www.naver.com
Eolasia.com	www.eolasia.com
MusicStation SkyOn	www.sky.fm

India Malaysia
Bluehyppo	www.bluehyppo.com

Philippines
Fliptunes	www.fliptunes.net
clubDAM	www.clubdam.com

Japan & Singapore
HMV Digital Japan	www.hmv.co.jp/digital
Jamster	www.jamster.com
Nokia Music Store	www.nokia.co.in
Naxos Digital Japan	www.naxos.com
Olio Music	www.oliomusic.com

Korea and Thailand
CCM Love	www.ccmlove.com
Dosirak	www.dosirak.com

AUSTRALIA & NEW ZEALAND
BigPondMusic	www.bigpond.com
ChaosMusic Digirama	www.digirama.co.nz
MP3.com.au	www.MP3.com.au
Mall Music	www.mallmusic.com.au
Mulemusic	www.mulemusiq.com
Nokia Music Australia	www.nokia.com.au
Optus Zoo Music	www.optuszoo.com.au
Ripit.com.au	www.ripit.com.au
Sanity.com.au	www.sanity.com.au

For excellent up-to-date information on the digital music market, legal dos and don'ts, trends, thoughts and statistics, check out: www.pro-music.org/Content

Bonus Resource 6: Pressing and Duplication Services

Here's a list of record pressing, CD duplication and media production facilities to help you get your product into physical formats.

UNITED KINGDOM

ACCURATE DISC DUPLICATION
Email: sales@accuratedisc.com

AUDIO SERVICES
Email: asl@audio-services.co.uk
www.audio-services.co.uk

BUMP STUDIOS
Email: info@bumpstudios,co.uk
www.bumpstudios.co.uk

BURNING MEDIA
Email: info@burningmedia.com
www.burningmedia.com

CINRAM
Email: uk.sales@cinrani.com
www.cinram.com

CLEAR SOUND & VIS1ON
Email: clive@c-s-v.co.uk

CYCLONE MUSIC PRODUCTS
Email: sales@cyclonemusic.co.uk
www.cyclonemusic.co.uk

DIRECT DUPLICATION SERVICES
Email: info@audiocopying.com
www.audiocopying.com

DISC MAKERS
Email: Sales@discmakers.co.uk
www.discmakers.co.uk

DOC DATA UK
Email: uksales@docdata.co.uk
www.docdata.co.uk

DOWNSOFT
Email: work@downsoft.co.uk
www.downsoft.co.uk

GOLDING PRODUCTS
Email: sales@goldingproducts.com
www.goldingproducts.com

HERE AND NOW DISTRIBUTION
Email: adrian@hereandnowdistribution.co.uk
www.hereandnowdistribution.co.uk

HILTONGROVE MULTIMEDIA
Email: info@hiltongrove.com
www.hiltongrove.com

ICC DUPLICATION
Email: sales@iccduplicacion.co.uk
www.iccduplication.co.uk

IDEAL MASTERING
Email: work@idealmastering.co.uk
www.idealmastering.co.uk

IMPRESS MUSIC
Email: feedback@impressmu5ic-uk.com

INDEPENDENT PRESSING COMPANY
Email: info@independentpressing.com

MEDIA HEAVEN
Email: info@mediahcaven.co.uk
www.mediaheaven.co.uk

MEDIA HUT
Email: j.mccabe@cdreplication.co.uk
www.cdreplication.co.uk

MEDIA SOURCING
Email: andrew@mediasourcing.com
www.mediasourcing.com

MULTI MEDIA REPLICATION
Email: info@replication.com
www.replication.com

NOISEBOX
Email: info@noisebox.co.uk
www.noisebox.co.uk

PORTALSPACE RECORDS
Email: info@portalspacerecords.com

PURE
Email: info@pure-music.co.uk
www.pure-music.co.uk

QUICK PRESS PRODUCTION
Email: info@quickpress.co.uk
www.quickpress.co.uk

REPEAT PERFORMANCE MULTIMEDIA
Email: info@repeat-performance.co.uk
www.repeat-performance.co.uk

RMS STUDIOS
Email: rmsstudios@blueyonder.co.uk
www.rms-studios.co.uk

SONOPRESS
Email: info@sonopress.co.uk
www.sonopress.co.uk

SOUND DISCS
Email: info@sognd-discs.co.uk
www.sound-discs.co.uk

SOUND PERFORMANCE
Email: sales@soundperformance.co.uk
www.soundperformance.co.uk

SOUND SOLUTION MASTERING
Email: soundsolutioncd@aol.com
www.soundsolutionmastering.com

SOUNDS GOOD
Email: sales-info@sounds-good.co.uk
www.sounds-good.co.uk

STANLEY PRODUCTIONS
Email: sales@stanleyproduction.co.uk
www.stanleysonline.co.uk

STREAM DIGITAL MEDIA
Email: info@streamdni.co.uk
www.streamdm.co.uk

STUDIO 7K
Email: info@studio7k.com
www.studio7k.com

TRIBAL MANUFACTURING
Email: sales@tribal.co.uk
www.tribal.co.uk

TWENTIETH CENTURY VIDEO
Email: sales@tcvideo.co.uk

VDC GROUP
Email: sales@vdcgroup.com
www.vdcgroup.com

XPRESSDUPLICATION
Email: info@xpressduplication.co.uk
www.xpressduplication.co.uk

ARGENTINA

EPSA MUSIC SA
Tel: +54 11 6778 7777

AUSTRALIA

AUSTRALIAN MUSIC MARKETING ABROAD
Tel: +61 3 9419 2828

BELGIUM

3.14
Tel: +32 2 762 77 76
Email: info@3.14.be
www.3.14.be

3.14 SPRL
Tel: +32 2 762 7776
www.3.14.be

B.I.E.
Tel: +32 2347 1620
www.bie.be

CARE4DATA SERVICES
Tel: +32 1137 0440

CINRAM
Tel: +53 750 873
Email: be.sales@cinram.com
www.cinram.com

VTV NV
Tel: +32 5 637 21 37

BRAZIL

BAND MUSIC SERVICIOS LTDA
Tel: +55 11 3742 8911

CANADA

ACME VINYL
Tel: +1 905 470 2937
Email: chad@acmevinyl.com
www.acmevinyl.com

BALL MEDIA
Tel: +1 519 756 7209
Email: info@ballmedia.com
www.ballmedia.com

CDMAN DISC MANUFACTURING
Tel: +1 800 557 3347
Email: info@cdman.com
www.cdman.com

CINRAM
Tel: +1 416 332 2924
www.cinram.com

DISQUES RSB
Tel: +1 514 342 8511
www.rsbdisc.com

MMS
Tel: +1 514 935 0410
Email: info@mmsdirect.com
www.mmsdirect.com

MUSIC MANUFACTURING SERVICES
Tel: 1 416 364 1943
Email: dave@mmsdirect.com
www.mmsdirect.com

OUTSIDE MUSIC
Tel: +1 416 461 0655
www.outside-music.com

RSB DISC
Tel: +1 800 361 8153
Email: info@rsbdisc.com
www.rsbdisc.com

COLOMBIA
CODISCOS SA
Tel: +57 4 255 7011

DENMARK

BC CONSULT & SALES
Tel: +45 216 691 02
Email: gdc@gdc.dk
www.gdc.dk

CD FACTORY
Tel: +45 70 20 12 94
Email: js@cdfactory.dk
www.cdfactory.dk

DCM DENMARK
Tel: +45 70 26 11 60

SDC DANDISC A/S
Tel: +45 87 45 45 45
www.sdc-group.com

TOCANO AS
www.tocano.com

FRANCE

19' PRODUCTION
Tel: +33 3 44 19 04 10
www.19production.com

A/D MASTERING
Tel: +33 5 56 92 09 20

ACD GROUPE FRANCE
Tel: +33 6 80 20 57 67

ART ET SON STUDIO
Tel: +33 1 48 06 70 40
Email: art-et-son.studio@worldonline.fr

BLUE COAST STUDIO
Tel: +33 04 97 21 33 33
Email: philippegdcm@wanadoo.fr

DISKKOPIE
Tel: +33 1 41 92 08 02
Email: friedensburg@diskkopie.de

GLOBE AUDIO SARL
Tel: +33 5 57 95 61 39
Email: globe-audio@wanadoo.fr
www.globe-audio.com

MAC AUDIO SYSTEM
Tel: +33 1 48 71 67 62
Email: macaudiosystems@wanadoo.fr

SGPS/3D CLASSICS
Tel:+33 1 55 43 84 34

STUDIO BLATIN
Tel: +33 4 73 34 12 30
Email: studioblatin@wanadoo.fr

TOPMASTER
Tel: +33 1 47 54 06 71
Email: topmaster@noos.fr

GERMANY

ALIVE AG
Tel: +49 221 709 043 00
www.alive-ag.de

B & B DATADESIGN
Tel: +49 2761 92 590
Email: landt@bb-datadesign.de

BAUER STUDIOS
Tel: +49 7141 2268 11
Email: eva@bauerstudios.de
www.bauerstudios.de

INCOM STORAGE GMBH
Tel: +49 228 979 770
www.incom.de

MMP MASTER MEDIA PRODUCTIONS
Tel: +49 2247 916810
www.master-media.net

OPTIMAL MEDIA PRODUCTION GMBH
Tel: +49 399 31 565 48
www.optimal-online.de

R.A.N.D. MUZIK
Tel: 688732
Email: info@randmuzik.de
www.randmuzik.de

SONOPRESS GMBH
Tel: +49 5241 805 200
Tel: +49 5241 735 43
www.sonopress.de

TOPAC MULTIMEDIAPRINT GMBH
Tel: +49 5241 80 5885
www.topac.de

ZYX MUSIC GMBH & CO KG
Tel: +49 6471 505 050
www.zyx.de

ITALY

1ST GROOVE
Tel: +39.045.580336
Email: marc@1stpop.net
www.1stpop.net

3S SERVIZIO SUPPORTI SONORI
Tel: +39 2 27 20 99 98
Email: info@tre-s.it

AUDIO & LIGHT SYSTEMS
Tel: +39 2 83 61 051

AUDIO VIDEO POINT LA VETRAIA
Tel: +39 2 89 40 40 19
Email: lavetraia@lavetraia.com

CONTACT MUSIC SERVICE
Tel: +39 11 73 28 84
Email: info@contactmusicservice.com

GDD MANUFACTURING
Tel: +39 2 92 91 881
Email: info@gddisk.com
www.gddisk.com

NATALI MULTIMEDIA
Tel: +39 55 73 74 711
Email: info@natali.it

POZZOLI
Tel: +39 2 95 43 41
Email: mail@pozzolispa.com
www.pozzolispa.com

SARABANDAS INTERNATIONAL
Tel: +39 2 44 78 933

SERINODATA
Tel: +39 825 99 81 55

JAPAN

AIRDRIVER
Tel: +31 3 5549 9563
Email: msagawa@e-lifemfg.co.jp

NETHERLANDS
C & T MULTIMEDIA FACILITIES
Tel: +31 10 467 2011
www.cdfacilities.com

COMPLETE MULTIMEDIA
Tel: +31 35 626 4444
www.cmmservices.nl

DOCDATA BENELUX
Tel: +31 41 667 4356
www.docdata.nl

MUSIC MARKETEERS
Tel: +31 20 420 0052
www.tmm.nl

NEXPAK
Tel: +31 49 259 0111
www.nexpak.nl

NEW ZEALAND

GALLO MUSIC GROUP
Tel: +27 11 340 9344
www.gallo.co.za

YFM
Tel: +27 11 88 07 070
www.yworld.co.za

PORTUGAL

MEDIA FASHION
Tel: +351 22 370 7270
www.mediafashion.com

SINGAPORE

COSMIC RECORDS
Tel: +65 687 511 54

SPAIN

CD POOL MUSIC
Tel: +34 91 644 00 84
Email: delfin@cdpoolmusic.com
www.cdpoolmusic.com

CONDOR CD
Tel: +34 97 645 7100
www.grupocondor.com

GRUPO GEMA
Tel: +34 93 718 4011
www.gemaod.com

MPO IBERICA SA
Tel: +34 91 643 1238
www.mpo.es

NOVODISC OD GROUP SA
Tel: +34 91 486 2760

POLISISTEM SA
Tel: +34 93 586 0303
www.polisistem.com

REVERSE
Tel: +34 932 1545 36

SWEDEN

AUDIODISC
Tel: +46 8-582 461 85
Email: info@audiodisc.se
www.audiodisc.se

DCM SWEDEN AB
Tel: +46 8 477 2000

SDC SWEDEN AB
Tel: +46 8 630 2100

UNITED STATES

A TO Z MUSIC SERVICES
Tel: +1 212 260 0237
Email: info@atozmusic.com

ARDENWOOD SOUND & DVD
Tel: +1 510 793 7511
Email: ardenwood@earthlink.net
www.ardenwoodsnd-dvd.com

ARMADILLO DIGITAL AUDIO
Tel: +1 818 754 1253
Email: steve@armadillodigital.com
www.armadillodigital.com

ARTIST DEVELOPMENT ASSOCIATES (ADA)
Tel: +1 888 782 2378
Email: info@artistdevelopment.com
www.artistdevelopment.com

ASSOCIATED AUDIO/VIDEO & DIGITAL SERVICES
Tel: +1 203 338 0699
Email: assocaudio@juno.com

ATLANTA MANUFACTURING GROUP
Tel: +1 866 230 9626
Email: info@amgcds.com
www.amgcds.com

AXIS CD
Tel: +1 800 237 1470
www.axiscd.com

BLUE HOUSE PRODUCTIONS
Tel: +1 301 589 1001
Email: info@bluehouseproductions.com

BOSTON DISC
Tel: +1 781 829 5050
Email: paul@bostondisc.com
www.bostondisc.com

BROOKSHOWARD PRODUCTIONS, Inc.
Tel: +1 323 874 3121
Email: salesdepartment@brookshoward.com

CALIFORNIAN REPLICATION
Tel: +1 714 960-2345
Email: info@californiareplication.com

CANAVERAL SKIES MUSIC
425 14th St., Suite C4, Brooklyn, 11215
NY, United States
Tel: +1 718 965 6562
Email: info@canaveralskies.com

CASS-A-TAPES
Tel: +1 816 767 0050
Email: cassette@swbell.net

CASSETTE AND CD EXPRESS
Tel: +1 615 244 5667

CD BABY
Tel: +1 503 595 3000
Email: cdbaby@cdbaby.com
www.cdbaby.com

CD LABS INC.
Tel: +1 818 505 9581
Email: cdlabs@pacbell.net

CHEAP CD DUPLICATIONS
Tel: +1 805 522 6556
www.cheapcdduplications.com

CINE MAGNETICS VIDEO & DIGITAL LABS
Tel: +1 914 273 7500
Email: bowen@cinemagnetics.com
www.cinemagnetics.com

CINRAM
Tel: +1 617 547 2828
Email: jackiewhelan@cinram.com
www.cinram.com

CLOCKWERKE SOUND & DUPLICATING
Tel: +1 440 331 2210
Email: clockwerke@aol.com
www.clockwerke.com

COMPACT DISC SERVICE
Tel: +1 800 599 9534
Email: info@cdsg.com
www.cdsg.com

COMPREHENSIVE MEDIA
Tel: +1 818 764 3855
Email: mailbox@compmediacorp.com
www.compmediacorp.com

COPYCATS CD DUPLICATION
Tel: +1 810 774 8144
Email: copycatscd@ameritech.net

CORPORATE DISK
Tel: +1 800 634 3475
dgimbel@disk.com
www.disk.com

CRAVEDOG CD MANUFACTURING
Tel: +1 503 233 7284
Email: info@cravedog.com
www.cravedog.com

CREATIVE SOUND CORP
Tel: +1 818 707 8986
Email: csound@csoundcorp.com
www.csoundcorp.com

DENON DIGITAL LCD
Tel: +1 706 342 3425
Email: micbro@denondigital.com

DERING
Tel: +1 717 283 0021
Email: ddering@dering.com
www.dering.com

DREAMS FACTORY
Tel: +1 804 358 2828
www.dreamsfactory.com

DUBHOUSE
Tel: +1 954-524-3658
Email: mike@thedubhouse.net
www.thedubhouse.net

ELS PRODUCTIONS
Tel: +1 800 927 3472
Email: customerservice@elsproductions.com
www.elsproductions.com

JEWEL RECORDING
Tel: +1 513 522 9336
Email: record@jewelrecords.com

JOES GRILLE
Tel: +1 303 442 1770
Email: sales@joesgrille.com
www.joesgrille.com

KABA AUDIO PRODUCTIONS
Tel: +1 415 883 5041
Email: paul@kabaaudio.com
www.kabaaudio.com

LIGHTNING HILL REPLICATORS
Tel: +1 310 827 7764
Email: sales@lightninghill.com

LION RECORDING SERVICES
Tel: +1 703 569 3200
Email: info@lionrecording.com
www.lionrecording.com

MAGNETIC AIR
Tel: +1 800 561 1815
Email: sales@cdexperts.com
www.cdexperts.com

MOON VALLEY MEDIA
Tel: +1 602 870 3987
Email: sales@moonvalleycassette.com
www.moonvalleymedia.com

MORPHIUS DISC MANUFACTURING
Tel: +1 410-662-0112
Email: mfginfo@morphius.com
www.morphius.com

NATIONAL RECORDING STUDIOS
Tel: +1 718 369 8273
www.tapes.com

OASIS DUPLICATION
Tel: +1 540 675 1500
Email: info@oasiscd.com
www.oasiscd.com

PLAY-IT PRODUCTIONS
Email: sergio@play-itproductions.net
www.play-itproductions.net

PHYLCO AUDIO DUPLICATION
Tel: +1 800 348 6194
Email: info@phylcoaudio.com
www.phylcoaudio.com

QUALITY CLONES
Tel: +1 323 464 5853
Email: qualityclones@sbcglobal.net

RECORD TECHNOLOGY
Tel: +1 805 484 2747
Email: reidm@recordtech.com
www.recordtech.com

RIMAGE
Tel: +1 952 944 8144
Email: info@rimage.com
www.rimage.com

SONOPRESS
Tel: +1 212 782 7668
Email: andrew@dapuzzo@sonopress.com
www.arvatodigitalservices.com

SONY DADC GLOBAL
Tel: +1 812 462 8100
Email: sklinger@disc.sony.com
www.sonydadc.com

Bonus Resource 7: Magazine Contacts

UNITED KINGDOM

24:7
Tel: +44 (0)1752 294130
Fax: +44 (0)1752 257320
Email: info@afterdarkmedia.net
www.outofhand.co.uk

AUDIO MEDIA
Tel: +44 (0)14 8046 1555
Fax: +44 (0)14 8046 1550
Email: mail@audiomedia.com
www.audiomedia.com

BILLBOARD
Tel: +44 (0)20 7420 6003
Email: billlboard@espcomp.com
www.billboard.com

BLUES & SOUL
Tel +44 (0)20 7402 7708
Fax: +44 (0)20 7224 8227
Email: editorial@bluesandsoul.com
www.bluesandsoul.com

BPM
www.bpmmagazine.net

BROADCAST
Tel: +44 (0)20 7505 8014
Fax: +44 (0)20 7505 8050
www.produxion.com

COMPUTER MUSIC
www.musicradar.com/computermusic.co.uk

DJ MAGAZINE
Tel: +44 (0)20 7042 4000
Email: editors@djmag.com
www.djmag.com

FAITH FANZINE
www.faithfanzine.com

FUTURE MUSIC
Tel: +44 (0)1225 442244
Fax: +44 (0)1225 462986
www.futuremusic.co.uk

GUIDE
Tel: +44 (0)20 7713 4152
Fax: +44 (0)20 7713 4346

I DJ
Tel: +44 (0)1 17 945 1913
Fax: +44 (0)1 17 927 7825
Email: adam@i-DJ.co.uk
www.i-DJ.co.uk

KNOWLEDGE
Tel: +44 (0)20 8533 9300
Email: rachel@knowledgemag.co.uk
www.knowledgemag.co.uk

M8
Tel: +44 (0)141 840 5980
Fax:+44 (0)141 353 1448
Email: listings@M8magazine.com

MIM PRO
Tel: +44 (0)20 8545 0955
Fax: +44 (0)20 8417 0466
Email: info@mim.dj
www.mim.dj

MIXMAG
Tel: +44 (0)20 7520 8625
www.mixmag.net

MOJO
Tel: +44 (0)20 7436 1515
Fax: +44 (0)20 7312 8296
www.mojo4music.com

MUSIC TECH
www.musictechmag.co.uk

MUSICWEEK
Tel: +44 (0)20 7921 8401
Fax: +44 (0)20 7921 8339
Email: ajax@musicweek.co.uk
www.musicweek.com

NIGHT
Tel: +44 (0)161 429 7803
Fax: +44 (0) 161 480 8896

NME
Tel: +44 (0)20 7261 5813
Fax: +44 (0)20 7261 5185
Email: krissi_murison@ipcmedia.com
www.nme.com

NOTION
Tel: +44 (0)20 7404 2244
www.planetnotion.com

ONE WEEK TO LIVE
Tel: +44 (0)20 7608 0974
Email: info@oreweektolive.com

OUR HOUSE
www.ourhousemag.com

PRO MOBILE
Tel: +44 (0)1 14 2447 548
Email: info@promobile.org.uk
www.promobile.org.uk

Q MAGAZINE
www.qthemusic.com

REMIX MAG
www.remixmag.com

RESOLUTION
www.resolutionmag.com

RWD
Tel: +44 (0)87 0774 5619
Fax: +44 (0)20 8367 6184
Email: editor@RWDmag.com
www.RWDmag.com

SOUL SURVIVORS
Tel: +44 (0)1732 844246
Email: anna@thesoulsurvivors.co.uk
www.thesoulsurvivors.co.uk

SOUND ON SOUND
Tel: +44(0)1954 789888
Fax: +44 (0) 1954 78989S
Email: sos.feedback@sospubs.co.uk
www.sospubs.co.uk/
www.soundonsound.com

SPILL
Email: chris@spillonline.com
www.spillonline.com

SPIN
www.spin.com/

STUDIO 69
Tel: +44 (0) I 16 262 6969
Email: kevin@69magazine.co.uk

TILLATE (FORMERLY M8)
www.tilllatemagazine.com

TIMEOUT
Tel: +44 (0)20 7813 3000
Fax: +44 (0)20 7813 6158
www.timeout.com/london

UNCUT
www.uncut.co.uk

UPDATE
Tel: +44 (0)20 7706 8003
Fax: +44 (0)20 7706 8280
www.dmcupdate.com

WAX POETICS
www.waxpoetics.com

WIRE
Tel: +44 (0)20 7422 5010
Email: editor@thewire.co.uk
www.thewire.co.uk

XLR8R
www.xlr8r.com

ARGENTINA

TECNOPROFILE MAGAZINE
Tel: +54 11 4392-3536
Fax: +54 11 4392-3536
Email: paola@tecnoprofile.com
www.tecnoprofile.com

CANADA

KLUBLIFE
Tel: +1 416 861 1826
Email: info@klublife.com
www.klublife.com

NOCTURNAL MAGAZINE
Tel: +1 416 588 1678
Email: andrew@nocturnalmagazine.net
www.nocturnalmagazine.net

TRIBE
Tel: +1 416 778 4115
Email: editor@tribe.ca
www.tribe.ca

VICE
Tel: +1 514 286 5224
Email: eddym@viceland.com
www.viceland.com

FRANCE

CODA MAGAZINE
Tel: +33 1 46 07 01 02
Fax: +33 1 46 07 01 03
www.codamag.com

ONLY FOR DJS
Tel +33 4 7768 6914
Fax +33 4 7770 1042
Email: iudovjc.rambaud@onlvfordj.fr
www.onlyfordj.fr

GERMANY

GROOVE MAGAZINE
Tel +49 30 44 31 20 20
Fax: +49 30 4431 20 70
www.groove.de

RAVELINE
Fax: +49 (0)2363-5676-94
Email: info@raveline.de
www.raveline.de

ASTAN
Tel: +49 02556 1821
Email: astanmagazin@t-online.de
www.astan-magazin.de

CHARTREPORT
Tel: +49 4131 26 85 62
www.chartreport.de

DE BUG
Tel: 49 030.2838 4458
www.de-bug.de

DER MUSICKMARKT
Tel: +49 89 741 26 400
www.musikmarkt.de

DTECT MAGAZINE
Tel: +49 04131 727 141
Email: contact@dtect-magazine.com

ENTERTAINMENT MEDIA
Tel: +49 89 451 143 91
www.mediabiz.de

MUSIK MEDIA
Tel: +49 2236 96217 38
Email: p.misic@musikmedi.de

ORKUS MUSIK MAGAZIN
Tel: +49 0711 420 67 04
Email: info@orkus-online.de
www.orkus-online.de

OUK
Tel: +49 0 70 71 – 36 00 80
Email: redaktion@ouk.de
www.ouk.de

ITALY

DISCOID DANCE MAGAZINE
Tel: +39 054 1307 333
www.discoid.it

NETHERLANDS

RELEASE MAG
Tel: +31 020 8510600
Email: info@id-t.com
www.id-t.com

SPAIN

GO MAG
Tel: +34 0934176867
Email: go@go-mag.com
www.go-mag.com

THAILAND

HYPE MAGAZINE
Tel: +66 84 – 911-6575
Email: russell@hype-magazine.com
www.hype-magazine.com

UNITED ARAB EMIRATES

INFUSION
Email: charlchaka@infusion.ae
www.infusion.ae

UNITED STATES

ALTERNATIVE PRESS REVIEW
Tel: +1 703 553 2945
www.altpr.org

AMERICAN SONGWRITER
Tel: +1 615 321 6096
Email: info@americansongwriter.com
www.americansongwriter.com

BILLBOARD INFORMATION GROUP
Tel: +1 646 654 4644
www.billboard.com

BLUE SUEDE NEWS
Tel: +1 425 788 2776
Email: shakinboss@aol.com
www.bluesuedenews.com

BPM CULTURE MAGAZINE
Tel: +1 310 652 8145

CLUB SYSTEMS INTERNATIONAL
Tel: +1 516 944 8372
Email: kmason@testa.com
www.testa.com

CMJ NEW MUSIC MONTHLY
Tel: +1 917 606 1908
Email: cmjmonthly@cmj.com
www.cmj.com

COMPUTER MUSIC
Tel: +1 510 653 3307
Email: mlevine@primediabusiness.com
www.emusician.com

DJ TIMES
Tel: +1 516 767 2500
Email: djtimes@testa.com
www.djtimes.com

DMA DANCE MUSIC AUTHORITY
Tel: +1 708 614 8417
Email: feedback@dmadance.com
www.dmaclub.com

DOWN BEAT
Tel: +1 630 941 2030
Email: editor@downbeat.com
www.downbeat.com

ELECTRONIC MUSICIAN
Tel: +1 510 653 3307
Email: emeditorial@primediabusiness.com
www.emusician.com

FEEDBACK
Tel: +1 512 301 6527
Email: damon@feedbackmagazine.com
www.feedbackmagazine.com

FILTER
Tel: +1 323 930 2882
Email: info@filtermmm.com
www.filter-mag.com

FLYER – NEW YORK
Tel: +1 718 330 1218
Email: info@flyernyc.com
www.flyernyc.com

FREEBASS
Tel: +1 323 651 0275
Email: mail@freebass.tv
www.freebass.tv

GLOBAL RHYTHM
Tel: +1 212 868 4359
Email: edit@globalrhythm.net
www.globalrhythm.net

HARP
Tel: +1 301 588 4114
Email: scrawford@harpmagazine.com
www.harpmagazine.com

HITS
Tel: +1 818 501 7900
www.hitsdailydouble.com

HM
Tel: +1 512 989 7309
Email: letters@hmmagazine.com
www.hmmagazine.com

INK 19
Tel: +1 321 253 0290
www.ink19.com

KEYBOARD MAGAZINE
Tel: +1 650 513 4300
Email: keyboard@musicplayer.com
www.keyboardmag.com

LATIN BEAT MAGAZINE
Tel: +1 310 516 6767
Email: info@latinbeatmagazine.com
www.latinbeatmagazine.com

LIGHTING DIMENSIONS
Tel: +1 212 204 1813
Email: djohnson@primediabusiness.com
www.lightingdimensions.com

LOTUS
Email: sergio@lotusmag.com
www.lotusmag.com

MAGNET
Tel: +1 215 413 8570
Email: magnetmag@aol.com
www.magnetmagazine.com

MASS APPEAL
Tel: +1 718 625 9033
Email: justin@massappealmag.com
www.massappealmag.com

MC2
Tel: +1 650 513 4300
Email: mc2mag@musicplayer.com
www.mcmag.com

MIX
Tel: +1 510 653-3307
Email: mixeditorial@primediabusiness.com
www.mixonline.com

MIX MAGAZINE
Tel: +1 510 985.3229
Email: remixhotel@primediabusiness.com
www.remixmag.com

MIXER
Tel: +1 212 843 0740
Email: dcmusa@aol.com
www.mixermag.com

MOBILE BEAT
Tel: +1 954 973 355
Email: ifox@mobilebeat.com

MURDER DOG
Tel: +1 707 553 8191
Email: infol@murderdog.com
www.murderdog.com

MUSIC BUSINESS REGISTRY
Tel: +1 818 995 7458
www.musicregistry.com

MUSIC CONNECTION
Tel: +1 818 755 0101
Email: contactmc@musicconnection.com
www.musicconnection.com

MUSICO PRO
Tel: +1 303 516 9118
www.musicopro.com

NEW AGE RETAILER
Tel: +1 800 463 9243
www.newageretailer.com

OUTBURN
Tel: +1 805 493 5861
Email: outburn@outburn.com
www.outburn.com

PERFORMER PUBLICATIONS
Tel: +1 617 627 9200
Email: editorial-ne@performermag.com
www.performermag.com

PERFORMING SONGWRITER
Tel: +1 615 385 7796
Email: editorsps@performingsongwriter.com
www.performingsongwriter.com

RADIO & RECORDS
Tel: +1 310 553 4330
Email: mailroom@rronline.com
www.rronline.com

REMIX
Tel: +1 510 653 3307
Email: remixeditorial@intertec.com
www.remixmag.com

ROCKRGRL MAGAZINE
Tel: +1 206 275 4622
Email: rockrgrl@aol.com
www.rockrgrl.com

ROLLING STONE
Tel: 212 484 1616
www.rollingstone.com

SINGER MAGAZINE
Tel: +1 585 385 9920
Email: greg@singermagazine.com
www.singermagazine.com

SLANG
Tel: +1 617 292 8099
Email: info@slangmedia.com

SOURCE
Tel: +1 212 253 3700
Email: editor@thesource.com
www.thesource.com

SPIN
Tel: +1 212 231 7400
Email: info@spin.com
www.spin.com

TIME OUT
Tel: +1 646 432 3000
www.timeoutny.com

Bonus Resource 8: List of International DJ Agencies

This is by no means an exhaustive list but is a good starting point for some of the main artist agencies. For a more comprehensive list (and for outside of the UK) simply search DJ Agencies in your web browser.

ALTERNATIVE MUSIC & EVENTS CO. LTD
3 Merrivale, Foxmoor Lane, Ebley,
Stroud, Gloucestershire GLS 4PP
Tel: +44 (0)1-153 825630
Email: bookings@alternativemec.co.uk
www.akernativemec.com

BULLDOZER MEDIA
8 Rowland Mews. Stepney Green,
London EI 3JT
Tel: +44 (0)20 7929 3333
Fax: +44 (0)20 7929 3222
Email: oliver@bulldozermedia.com
www.bulldozermedia.com

CEMENT (DEX-RAY) – WORLD DJ
103 Gaunt Street. London SEI 6DP
Tel: +44 (0)845 644 0705
Fax: +44 (0)207 403 5348
Email: amy@dex-ray.com
www.worlddj.com

CLASS A DJS
PO Box 1431, Croydon. Surrey CR9 6XG
Tel: +44 (0)870 746 9501
Fax: +44 (0)870 746 9504
Email: info@classauk.com
www.classauk.com

CODA
229 Shoreditch High Street,
London, E1 6PJ
Tel: +44 (0)20 7456 8888
Fax: +44 (0)20 7456 8800
www.codaagency.com

COFFEE ARTISTS
5 Weyhill Close, Maidstone,
Kent ME14 5SQ
Tel +44 (0)1622 222222
Fax: +44 (0)1622 222223
Email: gelli@coffeeartists.com
www.coffeeartists.com

CONNECTED DJS
16 Merchants House, 66 North Street,
Leeds LS2 7PN
Tel: +44 (0)1132 343343
Email: rich@connecteddjs.com
www.connecteddjs.com

CREATE MUSIC LTD
3 Palmerston Street, Hanley,
Stoke on Trent, Staffs STI 3EU
Tel: +44 (0)870 428 7434
Fax: +44 (0)870 428 7435
Email: andy@createmusic.co.uk

ECLECTIC BREAKS
Top Floor, Cross House. Cross Lane,
London N8 7SA
Tel: +44 (0)20 8340 1887
Fax: +44 (0)20 8340 0697
Email: info@eclecticbreaks.com
www.eclecticbreaks.com

EMINENCE LEISURE
18-24 John Street, Luton LU I 2JE
Tel: +44 (0)1582 817030
Email: info@eminenceleisure.co.uk

EXCESSION
Unit I I7,Westbourne Studios,
242Acklam Road.
London W10 SJJ
Tel: +44 (0)20 7524 7676
Fax: +44 (0)20 7524 7677
Email: tara@excession.co.uk
www.excession.co.uk

FLIPSIDE DJS
Hindol House, Beadles Lane. Oxted,
Surrey RH8 90J
Tel +44 (0) 1892 544 85I
Email: mfo@femaledjs.com
www.flipsidedjs.com

FLUID MANAGEMENT
Tel: +44 (0)7729 133396
Email: team@fluidmanagement.co.uk

FOREFRONT
Tel: +44 (0) 7540 725892
Email: charlie@forefrontagency.co.uk
www.forefrontagency.co.uk

FRESH ARTIST MANAGEMENT
1 Brookfield Yard, Sheffield S71 DY
Tel: +44 (0)870 990 9216
Fax: +44 (0)870 990 9217
Email: barry@freshdjs.co.uk
www.freshdjs.co.uk

FUNKED UP
8 Lilac Grove, Scourport On Severn
DY13 8SR
Tel: +44 (0)7743 427375
Email: rcds@clubbedup.co.uk
www.clubbedup.co.uk

GROOVE CONNECTION
11 Webbs Road. London,
London SWII IXJ
Tel: +44 (0)20 7223 4777
Fax: +44 (0)20 7223 4999
Email: info@grooveconneccion.co.uk
www.grooveconnection.co.uk

HEAD SPACE
26 Bresford Rd, New Maiden KT3 3RQ
Tel: +44 (0)7939 5434S2
Email: scott@headspacedjs.com
www.headspacedjs.co.uk

HYPER
Po Box 2222. Reading RG 1 4WH
Tel: +44 (0)870 445 0444
Fax: +44 (0)870 445 0 443
Email: info@hyperworld.net

INSANITY ARTISTS AGENO
8 Duncannon Street, London WC2N4JF
Tel +44 (0)845 644 6625
Email: info@insanitygroup.com
www.insanitygroup.com

INTERNATIONAL MANAGEMENT DIVISION
Unit 4c Bannon Court.
S4-S8 Michael Road,
London SW6 2EF
Tel: +44 (0)20 7371 0995
Email: rachel@imd-info.com
www.imd-info.com

ITB
1st Floor Ariel House,
74a Charlotte Street,
London, WIT 4QJ
Tel: +44 (0)20 7637 6980
Fax: +44 (0)20 7637 6978
Email: karey@itb.co.uk
www.itb.co.uk

LG4
PO Box 253, Edgware HA8 OXG
Tel: +14 (0)20 8908 6663
Email: prozakdj@gmail.com

MN2S MANAGEMENT
4-7 The Vineyard, Sanctuary Street,
London SEI IQL
Tel: +44 (0)20 7378 7321
Fax: +44 (0)20 7378 6575
Email: info@mn2s.com
www.mn2s.com

MOST WANTED
PO Box 305, Hayes. UB4 9SZ
Tel: +44 (0)8707 454940
Fax: +44 (0)8707 454941
Email: info@mostwanteduk.com
www.mostwanteddjs.com

OPTIMUM MANAGEMENT
PO Box 305, Hayes, Middlesex UB4 9SZ
Tel: +44 (0)8707 454940
Email: lee@mostwanteduk.com

OVEN READY PRODUCTIONS
Tel: +44 (0)7050 803933
Fax: +44 (0)7050 693471
Email: info@ovenready.net
www.ovenready.net

PARAGON
7 Riverside, 317 Southend Lane,
Catford, London SE6 3NF
Tel: +44 (0)7908 762512
Email: info@paragon-dj.co.uk
www.paragon-dj.co.uk

PRIMARY
10-11 Jockeys Fields, London WCIR 4BN
Tel: +44 (0)20 7400 4500
Fax:+44 (0)20 7400 4501
Email: mail@primary.uk.com
www.primary.uk.com

PURE DJS
2 Whiting Street, Sheffield,
S Yorkshire S8 9QR
Tel:+44 (0)1142 555768
Fax:+44 (0)1142 812788
Email: paul@puredjs.com
www.puredjs.com

REPRESENTS
Office 3 Bannon Court,
54-58 Michael Road,
London SW6 2ES
Tel: +44 (0)20 7384 2080
Fax: +44 (0)20 7384 2005

RRR MANAGEMENT
96 Wentworth Road,
Birmingham BI79 SYM
Tel: +44 (0)121 426 6820
Fax: +44 (0) 121 426 5700
Email: enquiries@rrrmanagement.com
www.rrrmanagement.com

SEDITION DJS
Second Floor, Arishi House,
20-22 Curtain Road, London EC2A 3NF
Tel: +44 (0)20 7247 5400
Fax: +44 (0)1992 850446
Email: info@seditiondls.com
www.seditiondjs.com

SPARKLE AGENCY
Royal Tunbridge Wells, Kent TNI 2FR
Tel+44 (0)1892 544 851
Email: bookings@sparkleagcncy.com
www.sparkleagency.com

STONE MANAGEMENT
IB Anderson Road, Birmingham,
West Midlands B67 5DR
Tel +44 (0)7976 269094
Fax:+44 (0)121 420 2502
stone_management@hotmail.com

STORM MANAGEMENT
166 Storm House, Twickenham TW2 6NW
Tel: +44 (0)20 8241 1302
www.stormanagement.co.uk

TEK-DJS & PROMOTION MANAGEMENT
Tel: +44 (0)7904 388675
Email: tom@tekdjs.wanadoo.co.uk

THERAPY MUSIC & MANAGEMENT
PO Box 8126. Newark NG24 4ZY
Tel:+44 (0)1636 605934
Fax: +44 (0)1636 605781
Email: sara@therapymusic.co.uk
www.therapymusic.co.uk

TIDY MANAGEMENT
Po Box 305, Hayes UB4 9SZ
Tel: +44 (0)8707 454 940
Fax: +44 (0)8707 454 941
Email: simon@mostwanteduk.com

TOP MUSIC AGENT
Studio 4 Willington Ave, Wenthworth
GU25 4QX
Tel: +44 (0)1483 722533
Email: will@topmusicagent.com
www.topmusicagent.com

TOP1 PROMOTIONS
The Flint Glass Works. 64 Jersey Street,
Ancoats Urban Village,
Manchester M4 6JW
M+44 (0)8709 107101
Email: info@top1.co.uk

UDJS
2nd Floor, Arishi House,
20-22 Curtain Road.
London EC2A 3NF
M +44 (0) 207 247 4121
Email: chloe@udjs.net
www.udjs.net

UK-DJS.NET
2 Dagonet Road, Bromley, Kent BRI 5LR
Email: office@uk-djs.net
www.uk-djs.net

UKCLUBDJ.COM
Glenfield,The Avenue, Bishops Waltham,
Southampton SO3 2IBP
Tel: +44 (0)1489 890060
Email: info@ukclubdj.com
www.ukclubdj.com

ULTRA DJ MANAGEMENT
42 City Business Centre, Lower Road,
London SEI6 2XB
Tel: +44 (0)20 7740 21 19
Fax: +44 (0)20 7394 1139
Email: cach@ultradj.co.uk
www.ultradj.co.uk

UMC ARTIST MANAGEMENT
PO Box 1401, Glen Parva,
Leicester LE2 8Zj
Tel:+44 (0)1 16 277 9777
Fax: +44 (0) I 16 277 3888
Email: tania@umcmanagement.co.uk
www.umcmanagement.co.uk

URBAN MANAGEMENT
11 Canal Buildings,
135 Shepherdess Walk,
London NI 7RR
Tel: +44 (0)20 7091 0080
Fax: +44 (0)20 7836 4224
Email: rod@urbandjs.net
www.urban-djs.net

URBAN AGENCY
Po Box 512, Rochester, Kent ME2 3WH
Tel: +44 (0)1634 300 046
Fax: +44(0)1634 715 230
Email: jon@urbantakeoverco.uk
www.urbantakeover.co.uk

UTOPIA
Southbridge House, Southbridge Place,
Croydon, Surrey CRO 4HA
Tel: +44 (0)870 444 8991
Fax: +44 (0)870 284 0629
Email: bookings@utopiadjs.com
www.utopiadjs.com

XTREMETALENT
PO Box 1034, Morden, Surrey SM4 6QX
Tel: +44 (0)870 787 3410
Fax: +44 (0)870 755 0634
Email: info@xtremetalent.co.uk
www.xtremetalent.co.uk

XTREME UK ARTIST MANAGEMENT
Xtreme UK, PO Box 43, Norwich,
Norfolk NR7 OLJ
Tel: +447730802000
Fax: +44I60366S6II
Email: paul@xtremeuk.biz

ARGENTINA

GLAMSITE AGENCY
Contact: Santiago
Tel: + 541145242590
www.glamsiteagency.com

MARTIN GONTAD
Buenos Aires
Email: mgontad@uolsinectis.com.ar

BELGIUM

DEEJAY BOOKING
144 Rue de Livourne, 1000 Brussels
Tel: +32 2 647 96 74
Fax: +32 2 644 18 20
Email: info@deejaybooking.com
www.deejaybooking.com

CANADA

BLOW MEDIA
38 Hollywood Avenue, Suite 109, Toronto
M2N 6S5
Email: info@blowmedia.com

PROMO ONLY
#150,3015 – 12 Street NE, Calgary, Alberta
T2E 7 J2
Tel: +1 403 226 6445
Fax: +1 403 226 6417
Email: info@promoonlycanada.com
www.promoonly.ca

FRANCE

FUTURIA
2 Rue Vivienne Bevand
Tel: +33 1 44 19 59 80
Fax: +33 1 53 29 95 30
Email: futuria@futuriaproduction.com

GERMANY

DANGEROUS DRUMS
Tostr: 177, 10115 Berlin
Tel: +49 030 726296335
Fax: +49 030 85603678
Email: info@dangerous-drums.de
www.dangerous-drums.de

KOMPAKT SHOP
Werderstr. 15-19, 50672 Cologne
Tel: +49 221 94995 170
Fax: 49 221 94995 150
Email: agentur@kompakt-net.de
www.kompakt-net.com

MFS/FLESH
Postfach 61 31 58, 10942 Berlin
Tel: +49 0 511 76 86 0 -15
Fax: +49 0 511 76 86 0 -55
Email: mark@mfs-brerlin.de
www.mfs-berlin.de

PEPPERMINT JAM
Boulevard der EU 8; 30539 Hannover
Tel: +49 0 511 76 86 0 – 15
Fax: +49 0 511 76 86 0 – 55
Email: sonia@peppermint-jam.com
www.peppermint-jam.com

MALAYSIA

PURE SUNSTANCE MANAGEMENT
27, Jalan Medang Tanduk, Bangsaria,
Bukit Bandaraya, Kuala Lumpur 59100
Tel: +60 02093 3688
Fax: +60 02093 3688
Email: info@substancemgmt.com

MALTA

FRESH MUSIC AGENCY
5, Ranceis, E.H Furse Street,
Msida MSD 04
Tel: +356 21344840
Fax: +356 21344840
Email: info@freshmusicagency.com

NETHERLANDS

I MANAGEMENT
PO Box 15503, 1001 NA Amsterdam
Tel: +31 020 428 31 70
Fax: +31 020 428 31 75
Email: info@Imanagement.nl
www.1management.nl

DJ BOOKINGS
PO Box 1320, 1500 AH Zaandam
Tel: +31 075 6144460
Fax: +31 06144462
Email: info@dutchdjagency.com

SOUTH AFRICA

DJSA
147 Linmeyer Garden Village,
Plinlimmon Road, The Hill ext,
Johannesberg, Gauteng 2197
Tel: +27 0114325597
Fax: +27 04325597
Email: Brenden@djsa.co.za
www.djsa.co.za

SWITZERLAND

WDB MANAGEMENT
Ch.D Arche 41 c 1870 Monthey
Tel: +41 244 725 528
Fax: +41 244 725 529
Email: josemanso@wdbmanagement.com
www.wdbmanagement.com

UNITED STATES

AGENCY GROUP
8490 Sunset Blvd. 403, Los Angeles,
CA 90069
Tel: +1 310 360 0071
Fax: +1 310 360 0721
Email: MikeMori@theagencygroup.com
www.theagencygroup.com

AM ONLY
55 Washington Street, Suite 658, Brooklyn,
NY 11201
Tel: +1 718 237 2428
Fax: +1 718 237 2429
Email: paul@amonly.com
www.amonly.com

BLUE COLLAR ENTERTAINMENT
615 Clayton Street, San Francisco,
CA 94117
Tel: +1 415 845 7013
Fax: +1 415 651 9498
Email: Andrew@blue-collarent.com
www.Blue-CollarEnt.com

BYASSIN INC
171 Sackett Street 1, Brooklyn,
NY 11231
Tel: +718 858 5222
www.byassn.com

CHAOTICA INC
32 East 31st Street, 9th Floor New York,
NY 10016
Tel: 212 725 6868

COLLECTIVE AGENCY
25 Peck Slip, 4th Floor, New York, NY
10038
Tel: +1 212 431 4740
Fax: +1 212 431 4714
Email: info@tca-web.com

DEF MIX PRODUCTIONS
928 Broadway. Suite 400 New York,
NY10010
Tel: +1 212 505 7728
Fax: +1716 731 7175
Email: info@defmix.com
www.defmix.com

DJL RECORD POOL
Medford, MA 02155
Tel: +1 781 396 0015
Fax: +1 781 396 2062
www.djlatino.com

EXSTUS – E
Contact: Bart Landry
5800 Brodie Lane 814, Austin 78745
Tel: +1 512 680 3541
Email: info@exstus-e.com

FUSED
PO Box 461, Sanborn, NY 14132
Tel: +1 716 583 2943
Fax: +1 716 731 7175
Email: trish@fusedmanagement.com
www.defmix.com

MAISON MUSIC
Tel: +1 514 845 9976
Fax: +1 716 982 9565
Email: ana@maison-music.com

PRODUCER ARTIST MANAGEMENT INC.
330 Clematis Street, Suite 215,
West Palm
Beach, FL 33401
Tel: +1 561 650 8191
Fax: +1 561 650 8119
Email: info@pamdjs.com

PROMO ONLY
257 S Lake Destiny Drive, Orlando, FL
32810
Tel: +1 407 331 3600
Fax: +1 407 331 6400
www.promoonly.com

RECORD POOL
Contact: Lewis Davidson
1881 Suite A, Drew Street, Clearwater, FL
33765
Tel: +1 727 799 3828
Email: lewis@therecordpool.com

RED ENTERTAINMENT GROUP
16 Penn Plaza, Ste 1750, New York,
NY 10001
Tel: +1 212 563 7575
Fax: +1 212 563 9396
Email: info@redentertainment.com
www.redentertainment.com

TJS DJS RECORD & CD POOL
1424 Capital Circle NW, Tallahassee, FL
32303
Tel: +1 850 878 3634
Fax: +1 850 877 3110
www.tjsdjs.com

RED LIGHT MANAGEMENT
Charlottesville 321 East Main Street,
Suite 500, Charlottesville, VA 22902
New York 44 Wall Street, 22nd Floor,
New York, NY 10005
Nashville, 39 Music Square East,
Nashville, TN 37203
Los Angeles, 9200 Sunset Boulevard, Los
Angeles, CA 90069
www.redlightmanagement.com

VITAL TALENT AGENCY
32 East 31st Street, Suite 9B, New York,
NY 10016
Tel: +1 212 725 5588
Fax: +1 212 725 6868

TM CENTURY INC
2002 Academy Ln, Dallas, TX 75234
Tel: +1 972 406 6842
Fax: +1 972 406 6890
Email: madams@tmcentury.com
www.tmcentury.com

Bonus Resource 9: Leading International Trade Events

www.wmcon.com – The Miami Winter Music Conference is one of the most publicised annual music gatherings in the world, respected as a pivotal platform for the advancement of the music industry.

www.sonar.es – The Sonar festival in Barcelona holds conferences at this respected international music, arts & multimedia event.

www.djtimes.com/thedjexpo – The DJ industry's best-attended, most successful trade show/exhibition. Each year, the Expo presents more than two-dozen educational seminars, an exhibit hall filled with the latest DJ, pro audio and studio gear, and three evenings full of sponsored events.

www.plasashow.com – Annual showcase of the music and entertaining industry's latest pro audio, DJ, lighting, stage engineering, AV and systems integration technology.

www.namm.org/thenammshow/2010 – The NAMM trade shows serve as a hub for people wanting to seek out the newest innovations in musical products, recording technology, sound and lighting.

www.amsterdam-dance-event.nl – Europe's main dance music conference, bringing together music business professionals from all over the world.

www.clubworldawards.com – Awards for the clubbing peaks of the previous year.

www.grammy.com – Home of the world famous music awards.

www.en.wikipedia.org/wiki/Music_festival – comprehensive list of all the main music festivals in the world.

Bonus Resource 10: DJ & Audio Equipment Manufacturers and Suppliers

www.pioneerdj.com – Pioneer DJ Products are the industry standard for professional DJs. Digital turntables, DVD turntables, CD players, mixers, and headphones.

www.allen-heath.co.uk – Professional audio mixing consoles for live, studio, broadcast, PA, installation, contractors.

www.kam.co.uk – Kam build DJ equipment and audio and lighting tools to help you release your creative potential.

www.vestax.com – Manufacturers of turntables, mixers, vinyl cutters and accessories.

www.behringer.com – Manufacturer of a wide range of professional audio equipment such as mixing consoles, compressors, and guitar amplifiers.

www.eclerdjdivision.com – Whether you play hip hop, deep house or minimal techno, ECLER designs and manufactures today's finest and most innovative DJ mixers.

www.stantonmagnetics.com – Stanton, makers of FinalScratch, professional DJ equipment, and accessories.

www.native-instruments.com – Native Instruments creates innovative hardware and software for music production and performance – for producers, guitarists, sound designers and DJs.

www.faderfox.de – Optimised controllers for LIVE & TRAKTOR; 2nd generation of micromodul.

www.ableton.com – Ableton Live is a complete music solution for Mac OS and Windows. Live covers the entire musical process, from inspiration to studio to stage. Create.

www.numark.com – Manufacturer of DJ accessories and audio equipment.

www.denondj.com – Welcome to Denon DJ. Mixers, media players, controllers, and CD/MP3 players for turntablists, Club DJs and Mobile DJs.

www.geminidj.com – Catalogue of Gemini's entire DJ product lineup, including LyteQuest lighting effects.

www.rane.com – Producers of top-end mixing consoles.

www.panasonic.com/consumer_electronics/technics_dj – Technics 1200, DJ mixing software, Technics turntables, audio recording, Technics speakers, music software.

www.reloopdj.com – Hardware controllers for Traktor DJs.

www.cortex-pro.com – The Cortex USB-compatible digital music controllers, the first of their kind, gives DJs the power to cue, play, manipulate, and even scratch digital files.

www.americandj.com – providers of DJ equipment

www.adjaudio.com – Professional DJ equipment and accessories.

www.ortofon.com – DJ cartridges.

www.citronic.com – DJ hardware

www.krksys.com – Manufacturer of studio monitors.

www.ikey-audio.com – Monitors, recorders, headphones, sound cards.

www.genelec.com – Active monitoring loudspeakers since 1978.

www.shure.com – World-renowned microphones, quality wireless systems, premium earphones and related audio products.

www.sennheiser.com – manufacturers of a wide range of headphones, microphones and wireless systems.

www.edirol.com – Group of field recorders by Roland.

www.scratchlive.net – Digital solution for Professional DJs. Hardware by Rane, Software by Serato.

www.m-audio.com – A leading provider of digital audio and MIDI solutions for today's electronic musicians and audio professionals.

www.propellerheads.se – Creators of the popular Reason, ReBirth, ReCycle software packages.

www.akai.com – Providers of audio products.

www.korg.com – Keyboards and modules, dance tools, digital recording, concert pianos, tuners, metronomes, effect processors.

www.novationmusic.com – Manufacturer of premium midi controller, synths and Automap.

www.hercules.com – DJ & Audio Products.

www.eks.fi – DJ controllers.

www.cakewalk.com – A world-leading developer of hardware and software for making music and recording digital audio.

www.thudrumble.com – DJ accessories.

www.spacetekusa.com – DJ gear, wall mounts and music equipment.

www.dmcworld.com – CDs and DVDs, DMC/Technics merchandise, The DMC World DJ Championships, DMC Update, DMC downloads, DJ pages.

www.slappa.com – CD cases, DVD cases and laptop backpacks.

www.sefour.com – DJ stands, DJ furniture, CDJ brackets and studio consoles.

www.ultimate-dj-gear.com – UDG record bags, DJ lights, slipmats, and t-shirts.

www.magma.com – PCI/PCI-X Expansion systems allows you to add up to 13 full-length PCI/PCI-X cards to a server/desktop and laptop.

www.decksaver.co.uk – Professional hard top covers protecting the Pioneer CDJ-2000/1000/900/800/400, DJM-600/700/800, Allen & Heath XONE-62/92/3D/4D & Vestax VCI-300/1000.

www.roadreadycases.com – ATA DJ cases, racks, stands and portable stage systems.

www.ministryofsound.com – Merchandise, music and more.

www.gloriousdj.com – DJ Mixstations.

www.skullcandy.com – Designer headphones, earbuds, and iPod docks.

www.jbl.com – Manufacturer of subwoofers, loudspeakers, component systems, and amplifiers for home and car.

www.rcf.it – Professional loudspeakers.

www.mackie.com – Professional audio gear.

www.prolight.co.uk/brand/w-audio – Professional sound systems.

www.cerwinvega.com – Manufactures audio speakers, subwoofers and amplifiers.

www.directproaudio.com – Pro audio loudspeakers.

www.samsontech.com – Distributors of Hartke Bass Systems and Zoom Signal Processing.

www.alesis.com – USB mixers, synths and keyboards, amps and live sound, audio processing.

www.dbxpro.com – Digital processors, noise reduction and EQ products.

www.diehard.proelgroup.com – Die·Hard: professional cables, stage boxes and connectors.

Bonus Resource 11: Specialist DJ Playlists

These genre-specific charts have been compiled by some of the world's most established and knowledgeable DJs within their scene, and from some of the leading music forums. They contain an overview of important tracks from specific music scenes within dance music. You should take them as a starting point only, as it would be an impossible task to list all the important records from the last four decades. They do, however, give you a good overview and introduction.

If you would like to discover more about any track (including catalogue numbers) then visit the online music database at www.discogs.com. This incredible site lists all the releases, artists and details for reference. It includes a marketplace where you can trade and exchange music, and many other superb features including the ability to build a Microsoft Excel spreadsheet of your own record collection.

Norman Jay – Soul, Funk and Rare Groove

The clued-up, passionate vinyl junkies at Norman Jay's 'Crate Diggers' forum have compiled this list of essential tracks. Not many people can lay claim to receiving an MBE from HRH Queen Elizabeth II for 'Services to DJing and Music', but Norman is one of them. His team of loyal supporters have helped provide you with a list of the best.

For bookings, chat and more info visit: www.normanjay.com

Archie Bell & The Drells – Strategy

Aaron Neville – Hercules

Average White Band – Stop The Rain

Banbarra – Shack Up

Bobbi Humphries – Jasper Country Man

Bobby Womack – How Could You Break My Heart?

Boiling Point – Let's Get Funktified

Brentford All Stars – Greedy G

Brick – Dazz

Brothers Johnson – Get The Funk Outta My Face

Bt Express – Do It 'Til You're Satisfied

Carl Davis & Chi-Sound Orchestra – Windy City Theme

Chuck Brown – Ashley's Roachclip

Creative Source – Who Is He & What Is He To You

Cymande – Fug

Donald Byrd – Dominoes

Dusty Springfield – Spooky

Eddie Harris – It's Alright

Eddie Jefferson – Psychadelic Sally

Edwin Starr – Easin In

Fatback Band – Ninja Walk

Fatback Band – Nycnyusa

Freda Payne – Unhooked Generation

Funk Inc – The Thang

Funkadelic – Knee Deep

Gary Bartz – Music Is My Sanctuary

Hank Ballard – From The Love Side

Ike & Tina – Bold Soul Sista

Jackson Sisters – I Believe In Miracles

James Brown – Stone To The Bone

James Brown & The Famous Flames – I Got You (I Feel Good)

James Mason – Sweet Power Your Embrace

Jean Knight – Mr Big Stuff

Johnny Guitar Watson – Superman Lover

Johnny Hammond – Fantasy

Johnny Pate – Brother On The Run

Kool & The Gang – Jungle Boogie

Kool & The Gang – Nt, Pts.1 & 2

Larry Youngs Fuel – Turn Off The Lights

Lee Dorsey – Night People

Leo's Sunship – Give Me The Sunshine

Linda Williams – Elevate Your Mind

Love Unlimited Orchestra – Strange Games & Things

Lyn Collins – Think (About It)

Maceo & The Macks – Soul Power '74

Magic Disco Machine – Scratchin'

Mandrill – Fat City Strut

Meters – People Say

Miami – Kill That Roach

Mickey & The Soul Generation – Iron Leg

Milton Wright – Keep It Up

Minnie Ripperton – Reasons

Ohio Players – Fire

Natalie Cole – Sophisticated Lady (She's A Different Lady)

Oliver Sain – Apricot Splash

Omar – It's So

Parliament – Tear The Roof Off The Sucker

Patti Jo – Make Me Believe In You

People's Choice – Do It Anyway You Wanna

Pleasure – Bouncy Lady

Ramp – Daylight

Reuben Wilson – Got To Get Your Own

Rhythm Makers – Zone

Ripple – I Don't Know What It Is

Roy Ayers – Brother Green (The Disco King)

Roy Ayers – Love Will Bring Us Back Together

Skull Snaps – It's A New Day

Sly & The Family Stone – Family Affair

Sonny Stitt – Slick Eddie

Soul Searchers – Ashley's Roach Clip

Steve Parks – Movin' In The Right Direction

Streisand And Gibbs – Guilty

The Headhunters – God Made Me Funky

The Honeydrippers – Impeach The President

The Jbs – Pass The Peas

The Jb's Givin' Up Food For Funk

The Last Poets – Sport

The Politicians – Free Your Mind

Tommy Stewart – Bump & Hustle Music

Tower Of Power – What Is Hip?

'T' P – Marvin Gaye Lays It Cool

Voices Of East Harlem – Wanted Dead Or Alive

War – Me & Baby Brother

Weldon Irvine – Walk That Walk, Talk That Talk

Whole Darn Family – Seven Minutes Of Funk

Willie Hutch – Aint That Mellow Mellow

Greg Wilson – Electro-Funk Roots

Greg Wilson's contribution to the dance music scene cannot be underestimated. His main club nights, at 'Legend' in Manchester and Wigan Pier were voted the top two in the North of England by readers of *Blues & Soul*, while he was named Best DJ. He also kicked off The Haçienda's first full-on dance night, the forerunner to 'Nude'.

Widely respected as the electro-funk originator and a true DJ talent with an incredible heritage, Greg can be found gigging around the world.

The chart below is a small selection of his early 1980's Black Underground Ingredients and also include the tracks he played on his superb Essential Mix on BBC Radio 1 (which was nominated Essential mix of the year). For more comprehensive charts and listings contact matt@nuphonic.co.uk. For bookings check out his superb site at: www.electrofunkroots.co.uk and http://www.myspace.com/djgregwilson

808 State – Pacific State (Greg Wilson mix)

Aretha Franklin – Rock Steady (Danny Krivit mix)

Atlantic Conveyor – We Are

Aurra – Such A Feeling (Parts II & III)

B.T (Breanda Taylor) – You Can't Have Your Cake And Eat It Too (Greg Wilson mix)

Banbarra – Shack Up

Brown – I Specialize In Love

Captain Rapp – Bad Times (I Can't Stand It)

Chic – I Want Your Love (Todd Terje mix)

Dc La Rue – Cathedrals (Greg Wilson mix)

DJ Divine – Get Into The Mix

Dolby's Cube – Get Out Of My Mix

Dr Jeckyll & Mr Hyde – The Challenge

Eddie Murphy – Boogie In Your Butt

Edit The Edit – Two Sides Of Sympanthy (PTA mashup/Greg Wilson mix)

Extra T's – E.T. Boogie

Firefly – Love (Is Gonna Be On Your Side)

Formula V – Killer Groove

G Force – Feel The Force

Geraldine Hunt – Cant Fake The Feeling

Gino Soccio – Try It Out

Goody Goody – It Looks Like Love

Gunchback Boogie Band – Funn

Gwen Guthrie – Seventh Heaven (Larry Levan mix)

Happy Mondays – WFL (Vince Clarke mix)

Incredible Bongo Band – Apache

Jazzy Dee – Get On Up

Kasso – Walkman

Last Rhythm – Last Rhythm

League Unlimited Orchestra – Things That Dreams Are Made Of

Loose Ends – Hangin On A String (Frankie Knuckles mix)

Magic Mike Crew – Magic Mike Theme

Metro Area – Dance Reaction

Mike T – Do It Anyway You Wanna

Nitro Deluxe – This Brutal House

P-Funk All Stars – Hydraulic Pump Pt III

Q – The Voice Of Q

Rafael Cameron – Boogies Gonna Get Ya (Francois K Mix)

Richie Scotti – Breaker

RJ's Latest Revival – Ultimate Masterpiece

Rose Royce – Do Your Dance

263

Rufus feat Chaka Khan – Aint Nobody (Frankie Knuckles mix)

Russell Brothers – The Party Scene

Sandy Kerr – Thug Rock

Shirley Lites – Heat You Up (Melt Down mix)

Sir Joe Quarterman – (I Got) So Much Trouble In My Mind (Barna Soundmachine mix)

Slyck – Bush Beat

Soul Searchers – Blow Your Whistle

Stevie Wonder – Superstition (Todd Terje mix)

Stockingcap – Wave Craze

Stone Roses – Fools Gold

Sugardaddy – Love Honey (Greg Wilson mix)

Talking Heads – Psycho Killer (Greg Wilson mix)

Teenage DJ – I Was A Teenage DJ (part 1) (Greg Wilson mix)

The Clash – Casbah Breakdown (Joey Negro mix)

The Commodores – Machine Gun (Situation mix)

The Gunchback Boogie Band – Funn

The Love Unlimited Orchestra pres. Mr Webster Lewis – Welcome Aboard

The Originals – Down To Love Town (Dimitri From Paris mix)

The Webboes – Under The Wear

Treacherous Three – Get Up

TW Funkmasters – Love Money

Tweet – Boogie 2nite

Vaughn Mason – Rockin' Big Guitar

Verycheri – 69 Cancer Sign

Visual – The Music Got Me

War – Me And Baby Brother

Warp 9 – Nunk

West Phillips – I'm Just A Sucker For A Pretty Face

X-Ray Connection – Replay

Young Dog Alien – Gotta Keep Workin It (Greg Wilson mashup)

Southport Weekender – Soulful/US House

The incredibly passionate, friendly and dedicated forum members from one of the world's most respected and revered Soulful-based events, Southport Weekender have raided their crates and memories to compile this list for you. It spans the Soulful sound of the House scene, again encompassing many of the main tracks that have shaped the movement. For information on this amazing event which takes place on the 1st weekend of May each year, or to join the active forums visit: www.southportweekender.co.uk

2 Dope – A Touch Of Salsa

27th Century – Turn It Up/Turn It Out

808 State – Pacific

A Bitcha Named Johanna – Freak It

A Guy Called Gerald – Blow Your House Down

A Guy Called Gerald – Hot Lemonade

A Man Called Adam – Bread, Love And Dreams

A Man Called Adam – Techno Powers

Adeva – In And Out Of My Life

Adeva – Promises

Adeva – Warning

Alan Oldham – House

Alexander Hope – Brothers & Sisters

Alexander Hope – Feel The Music

Alexander Hope – Never Can Get Away

Alexis P Suter – You Don't Know

Alison Limerick – Getting' It Right

Anto Vitale – Theorema Del Faya (Tea Party Mix)

Aphrodisiac – Just Before The Dawn

Aphrodisiac – Song Of The Siren

Armand Van Helden – You Don't Even Know Me

Arnold Jarvis – Inspiration

B.G Prince Of Rap – Take Control Of The Party

B.O.P. – Come On, Move With The Beat

Bang The Party – Release Your Body

Barbara Tucker – Beautiful People/Stay Together

Barbara Tucker – I Get Lifted

Bas Noir – Addicted To Luv

Bas Noir – Shoo-B-Doo

Bas Noir – My Love Is Magic

Basil Hardhaus – Make Me Dance

Basshook & Friends – Hear My Call

Be Be Winans – Thank You

Big Sister Aka Sabrynaah Pope – 100% Woman

Black Magic – Freedom (Make It Funky)

Black Rascals – Keeping My Mind

Black Science Orchestra – Where Were You

Blaze – How Deep Is Your Love

Bnc – House Aint Giving Up

Brand New Heavies – Dream Come True (Mixes)

Brand New Heavies – Stay This Way (Mixes)

C&C Music Factory – Pride

Carleen Anderson – Mama Said

Cassio – Baby Love

Ce Ce Rogers – Someday

Chez Damier – Can You Feel It

Chip E. – If You Only Knew

Chrissi I-Eece – You Should Know By Now

Club 69 – Let Me Be You Underwear (It's Working Dub)

Club Artists United – Sweet Chariot (The Kerri Mix)

Club Mcm & Marshall Jefferson Beat

Clubland – Hold On – Great Jones

Coco Steel And Lovebomb – Touch It

Code 718 – Equinox

Colour Blind – Nothing Better

Cookie Watkins – I'm Attracted To You

Corina – Now That You're Gone

Culture Beat – Cherry Lips

D Influence – Good Lover

D Influence – Good Lover (Influential House Mix)

D-Influence – No Illusions

D*Note – Garden Of Earthly Delights

Da Posse – Searchin' Hard

Da Posse – String

Darryl D'bonneau – Say You're Gonna Stay

Darryl James/David Anthony – You Make Me Happy (Todd Terry)

David D'or – Yad Anouga

Debbie Gibson – One Step Ahead

Deep Sensation – Better Love

Degrees Of Motion – Do You Want It Right Now

Degrees Of Motion – Soul Freedom

Devine Masters – Paradise

Dhar Braxton – Jump Back (Set Me Free)

Dina Carroll – We Are One

Dionne – Kisses – Cyren

DJ Pierre – Come And Fly With Me

DJ Pierre – I Might Be Leavin' U

Don Carlos – Alone
Don Carlos – Mediterraneo Ep
Donna Allen – He Is The Joy
Donnie – Cloud 9 (Quentin Harris Mix)
Dred Flimstone – From The Ghetto
Dv8 – C'mon
El Barrio – So Confused
Electribe 101 – Talking With Myself . . .
Equation – I'll Say A Prayer 4 U
Ex Girlfriend – You (You're The One For Me) Joey Negro Mix
Fantazia B – Free Yourself (David Harness)
Fire Island – If You Should Need A Friend (Fire Island Mix)
Fire Island – Grace Of God
Four On The Floor – Your Mind Is So Crazy
Frankie Knuckles – It's Hard Sometimes
Frankie Knuckles – Rain Falls
Frankie Knuckles and Jamie Principle – Your Love
Freestyle Orchestra Feat. D'borah – Keep On Pumpin It Up
Funky Green Dogs From Outer Space – Reach For Me
Funky People – Funky People
Gate Ah – The Shelter
Gerideau – Take A Stand For Love
Happy Head – Digital Love Thing
Hotline – Rock This House
Hunter Hayes – It's Not Over
Image – It's Just A Groove
Inner City – Pennies From Heaven
Interceptor – Together
Intuition Feat Keith Nunally – Greed
Ira Levi – Free Your Mind (Free Your Dub)
J Sinister – Diamond Life

J.M. Silk – Shadows Of Your Love
Jada – Love Is
James Howard – We Can Do It (Wake Up)
Jamie Principle – You're All I Waited For
Janet Rushmore – Lost In Love
Janice Christie – Taking Me For Granted
Jasper St Company – A Feelin'
Jay Williams – Sweat
Jay Williams – Sweat
Jeanette Thomas – Shake Your Body
Jellybean – Spillin The Beans
Jimi Polo – Better Days
Joe Smooth – Promised Land
Joey Negro – Everybody
Joey Negro – Cant Get High Without You
Johnson Righiera's University Of Love
Joi Cardwell – Run To You
Jomanda – Don't You Want My Love
Jomanda – The True Meaning (Of Love)
Jon Secada – Just Another Day
Jovonn – Turn And Run Away
Jsc – Solid Ground
K-Creative – To Be Free
K-Tronics Ensemble F/Double J. Flash – House Of Calypso
K-Yze – Stome
Karan Pollard – Reach Out To Me
Kathy Brown – Happy People
Kathy Brown – Can't Play Around (Maw Dub) (as well as original)
Keicha Jenkins – Goin' Through The Motions
Keith Nunally – Freedom
Keith Nunnally – Seasons Of Love
Kelly Charles – Falling In Love
Kim English – I Know A Place/Nitelife/Learn 2 Love

Kim English – Learn 2 Luv (Mood Ii Swing Vocal)

Kim English – Almighty

Kim English – Supernatural

King Amazin – Double Asunder

Kingsley O/Butch Quick – Keep It Up

Kot – Finally

Kym Mazelle – I'm A Lover

Leee John – Mighty Power Of Love

Liberty City – Some Lovin

Lil Louis – Club Loneley

Lil Louis – Do U Luv Me

Lil Louis – Nyce N Slo

Limelife – Cause You're Right On Time

Liz Torres – Don't Stop

Lood – Shout N Out

Louie Vega & Tony Humphries – Just Believe

M Fada – Jungle Flute

M&S/The Girl Next Door – Justify

M1 – Feel The Drums

Mariah Carey – Dreamlover

Marshall Jefferson – Open Our Eyes

Marshall Jefferson Pres. Truth – Open Our Eyes

Mass Order – Let's Get Happy

Mass Order – Take Me Away

Master C & J – In The City

Masters At Work – Our Mute Horn

Masters At Work – Cant Get No Sleep

Maw – To Be In Love

Maw Feat India – Love And Happiness

Meli'sa Morgan – Still In Love

Michael Watford – Luv 4 2

Michael Watford – Holdin' On

Michael Watford – Love Changeover

Michael Watford – So Into You

Mirage Feat. Gary L – Everything's Gonna Be Alright

Mk – Burning

Modern-Nique – Love's Gonna Get You (91 Remix)

Montego Bay – Everything

Moodymann – Joy (Pt 2)

Mr Fingers – Can U Feel It

Mr Fingers – Closer

My Friend Sam – It's My Pleasure

N-Joi – Anthem

Night Writers, The – Let The Music (Use You)

Nomad – I Wanna Give You Devotion

Nu Shooz – Time Will Tell

Numarx – Do It Good

Pacha – One Kiss (Joey Negro Remix)

Pandella – Pull Our Love Together

Park Avenue – Don't Turn Your Love

Paul Scott – Off The Wall

Phase Ii – Reachin'

Photon Inc. – Give A Little Love

Pin Up Girls – Take Me Away

Planet X – Once Upon A Dancefloor

Precious – Definition Of A Track

Queen Latifah – Come Into My House

Queen Latifah – How Do I Love Theee (Ext Club Mix)

R.E – A Man And His Flute

R.E./Lidell Townsell – Let's Hold On

Ragtyme Featuring Byron Stingily – I Can't Stay Away

Ralphi Rosario Featuring Xavier Gold – You Used To Hold Me

Red Light – Rhythm Formula Ep

Redd – Mr. Right

Reese Project – Direct Me (Joey Negro Remix)

Reese Project – I Believe

Rhythim Is Rhythim – Strings Of Life (Flam-Boy-Ant Mix)

Rhythm Doctor – Esoteric Chakra

Rhythm Section – Thrill Me

Robert Owens – I'll Be Your Friend

Robert Owens – Was I Here Before

Roberta Flack – Uh Uh Ooh Ooh Look Out (Here It Comes)

Rodeo Jones – Get Wise

Roger Sanchez F/Jay Williams – Spirit Lift You Up

Roqui – Lover

Rosie Gaines – I Want U (Hippie Torales Mix)

Round 2 – New Day

Rozlyne Clark – Dancing Is Like Making Love

Sabrynaah Pope – Shelter

Sabrynah Pope – It Works For Me

Shay Jones – When Love Calls

Shirley Murdoch – Let There Be Love

Simone – My Family Depends On Me

Simphonia – Can't Get Over Your Love

Simply Red – Something Got Me Started (Steve Hurley Remix)

Solution – Givin It I Got

Soul Boy – Harmonica Track

Soul Rebellion – Live At The Dive EP

Sound On Sound – Time To Feel (Eric Kupper Dub)

South St Player – Who Keeps Changing Your Mind (Has To Be The Sure Is Pure Mix)

St Etienne – Only Love Can Break Your Heart

Stardust – Music Sounds Better With You

Sterling Void – Runaway Girl

Sub Sub – Space Face

Subterrania Feat Ann Conuselo – Do It For Love

Sugarcubes – Leash Called Love

Sun, Sun, Sun – Curious

Swing 52 – Color Of My Skin

Sybil – Falling In Love

Syndicate 305 – I Promise

T Coy – Da E Mas

T.K Roberts – Closer To My Heart

Tammy Payne – Do You Feel It (Like I Do)

Tears Of Velva – The Way I Feel

Ten City – Fantasy (Maw Mix)

Ten City – My Piece Of Heaven

The Believers – Who Dares To Believe

The Beloved – The Sun Rising

The Daou – Surrender Yourself

The Nick Jones Experience – Music For The Neighborhood

The Nick Jones Experience – Wake Up People

The Overweight Pooch – I Like It

The Reese Project – The Colour Of Love

The Toy Factory – Singing For Money

Tito Puente – Ran Kan Kan/Yellow Label

Tony Moran – Same Sun, Same Sky

Tribal House – Motherland

U.P.I – The Love Thing

UBP And Michael Proctor – Love Don't Live (Ubp Classic Mix)

Ultra Nate – Deeper Love

Ultra Nate – How Long (Farley & Heller Remix)

Ultra Nate – Deeper Love (Missing You)

Underground Resistance Feat Yolanda – Livin for The Night

Urban Blues Project – Deliver Me/Bassline

Urban Rhythm Feat. Roberta Gilliam – Get Your Thing Together

Viola – Little Girl

Wag Ya Tail F/Lonnie Liston Smith – Xpand Ya Mind
Wall Of Sound – Critical
Whyte – Promises

Yasmin – Sacrifice
Yo Bots – I Got It
Yoland Reynolds – Children Of The World
Zoo Experience/Overjoyd – Follow The Vibe

Ralph Lawson – 'Back to Basics' House Top 100 1991–2007

Arguably one of the most respected underground DJs in the world, Ralph Lawson is the original resident (alongside James 'Boggy' Holroyd) at Dave Beer's seminal house night, Back II Basics (where he played the first ever record). Ralph is a hugely in demand international DJ who plays at all the world's top parties, and is also owner of 20:20 Vision (one of house music's longest running and most successful independent labels with an impressive roster of artists) and the originator behind 20:20 Sound System, who travel the world playing to packed out clubs and festivals, fusing cutting-edge technology with live instrumentation.

Here, Ralph shares 100 of the tried and tested tracks that have rocked Back II Basics and floors worldwide since 1991. A genuine visionary and king of the underground House scene, get more info on Ralph's 20:20 Vision label, Sound System and DJing at: www.2020recordings.com or myspace.com/2020soundsystem

2020soundsystem – The Chase
280 West – Scattered Dreams
33 1/3 Queen – Searching
Adonis – No Way Back
Adonis – Lost In The Sound
Angel Moraes – The Cure
Ame Strong – Tout Es Bleu (Fk Remix)
A:Xus Feat. Naomi – Baghdad Cafe (Mood Ii Swing Mix)
Basement Jaxx – Deep Jackin
Basement Jaxx – Flylife
Black Science Orchestra – New Jersey Deep
Boo Williams – A New Beginning
Bpt – Moody
Carl Craig – The Throw
Chez Damier And Ralph Lawson – A Dedication To Jos
Chicken Lips – He Not In
Chubby Chunks Vol1 – Testemant 1
Coco, Steel And Lovebomb – Feel It

Daft Punk – Muzique
Danny Tenaglia – Bottom Heavy
Daphne – When You Love Someone
Dave Angel – New Orchestrations Ep
Dave Angel – Tokyo Stealth Fighter (Carl Craig)
Deep Dish – Chocolate City Love Songs
De–Lite Feat Osc a Child – Wild Times (Mayday Mix)
DJ Gilb'r – Venus
DJum DJum – Difference
DJ Sneak – Title Tbc
Ernest St Laurent – Do Ya Dub
Ernest St Laurent – Be With Me
Faze Action – In The Trees
Fierce Ruling Diva – You Gotta Believe
Fk Ep – Hypnodelic
Fingers Inc – I'm Strong (Dub)
Fingers Inc – Bring Down The Walls
Fluke – Philly
Francois K – Time And Space

Freaks – The Creeps (Steve Bug Mix)
Fred Everything – For Your Pleasure
Flow – Another Time
Funky Green Dogs – Reach For Me
Future Sound Of London – Papua New Guinea
Gabrielle – Forget About The World (Daft Punk Remix)
Galaxy 2 Galaxy – Hi Tech Jazz
Global Communications – The Way
Happy Mondays – Stinkin Thinkin (Farley & Heller Remix)
Headstock – Highly Strung
I Cube – Disco Cubism (Daft Punk Remix)
Jay J – Freaks
Jago – I'm Going To Go (Remix)
Jedi Knights – Intergalactic Funk Transmission
Joint Venture – Master Blaster
Josh One – Contemplation
Julius Papp – Groove Asylum
Justice – Never Be Alone
Kenlou – The Bounce
Leftfield – Not Forgotten
Lfo – Lfo
L'homme Qui Valait 3 Milliard – Foxy Lady
Liberty City – If You Really Love Someone (Murk Remix)
Lil Louis And The World – I Called You
Lucy Pearl – Don't Mess With My Man (Mood Ii Swing Dub)
Mae I – Sweet Melody
Maw Presents People Underground – My Love

Mathew Johnson – Typerope
Mondo Grosso – Souffles H
M I Cara – Casa Beat
Mike Inc – We Call It Acid
My Bloody Valentine – Glider
My Friend Sam – It's My Pleasure
Nightmares On Wax – Dextrous
Paul Woolford – Erotic Discourse
Penn And Chus – From Madrid From Love
Pepe Bradock – Burning
Petra & Co – Just Let Go
Primal Scream – Loaded
Red Planet – Star Dancer
Rhythm Invention – Can't Take It
Rhythm Is Rhythm – It Is What It Is
Rozlyne Clarke – Dancing Is Like Making Love (Dub)
Saro And Black – We Were There
Schatrax – Mispent Years
Sessomato – Feelin' Moody
Sneak – Can't Hide From Your Bud
Stephan Grieder And The Persuader – Naked Women
The African Dream – All In The Same Family
Tim Harper – I Feel A Groove
Terence Fm – Feelin' Kinda High
Vicious Muzik Presents Frozen Bass – Volume 2
Virgo – In A Vision
Visnadi – Racing Tracks

Steve Bicknell – Classic Techno

There are few who have helped to shape a scene and continuously push the boundaries of music and promotion as much as Steve Bicknell. Revered globally as one of the world's most consistent, forward-thinking and innovative nights, his seminal 'Lost' has defined and motivated a new generation of clubbers, DJs, artists and producers with its legendary and global reputation.

Steve was first to book latter day luminaries such as Jeff Mills, Basic Channel, DJ Rolando, Richie Hawtin, Robert Hood and a host of other global visionaries for their first UK outing (and for many, their first foray outside of the US). This is on top of his hugely successful production career. To help you appreciate some of the building blocks of the electronic/techno scene, Steve has compiled 50 essential tracks. For bookings and more info check out: www.lost.co.uk

Aphex Twin – Analogue Bubblebath
Autechre – Autechre Singles Pack
Aztec Mystic – Knights Of The Jaguar
Basic Channel – Octagon
Basic Channel – Phylyps Trak
Chloce – Acid Eiffel
CJ Bolland – The Ravesignal
Daniel Bell – Losing Control
Donna Summer – I Feel Love
Dopplereffekt – Faschist Staat
Drexclya – The Unknown Aquazone
Elektrabel – Elektrabel
Innerzone Orchestra – Bug In The Bass Bin
Jeff Mills – Growth
Jeff Mills – Medium
Jeff Mills – Meeca
Jeff Mills – Cycle 30
Jeff Mills – The Bells
Joey Beltram – Energy Flash
Juan Atkins Model 500 – Planet Earth
Kevin Saunderson – Good Life
Klf – Grim Up North
Kraftwerk – Numbers

Kraftwerk – Trans Europa Express
Lil Louis – Blackout
Mad Mike – The Final Frontier
Mike Parker – Innervisions
Omar S – 111
Paperclip People – Remake (Basic Reshape)
Philius – Ph
Plaid – Not For Threes
Planetary Assault Systems –Planetary Funk Vol. 1
Plastikman – Spastik
Psyche – Crackdown
Rhythim Is Rhythim – Strings Of Life
Richie Hawtin – Fuse
Robert Hood – Minimal Nation
Robert Hood – Moveable Parts
S Robbers – Us Heritage
Sleeparchive – Recycled
Steve Bicknell – Why? And For Whom?
Suburban Knight – The Art Of Stalking
The Evader – No Hats Required
The Martian – Red Planet 4

The Seawolf – The Seawolf
Underground Resistance – Sonic

Various Artists – 1 7
X102 – Discovers The Rings Of Saturn

Nicky Blackmarket – Classic Jungle

This list is provided by Nicky Blackmarket, the legendary DJ, producer and don of all things Drum & Bass, who runs the pivotal Drum & Bass department at Black Market Records (BM Soho) in London's West End. Nicky has an unrivalled knowledge and enthusiasm for the scene and has shared so much with so many. Book him, contact him or learn more at: www.myspace.com/nickyblkmkt or www.bm-soho.com

Adam F – Brand New Funk
Adam F – Circles
Alex Reece – Pulp Fiction
Bad Company – Planet Dust
Bad Company – The Nine
Deep Blue – The Helicopter Tune
Def Con One – Time Is The Fire
Dillinja – Acid Trak
Dillinja – Twist 'Em Out
Dillinja – Grimey
DJ Die – Clear Skies
DJ Krust – Warhead
DJ Marky & XRS – Lk
DJ SS – Lighter
DJ Zinc – 174 Trek
DJ Zinc – Super Sharp Shooter
Dkay & Epilson – Barcelona
Ed Rush, Optical & Fierce – Cutslow (Lokuste Remix)
Goldie – Inner City Life
Jonny L – Piper
Konflict – Messiah
LTJ Bukem – Horizons
LTJ Bukem – Music
Mampi Swift – The One
Marcus Intalex & ST Files – How You Make Me

Feel
Moving Fusion – Turbulence
Nasty Habits – Shadow Boxing
Omni Trio – Renegade Snares
Origin Unknown – Truly One
Origin Unknown – Valley Of The Shadows
P Funk – P Funk Era
Peshay – You Got Me Burning
PFM – One And Only
Q Project – Champion Sound
R'n'Flex – Clingtone 2000
Ram Trilogy – Titan
Ray Keith – Chopper
Renegade – Terrorist
Roni Size – It's Jazzy
Roni Size/Reprazent – Brown Paper Bag
Roni Size/Reprazent – Share The Fall
Rufige Cru – Terminator
Shimon & Andy C – Body Rock
Shimon & Andy C – Quest
Shy FX – Bambaataa
Shy FX & T Power – Shake Ur Body
Shy FX & T Power – Don't Wanna Know
Trace – Sonar
Un-Cut – Midnight
Urban Shakedown – Some Justice

Everything You Need to Know about DJing and Success

DZine – Drum & Bass

Respected DJ, producer and all round D&B aficionado, 'DZine' has provided an impressive list to help you navigate the D&B scene, presenting a cross-section of styles from over the years. To book or contact DJ DZine contact: www.myspace.com/dzine89

808 State – Pacific (Grooverider Remix)
Alex Reece – Basic Principles
Alex Reece – Pulp Fiction
Alix Perez – Vanguard
Andy C – Roll On
Artificial Intelligence – Uprising
Bad Company – The Nine
Big Bud – Fantasy
Boymerang – Mind Control
Boymerang – Still
Breakage – So Vain
Bukem & Epshay – 19.5
Calibre – Crop It Down
Calibre – It's Over
D-Bridge & Instra:Mental – Blush Response
Danny Breaks – The Bear
Digital & Spirit – Phantom Force
Dillinja – The Angels Fell
DJ Crystl – Warpdrive
Ed Rush & Optical – Funktion
Ed Rush & Optical – Gas Mask
Goldie – Inner City Life
Hatiras – Space Invader (J Majik Remix)
High Contrast – Make It Tonight
Hyper On Experience – Lords Of The Null Lines (Foul Play Remix)

J Majik – Love Is Not A Game
J Majik – So Vain
JMJ & Richie – Universal Horn
Jonny L – Piper
LTJ Bukem – Horizons
M.I.S.T. – How You Make Me Feel
Metalheadz – Terminator
Nasty Habits – Here Come The Drums
Nasty Habits – Shadow Boxing
Noisia – The Tide
Omni Trio – Feel Good
Optical – To Shape The Future Remix
Peshay – Miles From Home
Pfm – One & Only
Photek – Ni Ten Ichi Ryu
Photek – Ufo
Roni Size – Brown Paper Bag
Roni Size & Reprazent – Trust Me
Sabre & Vicious Circle – Endless
Solid State – Just A Vision (M.I.S.T. Remix)
Source Direct – Call & Response
Studio Pressure – Jump
Uncut – Midnight (M.I.S.T. Remix)
Wax Doctor – Atmospheric Funk
Wax Doctor – Kid Caprice

Lisa Lashes' Essential Hard Dance Recommendations

Lisa Lashes has sustained her position as the world's No. 1 hard dance DJ for many years. Fanatical about the hard dance scene, she travels the world weekly to rock parties. Here she has compiled a list of tried and tested dancefloor bullets. Find out more about Lisa here: www.djlisalashes.com

99th Floor Elevators – Hooked
Ace Of Space – 9mm Is A Classic
Age Of Love – Age Of Love (Marcel Woods Mix)
Anne Savage – Real Freaks
Ben Johnson – Come 1 (Nick Sentience Epic Remix)
Benny Benassi – Satisfaction (Pez Tellet Mix)
Bk – Playing With Knives
Bk – Revolution
Bk & Nick Sentience – Flash
Bk & Phil Reynolds – (Instru) Mental
BK And Tissera – Zulu Nation
Bk Pres Razor Babes – Come On Baby
Blue Amazon – No Other Love
Brainbug – Nightmare
Chris C – Freefall
Commander Tom – Are Am Eye
Cortina – Higher
Cortina – Music Is Moving (Kumara Mix)
Cosmic Gate – Fire Wire
Crw – I Feel Love
Da Hool – Meet Her At The Love Parade
Dejure – Sanctuary
DJ Misjah & DJ Tim – Access
DJ Scott Project – U I Got A Feeling
DJ Shredda – Chainsaw (The Crow Mix)
Ed Real And Coalition – 20,000 Hardcore Members
Fergie & Bk – Hoover And Horns (Ingo Mix)
Fergie Vs Trauma – There Out To Get Me

Gridlock 3000 – Fantastic Things
Ian M – Dreamer
Jonah – Ssssst . . . (Listen)
Joy Kitikonti – Joyenergiser (Mauro Picotto Personal Mix)
Jurgen Vries – The Theme (Jamx Dumonde Mix)
Lab 4 – Candyman
Lee Haslam – Music Is The Drug
Lee Jeffry And Justin Bourne – Drop The Dime
Lisa Lashes – Looking Good (Lashed)
Lisa Lashes – We Came We Saw
Lisa Lashes – What Can You Do For Me?
Lisa Lashes – Unbelievable
Lisa Lashes And Anne Savage – The Crow
Lisa Pin-Up – Baddest Mutha
Lisa Pin-Up – Future Acid House (Prime Mover Mix)
Love Revolution – Give It To Me Baby (Jon Doe Mix)
Marco V – Loops And Tings
Marco V – Godd
Mauro Picotto – Lizard (Claxixx Mix)
Mauro Picotto – Pulsar (Picotto Tes Mix)
Megamind – Taub
Miss Behavin – Such A Feeling
Neon Lights – Bullet From & Gun
Nick Rafferty And The Coalition – U
Nrg – Never Lost His Hardcore
Pants And Corset – Malice In Wonderland
Paul Glazby – Beautiful

Everything You Need to Know about DJing and Success

Paul Glazby – Muthafucker

Paul Glazby – Hostile

Phatt B – And The Drum Machine

Praga Khan – Injected With A Poison (Bk & Nick Sentience Mix)

Push – Universal Nation (Dumonde Mix)

Quench – Dreams (Tony De Vit Mix)

Rob Tissera Vs Quake – The Day Will Come (Steve Hill Vs K-Series Mix)

Shiva – Dreams (Paul Glazby Remix)

Signum – What Ya Got 4 Me (Vocal Mix)

Signum Feat Scott Mac – Coming On Strong

Steve Morley – Reincarnations

Storm – Time To Burn (Nick Sentience Mix)

Tomcraft – Loneliness (Harder Mix)

Tony De Vit – The Dawn (Paul James Mix)

Tony De Vit – Are You All Ready

Tony De Vit – I Don't Care

DJ Dino Moran – World House Top 50

South Africa's finest house DJ selects 50 all time House bombs with that 'world' feel.

With successful productions and over 17 years' DJing experience alongside the biggest names at the best South African clubs and parties, Dino knows how to rock a crowd. For info and bookings visit: www.dinomoran.com

Africanism – Ve Ou La

Afro Madusa – Pasilda

Alex S – Senti Sabi

Awa Band – Timba

B.O.P – Victory Song

Bongo Loverz Feat Ursula Cuesta – La Fiesta

Bongo Mafin – Mari Ye Fefa

Carl Cox – Black Shaolin

Cesaria Evora – Carnival De Sao Vincent

Chus & Chebalos – Echoes

Claude Monet – Voodoo Bounce

Conga Squad – Ka Nzenze

Copyright – Warrior Dance

Danny Marquez & Ferry B – Afrocatalans

Danny Marquez & Hanna Hais – Jazz Samba

Datar – B

David Morales And Bad Yard Club – Da Program

Dennis Ferrer – Funu

Dino Moran With Milk & Sugar – Gumba Fire

DJ Gregory – Tropical Sound Clash

DJ Sneak – Que Pasa

Dubtribe Sound System – Nothing Is Impossible

Faze Action – Kariba

Grant Nelson – Ethnicity

Hardsoul & New Cool Collective – Bounson

Havanna Club – Babae

Hoxton Whores Feat Dina Vass – Come Be With Me

Junior Jack – E-Samba

Khaya – Cheza

Leftfield – Afro Left (Ext. DJ Mix)

M.A.W – Work

Magic System – Premier Gaou

Martin Solveig & Salif Keita – Madan

More Kante – Yeke Yeke

Olav Basoski – Rubato

Pepe Link – Kalakuta

Quicksound – Stop Fooling Around
Rasmus Faber Feat. Clara Mendes – Demanda
Raul Rincon – Indigenous People
Salome De Bahia – Outro Lugar
Samba La Casa – Friday Marshmello
Scientific Soul – Karibu Dance

Stephan M & Sammy K – African Journey
Sumo Feat Clarisse Muvemba – Nini
Sydenham & Ferrer – Lost Tribes Of Ibadan
Upz – Afrikawo-Man
Wawa – Sombrita
Yves Larock – Zookie

DJ Jafar – Classic Deep House Tracks

One half of Jafar & Touch, owner of the Artizan record label, promoter of many excellent parties and all-round good guy and top DJ, Jafar is one of the hardest working spinners on the circuit, always spreading his infectious positivity. Here is his selection of all-time deep grooves. For bookings and info check out: www.artizanmusic.co.uk

Azymuth – Space Jazz Carnival
Ben Watt – Lone Cat
Black Science Orchestra – New Jersey Deep
Black Science Orchestra – Save Us
Blaze – Lovelee Dae
Blaze – My Beat
Blue 6 – Music And Wine
Blue 6 – Sweeter Love
Carton – Can't Be Without (Chez Damier and Ron Trent Prescription Mix)
Chez Damier – Keep On
Chez Damier – Your Love
Dave Clarke – Southside
Dave Warrin – Shine On
Demarkus Lewis – I See You
Dennis Ferrer & Jerome Sydenham – Sandcastles
Dennis Ferrer – Soul Collectives Vol. 1-3
Derrick Carter – Squaredancing In A Round House
DJ Gregory – Attend 1
DJ Pierre – The Switch
DJ Sneak – You Can't Hide From Your Bud

DJ Spen – Disco Dreams Vol. 1 & 2
Eric Kupper – Presents Organika
Etienne De Cracy – Prix Choc
Everything But The Girl – 5 Fathoms
Francois K – Time And Space (Farley & Heller Mix)
Frank Roger & DJ Deep – In & Out E.P.
Fred Everything – 1 For Me
Fresh & Low Groovin You
Glenn Underground – Lounge Excursions
Global Communications – The Way
Guy Called Gerald – Voodoo Ray
Head Nodding Society – 'Nudge Up
Inland Knights – Situations
Inner City – Big Fun
Isolee – Beau Mot Plage
Iz & Diz – Love Vibe (Original and Jimpster Remixes)
Jafar & Touch Ft Rich Medina – The Undeniable Truth
Jam & Spoon – Stellar
Jaydee – Plastic Dreams
Jimpser – Message For The DJ

Johnny D & Nicky P – Wild Kingdom

Johnny Fiasco – Calmado

Jon Cutler – Its Yours (Chez)

Jt Donaldson – Do Dat

Julian Jabre – Gardens

Justin Martin – Sad Piano (Jimpster/Charles Webster Remix)

Kenlou – The Bounce (Maw)

Kerri Chandler – A Basement, A Red Light And A Feeling

Kerri Chandler – Atmosphere (The Lost Dubs)

Kerri Chandler – Trionisphere (The Whole Series)

Kevin Yost – Night Of A Thousand Drums

Lenny Fontana – Spread Love

Les Macons De La Musique – No Time To Lose (Johnny Fiasco's Dirty Hands Mix)

Linkwood Family – Miles Away Firecracker

Lisa Shaw – Always

Lo:Rise – 21st Century Blues (Charles Webster Dub Mix)

Martha Cinader – When The Body Calls

Masters At Work – I Can't Get No Sleep

Masters At Work – Love And Happiness

Mateo And Matos – Celebrate Life

Miguel Migs – Future Flight

Mike Dunn – God Made Me Funky

Mondo Grosso – Star Suite

Mood II Swing – Do It Your Way

Moodymann – I Can't Kick This Feeling When It Hits

Mr Scruff – Get A Move On

Musica Felix – Buzzing Fly

Nathan Haines Feat.Verna Francis – Earth Is The Place

Nu Mood Orchestra – Aphrodisiac

Nu Yorican Soul – The Nervous Track

Osunlade Pres Scuba Bambino – Decourage (Charles Webster Mix)

Osunlade – Touched My Soul

Papillon – Higher

Pepe Braddock – Burning

Playin' 4 The City – Backside

Poussez – Tell Me How You Do

Random Factor – Convergence

Rodamaal – Insomnia

Romanthony – Ministry Of Love

Ron Trent – Instant Coco

Rozzo – Into Your Heart

Salome De Bahia – Outra Lugar

Seafoam – Mumbo Jumbo

Seal – Violet (Scott Wozniak Mix)

Sebastian Barquet – Nuage

Spirit Catcher – Dirty Circuit

Spooky – Little Bullet

Stacy Kidd – Let Love Enter

Stargazer – Intergalactic Buffer

The Beloved – The Sun Rising

The Detroit Experiment – Think Twice

The Timewriter – Diary Of A Lonely Sailor

Theo Parrish – Moonlight, Music & You

Tortured Soul – Might Do Something Wrong

Trentemoller – Le Champagne

Underworld – Dark And Long

United Future Organisation – Flying Saucer (Kings Of Tommorrow Remix)

Veena Harlem – Break It Down

Vince Watson – Moments In Time

X-Press 2 – The Sound

Essential Trance Tracks by John '00' Fleming

A DJ career spanning more than twenty years from the ripe old age of fifteen has afforded John 00 the sort of experience that most other DJs can only dream of. Never afraid to push the boundaries in the projects that he turns his hand to, he is the owner of the hugely successful J00F recordings and hosts his own radio show on Ministry of Sound/DI.FM, the highly popular Global Trance Grooves.

A musical taste that transcends genres and his determination to seek out fresh, new, exciting music has resulted in John playing in almost every corner of the world and selling over one million CD compilations.

John's work has been recognised many times over the years with rankings in various charts including Tranceaddict and *DJ* Magazine. Here he selects a range of classic Trance-based tracks that continue to work clubs around the world. For bookings, info and gig listings check out: www.john00fleming.com and www.joof.co.uk

Airwave – Above The Sky
Astral Projection – Mahadeva
Ayla – Ayla (Part 1 Taucher)
BBE – Seven Days And One Week
Binary Finary – 1998
Blank & Jones – Cream
Body Sock – Full Moon
BT – Flaming June
BT – Godspeed
Chicane – Saltwater
Christian West – Eterna
Cygnus-X – The Orange Theme (Solar Stone Remix)
Delerium – Silence (DJ Tiesto Remix)
Digital Blonde – Legato + At Least One Other of his Many Many Anthems
DJ Tiesto – Urban Train
Dumonde – Tomorrow
Energy 52 – Cafe Del Mar
Faithless – Insomnia
Ferry Corsten – Indigo
Freefall – Skydive (Mara Remix)
Goldenscan – Sunrise (DJ Tiesto Remix)

Grace – Not Over Yet (Breeder's It Is Now remix)
Grace – Skin On Skin (Orange Mix)
Infect Mushroom – I'm the Superviser
John 00 Fleming – Free
Jones and Stephenson – First Rebirth
Li Kwan – Point Zero
Lost Tribe – Gamemaster
Lsg – Netherworld
Man With No Name – Teleport
Miika Muisma – Orion (Misja Helsloot Remix)
Mogwai – Viola
Nalin and Kane – Open Your Eyes
Nu NRG – Dreamland
Nu-NRG – Dreamland (Original Mix)
Oliver Prime – Radiance
Olmec Heads – Spiritualised (Astral Remix)
Patient Saints – Imperpetuum Mobila
Paul van Dyk – For an Angel
Planisphere – NYE
Push – Strange World
Push – Universal Nation
Solar Stone – Seven Cities

Solar Stone – Solarcoaster
Three Drives – Greece 2000
Tilt – Children
Tilt – I Dream (Ressurection Mix)
Transa – Transtar

Veracocha – Carte Blanche
Vibrasphere – Seven Days to Daylight Days
Way Out West – The Fall
X-Cabs – Neuro 99

Old Skool Hardcore

Here's a selection of tracks as compiled by the incredibly knowledgeable veterans on the forum
at www.hardcorewillneverdie.com, where you can also finds hundreds of classic archived mixes
from dance music legends.

2 Bad Mice – Bombscare
2-X-Treme – X-Treme Theme
33 1/3 Queen – Searchin'
4Hero – Mr Kirk's Nightmare
808 State – Pacific State
A.E.K. – X AmountOf Juice E.P.
Acen-Close Your Eyes
Acen – Trip To The Moon Pt.2
Altern-8 – The Vertigo E.P.
Aphrodisiac – Song Of The Siren
Baby D – Daydreaming
Baby D – Let Me Be Your Fantasy
Bassix – Close Encounters
Bizarre Inc – Playing With Knives
Body Snatch – Just 4 U London
Bug Kann & The Plastic Jam
Carl Cox – I Want You Forever
Cool Hand Flex – Whip Lash
Cybersonic – Technarchy
David Charlesworth – Energiser
Desired State – Dance The Dream
Dionne – Come Get My Love
DJ Red Alert & Mike Slammer – In Effect
DLivin – Why
Dragonfly – Visions Of Rage
Electribe 101 – Talking With Myself

Ellis Dee – Brock Out
Eon – Spice
Epitome Of Hype – Ladies With An Attitude
Family Foundation – Express Yourself
Fantasy U.F.O. – Fantasy
Fierce Ruling Diva – Floor Filler
Fingers Inc. feat. Larry Heard – Can You Feel It?
Forgemasters – Track With No Name
Frankie Knuckles – Tears
Frankie Knuckles – Your Love/Baby Wants To
Ride
Future Sound Of London – Papua New Guinea
G Double E – Fire When Ready
Genaside II – Narra Minds/Sirens Of Acre Lane
G Double E – Fire When Ready
GTO – Pure
Guy Called Gerald – Voodoo Ray
Human Resource – Dominator
Humanoid – Stakker Humanoid
Hypersonic – Dance Tones
Joey Beltram – Energy Flash
Kariya – Baby Let Me Love You
Joey Beltram – Energy Flash
King Bee – Back By Dope Demand
King Bee – Must Bee The Music
KLF – 3AM Eternal

LFO – LFO
Lil' Lois – French Kiss
Liquid – Sweet Harmony
Manix – Oblivion (Head In The Clouds)
Meatbeat Manifesto – Radio Babylon
Metalheadz – Terminator
Midi Rain – Crack Train
Midi Rain – Eyes
MK13 – Techzone
Naz a.k.a. Naz – Started Again E.P.
Nebular II – Séance/Anthema
Nexus 21 – Real Love
Nightmares On Wax – Aftermath/It's A Feeling
Nitro Deluxe – Let's Get Brutal
N-Joi – Adrenalin E.P.
Nomad – (I Wanna Give You) Devotion
Nookie – Gonna Be Alright (Cloud 9 Remix)
NRG – I Need Your Love
Omni Trio – I Need Your Love
Orbital – Chime
Patti Day – Right Before My Eyes
Petra & Co – Just Let Go)
Phuture Assassins – Shot Like Dis
Pressure Drop – Feeling Good
Project 1 – It's A Moment In Time
Psychotropic – Only For The Headstrong
Psychotropic – Hypnosis
Q Project – Champion Sound
Quadrophonia – Quadrophonia
Quartz – Meltdown
Raze – Break For Love
Rebel MC – Wickedest Sound
Rebel MC – Tribal Bass
Reece & Sanantonio – Rock To The Beat
Renegade Soundwave – The Phantom
Rhythm Section – Atomic E.P.
Rhythm Section – Midsummer Madness E.P.

Rum & Black – Slaves
Satin Storm – Lets Get Together
Secret Desire – White Light/Anna Lies
Shades Of Rhythm – Homicide/Exorcist
Shades Of Rhythm – Sounds Of Eden
Shut Up And Dance – Lamborghini
Shut Up And Dance – I'm Ravin' I'm Ravin'
SL2 – DJs Take Control/Way In My Brain
Silver Bullet – Bring Forth the Guillotine
Sonic Experience – Protein/M.T.S.
Sonz Of A Loop Da Loop Era – Far Out
Sonz Of A Loop Da Loop Era – Peace & Loveism
Sweet Exorcist – Test Four
Subject 13 – Eternity
T99 – Anasthasia
Tango – Killer
Tekno Too – Jet Starr
The Lost – The Gonzo
The Prodigy – Charly/Your Love
The Ragga Twins – Spliff Head
The Ragga Twins – Wipe The Needle
The Scientist – The Exorcist
The Scientist – The Bee
The Source feat. Candi Staton – You Got The Love
Tic Tac Toe – Ephemeral
Tight Control – Hardcore Piano
Toxic – The Toxic E.P.
Tricky Disco – Tricky Disco
Ultranate – It's Over Now
Unique 3 – Weight For Bass
Unique 3 – Rhythm Takes Control
Urban Shakedown – Some Justice
Xpansions – Elevation (Move Your Body)
X-Tatic – X-Tatic E.P.
Zero B – Module E.P.

Bonus Resource 12: Sample DJ Contract and Contract of Agreement for Services

Over the page you will find an example of a professional contract which you can adapt according to your own needs. You will also have to adapt your contract to reflect what you are able to request and expect, dependent upon your experience, ability to pull a crowd and reputation. If you visit www.musiclegalforms.com/cat-djresidency.html you can also download contracts.

Sample Contract of Agreement for Services

Your Name _____

Your Address _____

Your Phone & Email Contacts _____

The following letter sets forth and, when executed, shall constitute a binding agreement between _____, herein after referred to as 'Employer' and _____, herein referred to as 'the DJ', entered into this ___th day of_____ 20_____.

It is mutually agreed between the parties as follows:

The DJ agrees to perform for the Employer on the ___th day of _____ in the year of _____. This service shall be between the hours of _____ and _____ on the aforementioned date at _____ in _____. The DJ (or a designated representative of the DJ) shall be allowed into the club at least one hour prior to opening for sound check.

The Employer will compensate the DJ in the amount of _____ *(put the currency you are dealing in here)* of which 50% is due no later than 30 days prior to the engagement date as a deposit to secure the DJ's availability for the performance. Payments shall be made to _____ *(fill in your account details here)*. The remainder of the DJ's fee _____ *(enter amount in the currency here)* shall be paid in cash to the DJ prior to the start of the DJ's performance. The DJ shall have no obligation to perform under this agreement unless the DJ has received such fee set forth herein. The DJ shall have the right, but not the obligation to terminate this agreement immediately, at which time the Employer shall be liable for actual damages incurred by the DJ as of such termination date, including loss of earnings and expenses incurred. Any initial payment received by the DJ shall be deemed non-refundable pursuant of this paragraph.

For events where you need to travel and stay overnight to perform:

The Employer will provide at least one night of lodging at a hotel located within a reasonable distance to the event, which will be paid in full by the Employer prior to the DJ's arrival and check-in. The Employer will also provide 1 roundtrip ticket on the DJ's carrier of choice. The Employer will provide travel to and from the airport/station as well as travel to and from the event. All travel expenses shall be paid by the Employer in advance. *(Depending on what your DJ reputation is, you may be able to specify the type of hotel accommodation, airline and transport used to collect you from the airport/station and hotel).*

The DJ allows his name to be used in any promotion related to this event in the form of '_____'. The Employer agrees to include the URL _____ on all promotional materials including but not limited to flyers, print ads, posters and any and all forms of advertising concerning the event at which the DJ will be performing. The DJ shall be provided with a copy of any promotional items bearing his name in a timely fashion up to and including the date of service. The Employer agrees to allow the aforementioned promotional materials to be used by the DJ in the future as part of the website and portfolio of the DJ.

The DJ agrees to supply all musical needs for his performance. The Employer shall provide any music to be used outside the DJ's performance. The Employer will provide the following professional sound equipment and services, which shall meet or exceed standards customary in the industry for such equipment and services, so that the artist may satisfactorily perform under the provisions contained herein:

a) Two (2) Pioneer CD-J 1000's or two (2) CD-J 800's

b) One (1) Rane rotary mixer (MP2016), UREI 1620, Allen & Heath Xone, or Pioneer 500 DJM

c) A clean sounding booth monitor (located in front or to the left of the DJ at or above ear level)

d) Ample surfaces (tables and chairs) to keep records and CDs off the floor

e) Ample lighting

The DJ will provide his own headphones. Any recording of the DJ's set is not permitted without the DJ's prior written consent.

The DJ shall have the right to cancel this contract: a) in the event of illness; b) in the event of an 'Act of God'; c) in the event of an act of terrorism or war (whether or not declared) which occurs in the host city or which impairs the DJ's ability to travel to, from or within the host city; d) if necessary work permits and/or visas cannot be obtained by the DJ due to the fault of the Employer; and e) if the transfer of monies has not been received by the DJ from the Employer in accordance with this agreement. If the DJ elects to cancel this contract for any of the foregoing reasons, the DJ is no longer obligated to fulfil his duties at the performance, but is still entitled to his fees. In the event the DJ must cancel, the DJ agrees to notify the Employer immediately and aid in finding a replacement DJ for the event.

In the event the Employer cancels within sixty (60) days of the scheduled event, the DJ shall be compensated a total of 50% of his pay or _____ UK pounds for time and effort put into preparing for the event. If the Employer cancels the scheduled event within thirty (30) days of the scheduled event, the DJ shall be compensated his entire fee as set forth in this agreement. Should the Employer cancel more than sixty (60) days prior to the event, this contract shall become null and void.

This agreement is the entire agreement between the parties and shall not be modified, except by an instrument of writing, signed by each parties duly authorised to execute such modification. This agreement has been entered into in the country of _____, and the validity, interpretation and legal effect of this agreement shall be governed by the laws of the country of _____. All claims, disputes or disagreements which may arise out of the interpretation, performance or breach of this agreement shall be submitted exclusively to the courts of the country of_____.

This agreement shall be binding upon and inure to the benefit of the parties hereto and their respective heirs, representatives, successors and assigns.

Please indicate your acceptance and concurrence with the terms and conditions set forth in this agreement by executing the acknowledgement below and returning via facsimile the same to the other party.

DJ's Signature:_____ Date: _____

Employer's Signature:_____ Date: _____

Bonus Resource 13: Sample Invoice Template

Your Logo _____

Your Name _____

Your Address _____

Your Website _____

Your Email _____

Your Telephone Number _____

Invoice number _____

Date _____

Client name _____

Client address _____

_____

_____

Client Post/Zip code _____

Event Date _____

Event Type _____

DJ Services Cost

No name DJ £ _____

(Any other services/Equip etc) £ _____

Total £ _____

Please pay by **bank transfer** into named account beneath within 7 days for the above services rendered. *(or pre-agreed date as in contract)*

Bank: _____

Sort Code: _____

Account Number: _____

Account Name: No name DJ

Or into Paypal Address below:

Nonamedj@hotmail.com

If you are VAT registered (or the equivalent) you should also include your VAT number. At present the UK threshold for declaring yourself for VAT is annual turnover of £70,000 or above.

Bonus Resource 14: Build Your Own Website Quickly and Easily

Whereas you used to have to employ the skills of a professional web programmer to create a website for you, in the past couple of years there have been some exciting online developments giving you the tools to quickly and easily create your own site. You just need to know where to look.

The best of these sites have all created simple to follow video (and written) tutorials online (as well as the user-generated ones that you can find through your web-browser). Once you've decided which provider you're going to use, simply utilise their support and training resources and you'll have a site live in no time.

The pick of the bunch are:

1) www.Wix.com – If you want to create a 'flash' site, there are 100's of templates to choose from. Simple 'click, edit and drop' technology.

2) www.MoonFruit.com – Award winning software with 'drag and drop' editing. Add social networking tools, 3rd party content, images, MP3s and video.

3) www.Weebly.com – Very easy to use 'click and drag' functionality. There are numerous templates and you can add YouTube videos and audio.

4) www.Jimdo.com – Another great 'click and drag' template-based web creation platform. Lots of designs to choose from.

5) www.WordPress.com – Originally a blog-based facility, Wordpress's open source means 1000's of developers around the world are constantly creating 'plug-ins' that you can add to your Wordpress site for free, such as SEO tools and different 'skins/themes'.

6) www.Podomatic.com – If you want a simple site to share podcasts and music mixes you'll be up and running in minutes

7) www.SoundCloud.com – Rapidly becoming the favoured choice for DJs and musicians to share music, mixes and audio. You don't have your own site but you have your own account and file storage.

8) www.MixCloud.com – Similar in layout and facility to SoundCloud.

9) www.apple.com/ilife/tutorials/#iweb – All Apple Mac computers come with the iLife software installed, which contains iWeb, a very simple program for creating professional looking sites.

10) www.madebyanalogue.co.uk – Excellent for professional design.

11) www.Artisteer.com – One of the first web-design automation products that instantly creates fantastic looking, unique website templates and blog themes for Joomla,Wordpress, Blogger and Drupal.

12) www.tumblr – Instant, attractive blog sites created.

If you would prefer someone else to create a site for you, I recommend that you sign up to www.elance.com and post a project brief. This one resource is rapidly shifting the way that business is done and is not only saving me time, but money, effort and stress. For a good overview of how elance can work for you I recommend: http://www.amazon.com/4-Hour-Workweek-Escape-Live-Anywhere/dp/0307353133

It's free to post a project on elance (they make their money by taking a small percentage from the winning service provider's fee) and in a matter of hours you will have people from all over the world bidding for your project. It's a transparent system like eBay – you can see everyone's portfolio of work, their earnings to date and their feedback score on critical areas such as price, communication, deliverability and competence. There are 1000s of service providers all over the world who will be able to deliver your project at very competitive prices and you simply interview (online) or select one that feels right for you.

A good tip to include in your project brief, to help get the best possible price and to eliminate potential service providers not up to the task, is to include the sentence: 'This is a very simple task for a candidate with the relevant skills. Only provide your very best quote and please, no time-wasters. All rights pertaining to the design of this site remain the intellectual property and copyright of the client and will need to be signed in an agreement stating so'.

If you are setting up your own website you firstly need to buy a domain name. A domain is your website name, e.g. www.yourname.com. Think of your domain name as your house number. If you don't have a house number then it will be difficult for the postman (or your friends) to find you. To check availability and to reserve your domain name I'd recommend that you go to 123reg (http://bit.ly/123Reg). Once you have your domain name, it's now time to purchase your hosting space (with Wix, MoonFruit, Podomatic, Soundcloud and Mixcloud the basic hosting is provided for you). Imagine hosting as your piece of land to build your house on (your website). Once you have your hosting (land), you are now in a position to build your website (your house). Go to HostGator to buy your hosting space at: http://bit.ly/HostgatorWebSite.

Now that you have your domain name and (if you need it, your hosting) you can now create your site using your preferred program. It's a matter of personal preference, but we are fortunate that today we have so many tools to make web design and editing accessible to the part-time hobbyist.

These last two pages alone are worth hundreds of pounds in value if you utilise the information correctly. Act on what I have shared with you and I guarantee you success.

Bonus Resource 15: Marketing Tools and Sites to Help Promote Your Music

Following is a list of some superb sites that will really help you get more from the internet. Many of these are 'insider secrets', so enjoy discovering the powerful tools on offer here.

www.getresponse.com – An easy email marketing software that delivers your email campaigns, online surveys, newsletters, follow-ups and autoresponders.

www.aweber.com – Email marketing software helping businesses automate email follow-up and newsletter delivery.

www.dropbox.com – The easiest way to store, sync and share files online. Used by producers, record labels and musicians for distributing their promos along with digital reaction sheets.

www.transmissionfm.com – DJ promotion network with free mix hosting, user profiles, mixes for download, and on-demand and live online streaming radio.

www.clickbank.com – Clickbank is the internet's leading retailer of digital products. Whether you're looking to sell, promote or shop for digital goods.

www.cj.com – Commission Junction is a global leader in affiliate marketing, online marketing, and search engine marketing.

www.eyejot.com – Eyejot is an easy way to send and receive video email for free. No download or installation is required. Send a webcam message or uploaded video file to any email address.

www.cafepress.com – Turn your designs into merchandise. No minimum orders and drop shipping around the world. You can design it, or sell it on CafePress.

www.wix.com – Create a free website with Wix.com. Use Wix free website builder to design stunning Flash website designs with drag-and-drop system.

www.wordpress.com – One of the best open source platforms for beginner web builders.

www.weebly.com – Create a free website or blog in minutes by using a simple drag-and-drop interface.

www.moonfruit.com – Moonfruit offers a free website builder that creates beautiful websites simply with no ads and no catches.

www.phpbb.com – Create a forum on your website and help drive traffic and discussion within a community.

www.marketerschoice.com – Features the best shopping cart software and ecommerce shopping cart service available.

www.ezs3.com – Amazon's S3 hosting. Enables you to put video on your sites with no issues at all. Fast, reliable, and easy.

www.gotomeeting.com/fec/webinar – Conduct webinars/online meetings for up to 1000 people

www.ekmpowershop.com – Easy, efficient way to set up an online store.

www.fotolia.com – Buy and sell royalty-free stock photos. Source of images for your design work.

www.animoto.com – Turn your still images into striking, unique promotional tools.

www.istockphoto.com – Select from 1000s of images for your design work.

www.befunky.com – Great tool for adding professional, designer effects to your images for free.

www.photobucket.com – Image hosting, free photo sharing and video sharing. Upload your photos, host your videos, and share them with friends and family.

www.moonpig.com – Personalised designs online.

www.slide.com – Turn your images into impressive presentations.

www.goodprint.co.uk – Handy site for designing your own business cards, letterheads, compliment slips, postcards and labels online. You can also upload your own design. They provide worldwide shipping and unique template designs.

www.pressbox.co.uk – Free press release distribution and news.

www.xtranormal.com – Turn your ideas into animated videos. If you can type, you can create a professional, tailor-made video.

www.whatthefont.com – Upload a sceenshot of a font and this software will tell you what font it is.

www.bradcallen.com/our_products.php – Loads of great web tools are available from this site.

www.elance.com – Outsource your projects or tasks to expert programmers, designers, coders, writers, developers, translators, marketeers, researchers and admin contractors with tested skills.

www.rentacoder.com – Rent a Coder is an international marketplace where people who need custom software developed can find coders in a safe and business-friendly environment.

www.agentsofvalue.com – Outsource IT and basic admin work for very competitive rates.

www.1websiteseo.com – Search engine optimisation specialists.

www.kunaki.com – DVD manufacturing, publishing, distribution and fulfilment.

www.lulu.com – Turn your document into a physical book for sale and distribution.

www.surveymonkey.com – Stay in the loop – create online surveys for your database and customers.

www.gbbo.co.uk – Getting British Business Online is a joint initiative by Google, Enterprise UK, BT, e-skills UK and many other partners to help small businesses.

www.uk.tilllate.com/en/all – The world's biggest nightlife community. Promote your events and leave reviews and photos.

www.dontstayin.com – Add events, reviews, photos to promote your event.

Bonus Resource 16: Social Networking Site Links and Tips

Social networking is probably the most effective online marketing tool that you can utilise to promote your business at no cost at all. One thing is for sure, the most successful online people, businesses and services have all embraced social networking according to what its real purpose is which is enabling people to interact and connect regardless of distance, time and place.

Here's a list of the most popular sites followed by a few considerations.

www.facebook.com
www.myspace.com
www.twitter.com
www.bebo.com
www.friendster.com
www.hi5.com
www.orkut.com
www.perfspot.com
www.zorpia.com
www.netlog.com
www.linkedin.com

1) Remember what your objective/goal is. If you want to market yourself in a certain way, the content, information and images that you share should all be consistent and support your objective.

2) Don't be naïve. Realise that what may be a 'private laugh between friends', be it a comment, photo or shared link, becomes 'public domain' once shared on many of these sites, often remaining online in cyber world for years and years to come. Does it suit you to have certain private moments shared globally?

3) Beware the increasing trend of prospective partners, friends and, more importantly, employers using these platforms as a simple, cost-effective and 'telling' way to do background checks. It can either work for or against you.

4) Don't post obscenities or copyrighted material.

5) Remember your manners.

6) Do not take it badly if someone declines or ignores your invitation to connect. That's their option. They have their own personal reasons, and don't make assumptions as to what they are.

7) Join social networking sites that cater to your preferences and whose members will have potential use for your services.

8) Try and remain consistent, positive and constructive in your posts – remember all we have said about people wanting to do business with likeable, capable and positive people.

9) Don't advertise using a pushy market strategy. 'Soft selling' is more welcome.

10) Your site should contain all the relevant information about you and your services. Don't overdo your member profile.

11) Give away free mixes, post articles and share links.

12) Make your page reader-friendly.

13) Join and participate actively in live discussions and forums. Aside from making your presence known, you can establish your particular expertise in a field. In a short period of time, you may have other members heading to your site and checking you out.

14) Do update your site regularly. There is no greater reason why people will visit your site than for the simple fact that it contains the latest and juiciest information that is related to your area of knowledge, services and products.

15) Check your site all the time for messages left by the other members. You should never forget to reply to these messages, to show your respect to people who've taken the time to communicate with you.

16) Don't forget to establish long-term relationships by visiting the other members' sites and pages, showing the same courtesy they have shown by visiting your site. The more people you help achieve their goals, the more people will help you achieve yours.

17) Be aware of the time spent on these sites and don't let them become a substitute for real human connection and interaction. Limit your time on them and stay 'on purpose' in your usage. Mindless browsing can actually be a destructive form of procrastination. Plan your work and work your plan.

Here are some additional tools and sites to help you improve your MySpace templates and layouts

http://www.freelayouts.com/myspace-layouts

http://www.myspacelibrary.com

http://www.pyzam.com/ – over 3000 MySpace templates

http://www.createblog.com/myspace-layouts

http://www.profilepimpz.com

http://www.myspace-pimper.net

http://www.pimperz.com

http://www.tikistadium.com/layoutpimper

Bonus Resource 17: Sources of Wisdom and Inspiration

There's a wealth of empowering insight, ideas and knowledge that rarely gets shared in the mainstream media or the classroom. These kinds of resources have had a huge impact on my life, so I've included an introductory list of recommended links if this interests you.

www.bit.ly/RamplingRecommendedInspiredReading – Many links to my recommended inspired reading and audio.

www.learnhowtobeadj.com – Sign up to receive free insights and tips. Also, my team and I are available for DJing training, internet-business training, motivation, coaching and speaking engagements, be they for private events, at schools and colleges or for workshops. Email us at: info@learnhowtobeadj.com

www.ted.com – Fantastic resource with hundreds of ten-minute lectures from the world's leading thinkers.

www.tut.com – Sign up for inspiring, personalised daily quotes. Created by Mike Dooley who featured in *The Secret*.

www.hayhouseradio.com – Radio for your soul. Louise Hay's internationally respected online radio site, home to many of the world's best, including Wayne Dyer, and Cheryl Richardson.

www.drwaynedyer.com – Official site of 'the father of motivation', Dr. Wayne Dyer. His words and thoughts have inspired millions around the world and helped people find happiness. Essential reading and listening.

www.thesecretlawofattractiontool.com – Learn how to attract your goals into your life with this proven and simple technique. Hugely powerful.

www.brainbullet.com – Make changes in your life effortlessly and smartly. This is powerful, customisable software that enables you to fire off subconscious messages on your computer screen to help you make the changes you've been meaning to. If you're looking at your screen, double up and make it productive.

www.inventionthroughintention.com – Everything starts with an intention. Invention through Intention helps you tap into this power.

www.chrishoward.com – Internationally acclaimed lifestyle and wealth strategist. For almost two decades, Chris has researched the success strategies of the world's greatest business, philanthropic and spiritual minds.

www.harveker.com – Arguably the world's leading 'wealth mindset coach'. Using the principles he teaches, T. Harv Eker went from zero to millionaire in only two-and-a-half years. He combines a unique brand of 'street-smart with heart'.

www.tonyrobbins.com – For over thirty years, Anthony Robbins has dedicated his life to helping shape the most successful people in the world and is sought after as a coach to heads of state, leading athletes and top CEOs in addition to his work contributing to youth and prison work.

www.abraham-hicks.com – The source material for the Law of Attraction that has captured imaginations worldwide.

www.hazelden.org/register – Sign up for daily inspiring quotes.

www.abraham.com – Jay Abraham is one of the world's leading marketeers, coaching the best of the best.

www.essence-foundation.com – One of the world's best personal development course providers. Life-changing, experiential weekends.

www.alternatives.org.uk – Talks and workshops on holistic and alternative spirituality.

www.insightoftheday.com – Start the day with a positive message and have positive results.

www.learnoutloud.com – A one-stop destination for audio and video learning with over 20,000 educational audio books, MP3 downloads, podcasts, and videos.

www.youtube.com/user/aSecretAgent – With over 10 million views on this channel alone, *The Secret* by Rhonda Byrne is part of today's zeitgeist. Watch the free twenty-minute trailer at this channel.

www.youtube.com/user/Successuniverse – Inspiring quotes and thoughts including summaries of influential, bestselling books such as *The Secret* and the *Tao Te Ching*.

www.youtube.com/user/Jedi87 – A wealth of inspiring and educational uploads from this YouTube user.

www.youtube.com/user/prussell117 – Visionary Peter Russell's channel.

www.youtube.com/user/NullClothing – Visit the zeitgeist uploads that have attracted over 9 million views.

www.youtube.com/user/FranklinCoveyVideos – Top training from Stephen Covey's channel.

www.youtube.com/watch?v=FLXsilXdLR0 – 5-minute summary of highly influential bestselling book *The 7 Habits of Highly Effective People*.

www.youtube.com/user/HayHousePresents – Hay House channel with some of the world's leading thinkers.

www.youtube.com/user/EckhartTeachings?feature=chclk – Home to Eckhart Tolle and his empowering ideas on presence.

www.youtube.com/user/MindliftTV – Inspiring online channel.

www.youtube.com/user/LightbridgeMedia#p/u – Inspiring interviews and links.

www.youtube.com/user/IntentVideo – Uplifting video channel.

www.spiritualcinemacircle.com – The inspirational films from Spiritual Cinema Circle are compelling, uplifting stories about courage, love, family and truth-seeking.

www.bit.ly/IntroductionToEFT – Get more energy, enhance confidence and overcome limiting habits with this simple and powerful technique.

www.bit.ly/StopSmokingWithEFT – Quit smoking with the simple yet powerful EFT (Emotional Freedom Technique).

WELL DONE. THE FACT YOU HAVE GOT THIS FAR PROVES THAT YOU ARE AN ACHIEVER.

The simple fact that you have completed this book means that you are in the top 5% of people, who tend to be the same 5% of people who enjoy great success in life. You've proved to yourself that you really possess the qualities, persistence and determination to succeed.

I'd love to hear about what you found most valuable in this book: what were your highlights and what constructive feedback can you share? Have I missed out ideas, links or topics that you'd like to see in an update? I need your feedback so that future editions can be even better.

Remember to share any insights that you have had with others: if something has made a positive impact on your life, the chances are it will do the same for someone else. And please do let me know about your successes. Success really is a journey and not a destination, so make sure you enjoy the daily process of 'becoming more' and get in touch at: http://bit.ly/DannyRamplingBookFeedback. I listen to all constructive feedback and will update future editions of the book to include people's suggestions.

I have also created a special bonus resource for people who have invested in this book. This includes links to tutorials, opportunities to ask me questions directly via live conference calls and loads of active links to help you on your journey. You can access this via www.learnhowtobeadj.com or www.dannyrampling.com.

Also, make sure that you sign up to receive regular tips and links from me. I send out inspiring ideas, music-related links and insights a few times a month. Sign up for free at: www.learnhowtobeadj.com. You can also join my Facebook group or you can stay in touch by emailing me at: info@learnhowtobeadj.com.

Thank you for allowing me to share . . .

Wherever you are reading this right now I wish you every success and happiness.

With gratitude, love and respect,

Danny Rampling

London, 2010

Acknowledgements

I'd like to take this opportunity to thank my fantastic team who have contributed to the creation of this book.

First and foremost to my business partners and co-authors Ben Brophy and Jerry Frempong, for their tireless commitment to all our projects and for their genuine spirit of contribution and giving. It's been a lot of fun: www.BigBenBrophy.com and www.JerryFrempong.com

To Andy 'Touchfingers' Baddaley for his encyclopaedic technical music knowledge and his incredible advice and contribution to Section 1 of this book, for being able to make the complex simple, and for his unsurpassed level of professionalism, enthusiasm and dedication.

To the ever helpful, excellent and reliable Barry Darnell and Tez Humphries at one of the UK's best design agencies, our chosen partners for artwork: www.madebyanalogue.co.uk

To Sam Harrison, Liz Somers, Jodie Mullish, Barbara Phelan, Anya Wilson and all the team at www.aurumpress.co.uk for your belief, support and vision for this project and for helping me realise a dream.

To my publishing agent Matthew Hamilton (and the team at www.aitkenalexander.co.uk) who secured the publishing deal for this book. Thank you for your consistent belief and support.

To all the extremely passionate and clued-up contributors to the superb 'Essential Music Lists' in the bonus resources section: The Forum members of 'Southport Weekender'; Norman Jay's 'Good Times' Crate Diggers'; and the 'Hardcore Will Never Die' collective. To the incredibly helpful Greg Wilson, Ralph Lawson, Nicky Blackmarket, Steve Bicknell, Lisa Lashes, John '00' Fleming, Alex Gold, DJ Dino, Jafar, Dzine and Jason Fakeerah.

To Christian Aindow for his time, support and dedication to image creation and DVD production, assisted by Toby Dibert and Tom Gilfillan: www.ChristianAindow.com

To Ian Bavill of www.yearendaccounting.co.uk for his accounting knowledge.

To Tone of Funktion One sound systems for his audio expertise: www.funktion-one.com

To Adam Laurie and Phill Robinson of www.funknaughty.com for their insight and contribution to the digital market.

To two of the world's best internet coaches, who have helped open exciting doors of unlimited possibility, Simon Coulson and David Cavanagh: www.bit.ly/SimonCoulsonInternetCoaching; wwwbit.ly/GettingStartedOnTheInternetCoaching

To Sharron at www.mn2s.com, my booking agent.

To Hayes, Rachel and Sam at IMD for your support over the years.

To Mark Moore, Chris Lopez and Dan Reid for all of the fantastic moments captured and shared through the lens.

To Sean Billington and Gillian McCann for casting their eagle eyes.

To Kevin A. Dean of WSI Net Advantage for his tips on website promotion.

To Simon Hinton of Passion PR and Lucy Wills of Globefox.

To our wonderful team across at Amazon (who handle and manage our shop of music, books, merchandise and DVDs), and to our CafePress Partners who handle our clothing and T-shirts.

To Jim Jomoah and Jamie Griffiths (DJ J-Me) for their experience and insight.

To Pete Tong, David Morales, Gordon Mac, Dave Lee (Joey Negro), Simon Dunmore, Marc Marot, Danny Newman, Alex Gold, Mark Brown, Tim Deluxe and Mat Playford for sharing generously their wealth of experience.

To all my teachers around the world, whose ideas have inspired me and stretched my mind to help me live the life of my dreams, and for enabling me to share a small amount of what I have learned with others globally through this book.

To all the amazing party people, DJs, magazines, journalists, producers, promoters, venue owners, music industry friends, contacts, associates and acquaintances I have had the pleasure of meeting so far on my incredible journey. You know who you are and I appreciate all of your support and the time we've spent together. Thank you.

And last but by no means least to my incredible son, Claudio Rampling, future global DJ. I love you dearly and dedicate this book to you.

Danny Rampling

London 2010

'It takes teamwork to make the dream work'

Index

Page numbers in *italics* refer to illustrations.